P9-AOW-639

COMPARATIVE STUDY OF POSTPOSITIONS IN MONGOLIAN DIALECTS AND THE WRITTEN LANGUAGE

HARVARD-YENCHING INSTITUTE STUDIES
XII

COMPARATIVE STUDY OF POSTPOSITIONS IN MONGOLIAN DIALECTS AND THE WRITTEN LANGUAGE

BY
FREDERICK HOLDEN BUCK

HARVARD UNIVERSITY PRESS
CAMBRIDGE, MASSACHUSETTS
1955

DISTRIBUTED IN GREAT BRITAIN BY
GEOFFREY CUMBERLEGE
OXFORD UNIVERSITY PRESS
LONDON

Library of Congress Catalog Card Number 55-5384

PRINTED IN THE UNITED STATES OF AMERICA

FOREWORD

This volume, the twelfth of the Harvard-Yenching Institute Studies, is financed from the residue of the funds granted during the war by the Rockefeller Foundation for the publication of Chinese and Japanese dictionaries. This series is distinct from the Harvard-Yenching Institute Monograph Series and consists primarily of bibliographical studies, grammars, reference works, translations, and other study and research aids.

PREFACE

Recent years have witnessed a growing interest in the field of Mongolian studies. Materials for extending the linguistic knowledge of Mongolian in the West have greatly increased through the efforts of such outstanding Mongolianists as Ramstedt, Pozdneev, Rudnev, and Kotwicz. In 1929 there appeared the introduction and phonology of Vladimircov's *Comparative Grammar of the Mongolian Written Language and the Khalkha Dialect.* Unfortunately, the additional volumes, which were to have covered morphology, syntax, and semantics, remained unfinished. During the 1930's several important works on other Mongolian dialects were published. These included Professor N. N. Poppe's comparative studies of the Buriat and Dagur dialects. During the same period and thereafter, the Reverend Antoine Mostaert introduced a series of studies on the Ordos dialect which included transcribed oral texts, grammatical commentaries, and an Ordos dictionary. These were supplemented by other dialect studies, such as, G. J. Ramstedt's Kalmuk dictionary and A. de Smedt and A. Mostaert's grammar and dictionary of the Monguor dialect. All of these publications provide new material for developing a comparative grammar of Mongolian.

Some of the books and many of the important articles dealing with linguistic features of Mongolian dialects are not easily accessible to the general scholar. One purpose of this study is to bring together some of the significant points discussed in these scattered works. No attempt has been made to carry out a complete synthesis of all of them. In fact, only some features are given and those in outline form, the purpose being to provide background material for a limited study of syntax.

Since the type of construction which I have called a postpositional phrase is the main subject of this study, the material leading up to it deals briefly with some features of comparative phonology and morphology. The postpositional phrase itself is a characteristic one in Mongolian, and it is a fairly simple matter to isolate the phrase from the complete syntactical situation. Rather than attempt to arrive at statements covering all grammatical phenomena, it has seemed preferable to bring together the historical and dialectal examples and let them, in a sense, speak for themselves.

In carrying out this procedure, I have chosen to designate certain words in Mongolian as adverbs and postpositions, even though they are, for the most part, of the same form-class as nouns, their distinguishing features being syntactical rather than morphological. Hence, as my interest has centered primarily on the comparative aspects of postpositional constructions, the terms adverb and postposition are used only as they apply to the situation in Mongolian. These words have at one time or another been called "particles," "defective nouns," "petrified nouns," or "nomina auxiliaria," and their verbal counterparts have been called "petrified gerunds" or "verba auxiliaria." Indeed, some linguists have pointed out that the division within non-verbal word matter, which is so strongly felt in Indo-European languages, does not exist in the Turkic and Mongolian languages.

However, these so-called adverbs and postpositions do occur in Mongolian in predictable syntactical patterns, and in a few instances their phonological development is different from that of ordinary nouns. As such they merit special attention both from the descriptive and historical points of view.

Chapter six contains a lexicon of postpositions with various examples of their usage from as many old and modern sources as were available to me. Some of the examples, however, do not necessarily show the word in its postpositional usage, since it was also desired that in some cases the extent of usage be shown. In these cases, the example cited is usually preceded by the sign "Cf."

Unfortunately, I have been unable to use two works on Mongolian syntax which would have undoubtedly helped me a great deal, namely, *Sintaksis mongol'skih yazïkov* (Moscow, 1934) and *Sintaksis buryat-mongol'skogo yazïka* (Ulan-Ude, 1940), both by G. D. Sanžeev. I do owe, however, a great debt to the authors of the studies mentioned above.

It is a pleasure to acknowledge my gratitude to the Reverend Antoine Mostaert, C.I.C.M., Scheut Mission, Arlington, Virginia, and to Professor N. N. Poppe, University of Washington, Seattle, Washington, for the explanations and examples of Mongolian grammar with which they have kindly supplied me on various occasions both orally and by correspondence. I have included some of their commentaries by correspondence on certain features of the Mongolian language in order to make available to others the remarks in their original form. They are, however, in no way responsible for the use to which I have put them in dealing with the general subject matter.

I am also indebted to Professor Francis W. Cleaves for the opportunity I have had to study under him thirteenth and fourteenth century Mongolian texts.

I am particularly grateful to Professor Joshua Whatmough, in that this doctoral dissertation is the outgrowth of several years of valuable study in the Department of Linguistics under his guidance.

For the publication of this dissertation as Number XII of the Harvard-Yenching Institute Studies, I wish to thank both the Director of the Institute, Professor Serge Elisséeff, and its Board of Trustees.

Needless to say, while making these acknowledgments, I assume at the same time responsibility for all errors of fact or judgment in my work.

Cambridge, Massachusetts
January, 1954 F. H. B.

CONTENTS

PLATES

LIST OF ABBREVIATIONS

The abbreviations for the sources are listed alphabetically with the exception of a few which are indicated by their chronological date.

(1335) Cleaves, F. W., "The Sino-Mongolian Inscription of 1335 in Memory of Chang Ying-jui," *HJAS* 13(1950).1-131.

(1338) Cleaves, F. W., "The Sino-Mongolian Inscription of 1338 in Memory of Jigüntei," *HJAS* 14(1951).1-104.

(1346) Cleaves, F. W., "The Sino-Mongolian Inscription of 1346," *HJAS* 15(1952).1-123.

(1362) Cleaves, F. W., "The Sino-Mongolian Inscription of 1362 in Memory of Prince Hindu," *HJAS* 12(1949).1-133.

(Arγun 1289) Kotwicz, Wł., "En marge des lettres des il-khans de Perse retrouvés par Abel Rémusat," *Collectanea Orientalia* 4(Lwow, 1933). (Professor Francis W. Cleaves had the Letter of Arγun to Philippe le Bel of France, dated 1289, photographed in 1948.)

(Arγun 1290) Pelliot, Paul, "Les Mongols et la Papauté," extrait de *la Revue de l'Orient Chrétien,* 3e série, T. III (XXIII), Nos 1 et 2 (1922-23), pp. 3-30. Listed on pages 2 and 3 of the reprint: 5o Une lettre mongole d'Arghun, daté de 1290. (Professor Francis W. Cleaves had the Letter of Arγun to the Pope, dated 1290, photographed in 1948).

(AYM) Haenisch, Erich, "Die viersprachige Gründungsinschrift des Tempels An-yüan-miao in Jehol v. Jahre 1765," *Abhandlungen der Geistes-und Sozialwissenschaftlichen Klasse,* Jahrgang 1950, Nr. 15, Akademie der Wissenschaften und der Literatur (Wiesbaden, 1950).

(BE) Heissig, Walter, *Bolur Erike "Eine Kette aus Bergkristallen" (eine Mongolische Chronik der Kienlung-Zeit von Rasipungsuγ, 1774/75)* [= *MS* Monograph X], Peking, 1946.

(BM) Poppe, N. N., *Grammatika buryat-mongol'skogo yazika* (Moscow-Leningrad, 1938).

(BMS) Tšeremisov, K. M., and Tsïdendambaev, Ts. B., *Buryat-mongol'sko-russkiy slovar'* (Gosudarstvennoe Izdatel'stvo Inostrannïh i Nacional'nïh Slovarey, Moscow, 1951).

(Buriat) Examples of Buriat speech supplied personally by Professor Poppe.

(ČQ) *Činggis qaγan-u čadig,* first edition (Peking, 1925).

(CSN) Classical script newspaper, *Ünen* "Truth" (Ulan Bator, 3 July 1944).

(ČT) Žamcarano, C. Ž., *Mongol'skie letopisi XVII veka* (Moscow-Leningrad, 1936). This contains the *Čaγan Teüke* "The White History."

(Dagur) Poppe, N. N., *Dagurskoe narečie* [=Materialï Komissii po Issledovaniyu Mongol'skoy i Tannu-tuvinskoy Narodnïh Respublik i Buryat-Mongol'skoy ASSR, v. 6], Leningrad, 1930.

(DM) Smedt, A. de, et Mostaert, A., *Dictionnaire monguor-français* (Pei-p'ing, 1933).

(DO) Mostaert, A., *Dictionnaire ordos,* vols. I-III (Pei-p'ing, 1941-1944).

(Doc. A) Letter of Prince *Sangba* of the *J̌arūd* of 1892. An unpublished letter in the collection of Professor Francis W. Cleaves.

(Doc. B) Letter of Prince *Üdei* of the *Qorčin,* dated 1891. An unpublished letter in the collection of Professor Francis W. Cleaves.

(Doc. C) Letter of *Funiyangγa* and others of the *Naiman,* dated 1895. An unpublished letter in the collection of Professor Francis W. Cleaves.

(DzDz) Bambaev, B. B., "Otčet o komandirovke v Mongoliyu letom 1926 goda," *Predvaritel'nïy otčet lingvističeskoy ekspedicii v Severnuyu Mongoliyu za 1926 god* (Izdatel'stvo Akademii Nauk SSSR, Leningrad, 1929). This contains the poem *Eriin Sain Dzaan Dzaluudai.*

(EBQ) Poppe, N., "Zum Khalkhamongolischen Heldenepos," *AM* 5(1928).183-213. This contains the epic poem *Enxe Bolot Xaan.*

(EE) Pozdneev, A. M., *Mongol'skaya letopisъ „Erdeniynъ-yin erike". Podlinnïy tekst sъ perevodomъ i poyasneniyami, zaklyučayuščimi vъ sebe materialï dlya istorii Halhi sъ 1636 po 1736 g.* (St. Petersburg, 1883).

(Geserica) Poppe, N. N., "Geserica. Untersuchung der sprachlichen Eigentümlichkeiten der mongolischen Version des Gesserkhan," *AM* 3(1926).1-32, 167-193.

(HB) Rudnev, A. D., *Hori-buryatskiy govor. Opït issledovaniya, tekstï, perevod i primečaniya. Vip. I-III* (Petrograd, 1913-1914).

(HsCh) Yüan edition of a Chinese and Mongolian text of the *Hsiao-ching,* photographed by Professor Francis W. Cleaves in 1946 (unpublished). See Bibliography in appendix.

(Hy) Lewicki, Marian, *La langue mongole des transcriptions chinoises du XIVe siècle. Le Houa-yi yi-yu de 1389.* [= Travaux de la Société des Lettres de Wrocław, Seria A. Nr. 29], Wrocław, 1949.

(K) Kovalevskiy (= Kowalewski), Osip, *Mongol'sko-russko-francuzskiy slovar'* (Kazan', vol. I, 1844; vol. II, 1846; vol. III, 1849).

(KD) Ramstedt, G. J. *Kalmückisches Wörterbuch* (Helsinki, 1935).

(Kh) Poppe, Nikolaus, *Khalkha-mongolische Grammatik, mit Bibliographie, Sprachproben und Glossar* (Wiesbaden, 1951).

(Kh [Rudnev]) Žamcarano, C., i Rudnev, A. D., *Obrazcï mongol'skoy narodnoy literaturï. I. Halhaskoe narečie (lith.,* St. Petersburg, 1908).

(Khalkha) Examples of Khalkha speech supplied personally by Professor Poppe.

(KhM) Ramstedt, G. J., "Über die Konjugation des Khalkha-mongolischen," *Mémoires de la Société Finno-Ougrienne* 19(1903).

(KhN) "Khalkha newspapers," i.e., modern script newspapers, the language of which is based largely on the Khalkha dialect. (1) *Tšoibalsantš* "Partisan of Choibalsang" (Dund Gow' Aimag, 7 May 1949). (2) *Tsölööt Mongoləin Emegteitšüüd* "Women of Free Mongolia" (Ulan Bator, 22 May 1948). (3) *Xödölmör* "Work" (Ulan Bator, 1 January 1949).

(MKB) Poppe, N., *Učebnik mongol'skogo yazïka (Mongol kele biçig suralcakada yzeke debter),* Leningrad, 1932.

(Mogholica) Ramstedt, G. J., "Mogholica. Beiträge zur Kenntnis der Moghol-Sprache in Afghanistan," *JSFOu* 23.4(1906).I-III, 1-60.

(Monguor) Smedt, A. de, et Mostaert, A., *Le dialecte monguor parlé par les Mongols du Kansou occidental, IIe Partie, Grammaire* (Peking, 1945).

(MSM) Poppe, N., *Mongol'skiy slovar' Mukaddimat al-Adab,* Parts I-III (Moscow-Leningrad, 1938-1939).

(NB) See *(DzDz).* This refers to the oral text of *Nitsügen Boroldžoi.*

(O) Mostaert, A., "Ordosica," *Bulletin No. 9 of the Catholic University of Peking* (Peking, 1934).

(Ǒljeitü 1305) See *(Arγun 1289)*.

(Ordos) Examples of Ordos speech supplied personally by the Reverend Antoine Mostaert.

(OS) Mostaert, A., "L' 'ouverture du sceau' et les adresses chez les Ordos," *MS* 1(1935-1936).315-337.

('P) Poppe, N. N., *Kvadratnaya pis'mennost'* (Moscow-Leningrad, 1941).

(QQK) Rinčin (= Rinčine), *Qan qan-köbegün qoyar* [= A translation of a story by Maxim Gorky forming part of the series *Eworöpe dakin-u uran ǰokiyal*], Ulan Bator, 1948.

(R) Rinčine, A. R., *Kratkiy mongol'sko-russkiy slovar'* (Moscow, 1947).

(SH) Shiratori Kurakichi 白鳥庫吉, *Onyaku Mōbun Genchō Hishi* 音譯蒙文元朝秘史 *A Romanized Representation of the Yüan-ch'ao pi-shih (A Secret History of the Mongols in its Original Mongolian Sound)*, Tōyō Bunko Publications Series C, Volume VIII (Tokyo, 1942).

Haenisch, Erich, *Manghol un niuca tobca'an (Yüan-ch'ao pi-shih). Die geheime Geschichte der Mongolen, aus der chinesischen Transkription (Ausgabe Ye Tê̆h-hui) im mongolischen Wortlaut wiederhergestellt* (Leipzig, 1935).

(SK) Jülg, Bernhard, *Mongolische Märchen-Sammlung (Die Neun Märchen des Siddhi-kür ... und die Geschichte des Ardschi-Bordschi Chan)*, (Mongolisch mit deutscher Übersetzung, etc.), Innsbruck, 1868.

(SME) Cleaves, F. W., "The Sino-Mongolian Edict of 1453," *HJAS* 13(1950). 431-446.

(SMY) Todaev, B. H., *Grammatika sovremmennogo mongol'skogo yazïka* (Izdatel'stvo Akademii Nauk SSSR, Moscow, 1951).

(ST) Šmidt (= Schmidt), I. Ya., *Geschichte der Ost-Mongolen und ihres Fürstenhauses, verfasst von Ssanang Ssetsen Chungtaidschi der Ordus. Aus dem Mongolischen übersetzt und mit dem Originaltexte, nebst Anmerkungen, Erläuterungen und Citaten aus anderen unedirten Originalwerken herausgegeben von . . .* (St. Petersburg, 1829). In Mongolian the history is popularly called *Sira Teüke* "The Yellow History." Its actual title is *Erdeni-yin tobči*.

(Teheran) Pelliot, Paul, "Les documents mongols du Musée de Ṭeherān," *A͟thār-é-Īrān* 1(1936).37-44. The documents are numbered I, II, and III.

(TOO) Mostaert, A., *Textes oraux ordos, recueillis et publiés avec introduction, notes morphologiques, commentaires et glossaire* (Peking, 1937).

(TT) Poppe, N. N., *Letopisi Horinskih Buryat. Vip. I* [= Trudï Instituta Vostokovedeniya IX], containing the chronicle of *Tegülter Tobo (TT)* dated 1863 (Moscow-Leningrad, 1935).

(ÜD) Šmidt (= Schmidt), I. Ya., *Grammatik der mongolischen Sprache* (St. Petersburg, 1831). The reference is to the story from *Uliger-ün dalai*, pp. 129-142.

(Vladimircov) Vladimircov, B. Ya., *Mongol'skiy sbnornik razskazov iz Pančatantra* (Petrograd, 1921). The reference is to the story *Muur-yin qudal üges kemegsen anu* which is found on p. 75. See n. 127.

(WM) Bleichsteiner, R., und Heissig, W., unter Mitwirkung von W. A. Unkrig, *Wörterbuch der heutigen mongolischen Sprache mit kurzem Abriss der Grammatik und ausgewählten Sprachproben* (Wien-Peking, 1941).

(WY) Poppe, N. N., *Letopisi Horinskih Buryat. Vip. I* [= Trudï Instituta

Vostokovedeniya IX], containing the chronicle of *Wangdan Yumčung (WY)* dated 1875 (Moscow-Leningrad, 1935).
(Žamcarano) Žamcarano, C. Z., *Mongol'skie letopisi XVII veka* [= Trudï Instituta Vostokovedeniya XVI], Moscow-Leningrad, 1936. The reference is to p. 93 of the *Altan Tobči* of bLo.bzan bsTan.'jin. See n. 127.

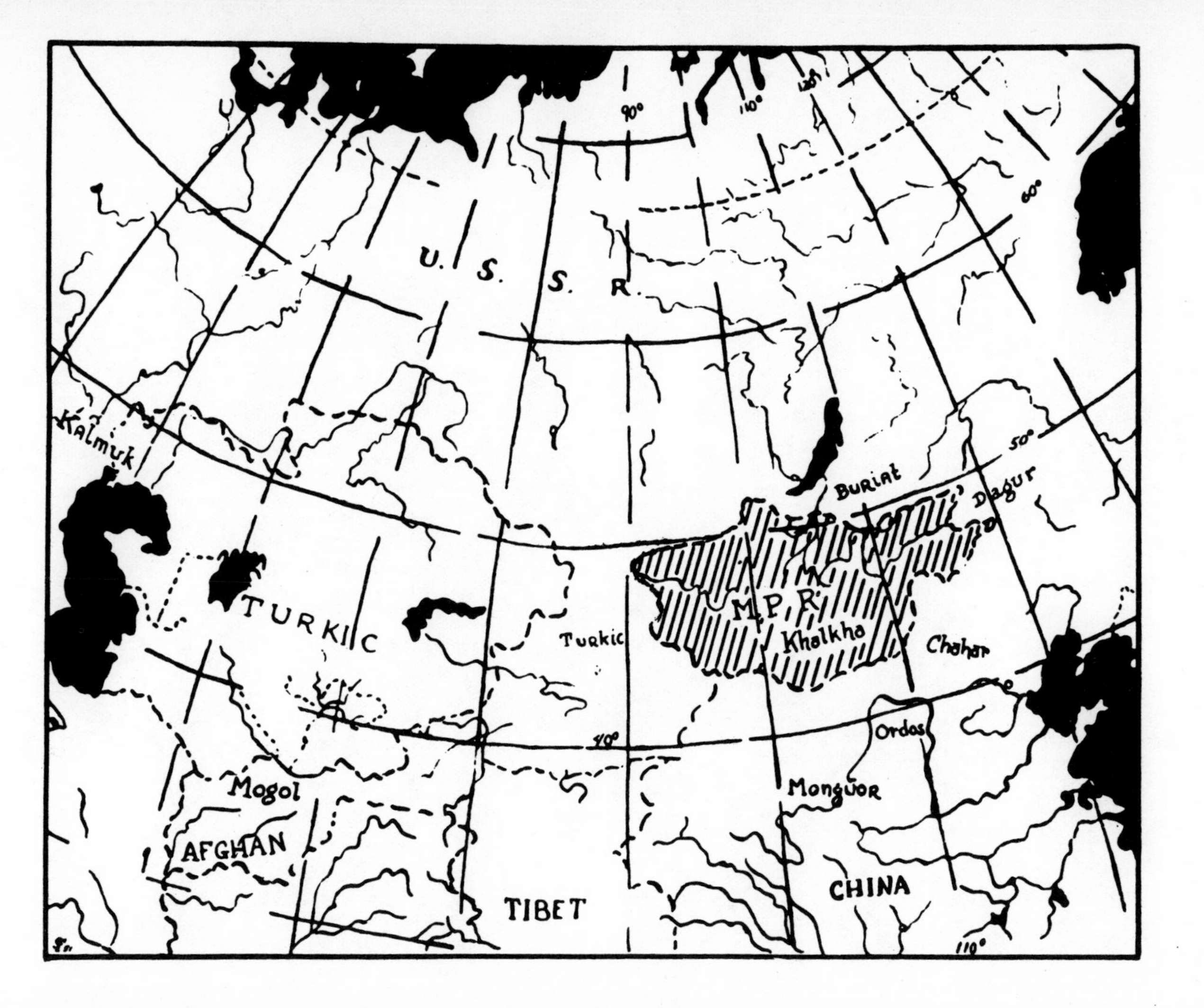

Central Asia

I

INTRODUCTION

GENERAL REMARKS

Although the subject of this study falls within the province of syntax, some introductory material is necessary to make clear the problems presented in the examples given in later chapters. Moreover, the sources of information concerning the Mongolian language are not numerous. The studies which have been made are located in different publications which are scattered both as to time and place. The purpose here is not to make a complete synthesis of all this material, but to bring together a sufficient amount of it to lessen the burden of the reader who has not studied Mongolian. Furthermore, there are also a few facts of a non-linguistic nature which are, in varying degrees, related to the general subject of Mongolian. These may well be presented at this point.

The statistical material concerning those areas where the Mongols live is very scant, since systematic compilations are few and not easily available. By comparing several sources, it has been estimated that between three to four million Mongols lived in various parts of Asia between the first and second World Wars. The Mongols in Outer Mongolia are generally estimated at somewhat less than a million. According to Skačkov,[1] there were approximately 1,500,000 Mongols in Inner Mongolia in 1934. This estimate includes Suiyuan, Chahar, Jehol, and Ningsia. In areas outside of Jehol and in Manchuria there are at least 900,000 more Mongols.[2] In the 1930's it was estimated that there were about 400,000 Mongols in the Soviet Union, about twenty per cent of whom were Volga Kalmuks.[3] The Kalmuk Republic was liquidated in 1943. Poppe lists about 350,000 Buriats as living in the Lake Baikal area.[4]

Outer Mongolia encloses the area which was the homeland of the Turco-Mongolian nomads who, from time to time, overran adjacent territories even to the extent of entering Europe. The Mongols founded a world empire under Činggis Qan in the thirteenth century, and, after its dissolution in the fourteenth century, the Mongols of the empire were divided into three main groups – the Northern

Mongols in Outer Mongolia, the Southern Mongols in Inner Mongolia and the Western Mongols in Sinkiang and Ch'ing-hai. Their organization was originally based on the patriarchal clan, where the leadership was personal and the law was common to all clans. From the sixteenth to the eighteenth centuries the simpler organization developed into what Vladimircov[5] calls "nomadic feudalism," eventually reaching its peak of development under Manchu suzerainty. With the Chinese revolution of 1912 begins the period of decline of the older organization.

Since the ties with the Manchu throne were rendered inoperative at the time of the abdication, the Mongols of Outer Mongolia considered themselves independent politically from China. Inner and Outer Mongolia became politically separated, as they had been economically (i.e., with cattle-raising north of the Gobi Desert and farming south of it). During the twenties and thirties a semi-independent literary movement grew up in the Lake Baikal area among the Buriat Mongols and at Ulan Bator,[6] capital of Outer Mongolia.

Literacy has never been very high in Central Asia. The spread of Lamaism in the fourteenth century created a situation whereby an increasing number of the male population became lamas, and in so doing they formed the basis of a literate class, although religious scripture was more apt to be studied in Tibetan rather than in Mongolian. This was the situation prior to the Chinese revolution. Under the Mongolian People's government (Communist), it has been claimed recently that the percentage of Mongols in Outer Mongolia who can read is as high as 55.5 per cent.[7] Ma Ho-t'ien,[8] a Chinese official who was sent to Outer Mongolia as an observer during the mid-twenties, comments that the Mongols were enthusiastic about their new schools and that they considered themselves to be in advance of the Chinese. Ma, however, considered the standards of the People's University to be the equivalent of a Chinese normal school. The Minister of Education, Batu Khan, was a Buriat. The courses consisted of general subjects, education, politics, and law. The state library at Ulan Bator contained some several thousands of volumes.

The Mongolian revolution took place under the merged leadership of Suke Bator and Choibalsang. After the death of the religious leader, Jebsun Damba Hutukhtu, in 1924, the ties with the past became even more remote. The constitution of the same year nationalized land, mineral wealth, forests, and granted a state monopoly of foreign trade. These changes were accompanied by a succession of intrigues and outbreaks which indicate considerable resistance to the changes. One revolt occurred at the time of the confiscation of princely and ecclesiastical property during 1931 and 1932. In the long run, pro-Russian groups under Marshal Choibalsang won out.

ALPHABETIC HISTORY

According to Diringer,[9] alphabetic writing had a period of expansion at the time of the Hyksos (1730-1580 B.C.). Its expansion was due to the fact that its origin was popular rather than theocratic. Of the various alphabets evolved from the Near East, the Syro-Palestinian was destined to become the model for a number of Asiatic scripts. Christianity spread through Central Asia via Edessa in northwestern Mesopotamia. After the Council of Ephesus (431 A.D.), which condemned the Nestorian doctrine, the Syriac Church was split into a Western and an Eastern branch. Syriac became an important language in the East Roman Empire, and the Eastern branch of the Syriac Church had great importance in the history of writing. The Nestorian alphabet followed the path of the doctrine. By the time of Marco Polo, the trade routes from Baghdad to Peking were lined with Nestorian bishoprics. The Syriac version of the Bible dates from 200 A.D. The Syriac script, known as *Estrangelo* ("evangelical writing"), became the model for the Sogdians, who spoke an Iranian dialect. From the latter, the alphabet spread to the Uigurs, a Turkic people, and thence, to the Mongols. The Uigurs used the Sogdian script, writing it vertically instead of horizontally. This alphabet, with a few minor modifications, is the one which has survived among the Mongols up to modern times.

The earliest example of Mongolian written with this script is on the stone which was set up between 1220 and 1225 in honor of Yisüngge. It consists of five lines of Uigur script. The Naiman Turks, whom Činggis Qan had conquered previously (1204 A.D.), seem to have known this script already. Tata[r] Toŋ-a, a learned Uigur in the service of the Naiman court, had charge of the seal and of accounts. Činggis Qan, impressed by his attainments, ordered him to teach his prince-sons how to write the national language (i.e., Mongolian) by means of Uigur letters.[10] Since the original dialect upon which the writing was based is not known, and since, from the fourteenth century on, tradition set the standard for orthography, it became a literary dialect corresponding to, but differing somewhat from, known spoken dialects. Buddhist elements were later incorporated into the literary style. These came from Tibetan, with the result that spelling was also influenced in the case of literary loan-words.

When Qubilai Qaγan made Daidu (Peking)[11] his capital, it was decided that a national alphabet should be created in order to facilitate the writing of the various languages within the Mongolian empire. It was also to be the "national" script of the Mongols, just as the Liao and Chin dynasties had created their own scripts. The aim and scope of the undertaking are described in the Edict of 1269, recorded in the *Yüan tien-chang* 元典章. 'Phags-pa Lama was named as the one responsible for the execution of this task. The alphabet he created, known as the 'Phags-pa alphabet,[12] was based on the Tibetan square script and was written in vertical columns from left to right. As it turned out, this system of writing was sparsely used owing to the convenience of the Uigur script, which was well established. It was used, however, in the Imperial Chancery during the Yüan dynasty. The extant examples of any length are inscriptions, covering the years from 1276 to 1352.[13]

As for the Uigur script, whose tradition has been continuous up to the present, by the seventeenth century spoken language elements began to replace words no longer understood. These were often archaized to fit the canons of spelling. The remaining archaic elements became regularized and fixed. This literary language is known as the "New Written Language." In the seventeenth and eighteenth centuries, printing in Peking and in South Mongolia helped to standardize the spelling and grammar. Most printing was done from engravings on wood. There were many dictionaries and some grammars. During this period the great Buddhist works were translated from Tibetan, such as the *Kanjur* in 108 volumes (1624) and the *Tanjur* in 225 volumes (1724). This remained the written language for the Khalkha, Barga, Buriat, and Kobdo Oirat Mongols up to recent times. There were, however, Mongols outside of this area to whom the written language was not known. When a church mission was founded in Transbaikal in 1681, the Buriats of that area did not know the Mongolian written language. It was not until 1712 when Buddhist missionaries entered Buriat Mongolia to spread the teaching of Buddhism that the Buriats came to know the Mongolian written language. In the western Buriat area the Mongols remained unaffected by this Buddhist expansion, and they practised Shamanism to a greater extent and for a longer period of time. The earliest literacy among these Mongols grew out of an acquaintance with the Russian alphabet. Hence, these Western Buriats were the earliest and most persistent advocates of the use of a western alphabet for the writing of Mongolian.[14]

These experiments with the Latin alphabet began with Baradin's publication of *Buriaad zonoi uran eugeiin deeje* [*Selections from Buriat Popular Literature*] in 1910. Other Buriats were interested in this development, but it never received widespread support at that time. It was not until after the Chinese and Mongolian revolutions that a concerted effort was made to adopt wholesale a western alphabet. The Latin alphabet was the first to be introduced as the basis for a modern literary script, but by 1941 the Russian alphabet had taken its place, as it had done in the case of the Turkic languages spoken to the west of the Mongols.

The periods and types of alphabetic change may be summarized as follows:

1) *Ca.* 1204. Uigur script.
2) 1269. 'Phags-pa script.
3) 1648. Oirat script, invented by Za-ya Pandita in the seventeenth century, based on Uigur, and used by the Western Oirats.
4) 1920. Russian alphabet used by the Kalmuks, later replaced by the Latin alphabet.
5) 1931. Latin alphabet adopted by the Buriats, Khalkhas, and Kalmuks.
6) 1937. Russian alphabet adopted by the Buriats and Kalmuks.
7) 1941. Russian alphabet adopted by the Khalkhas of Outer Mongolia.

In the last thirty years a large number of new terms have become current in Mongolian. They reflect the impact of European and Russian culture on Central Asia. A Scientific Committee was founded in Outer Mongolia along with the founding of the Mongolian People's Republic in 1924. The new literature abounds in new economic, political, and technical terms.

TRANSCRIPTION SYSTEMS

From the foregoing it is apparent that one of the difficulties in citing historical materials in Mongolian is the variety of systems of writing among the Mongols themselves both past and present. To this must be added the variety of transcriptions used by different linguists at different times in order to record living speech. In the following examples mechanical transcriptions have been used for the former written language and for the modern written language.

For the New and Old Written Languages (= former written language), the mechanical transcription is that used by *HJAS*. This is a mechanical substitution letter for letter, with the exception of four Mongolian letters which are further differentiated in the mechanical transcription, resulting in one of two possible substitutions per letter in each case. The choice of letter is based upon distinctions found in spoken dialects or reconstructions based on comparative studies.[15] The *Tablica* of the Mongolian alphabet, on page six, shows the substitutions made for the transcription and also the original Mongolian letters.[16] As may be seen

ТАБЛИЦА VII

монгольский алфавит.

Название букв и их механическая транслитерация согласно основному значению.		Начальные.	Средние.	Конечные.	Древнее значение.	Современное халхаское произношение.	Mechanical Transcription
āleph	ʼ	[illegible]	[illegible]	[illegible]	*a*	a ȧ	a
—	ʼ	[illegible]	[illegible]	[illegible]	*e*	e ė ȯ ẏ	e
yod	*y*	[illegible]	[illegible]	[illegible]	*i*	i	i
waw	*w*	[illegible]	[illegible]	[illegible]	*o u*	о у	o/u
—	*w*	[illegible]	[illegible]	[illegible]	*ö ü*	ȯ у	ö/ü
nūn	*n*	[illegible]	[illegible]	[illegible]	*n*	н	n
nūn + kāph	*nk*		[illegible]	[illegible]	*ng*	ң	ng
ḥēth	*γ*	[illegible]	[illegible]		*q* > *χ*	х	q
—	*γ*	[illegible]	[illegible]	[illegible]	*γ g*	ҕ ґ ґ k	γ
pē	*p*	[illegible]	[illegible]	[illegible]	*p b w*	б w б w п	b
Новая монг. буква.		[illegible]	[illegible]		(*p*)	п'	p̣
šīn	*š* (*s*)	[illegible]	[illegible]	[illegible]	*s*	с	s
—	*š*	[illegible]	[illegible]	[illegible]	*š*	ш	š
taw, dāleth	*t δ*	[illegible]	[illegible]	[illegible]	*t d*	т' д	t/d
lāmedh	*l*	[illegible]	[illegible]	[illegible]	*ł l*	л л l l	l
mēm	*m*	[illegible]	[illegible]	[illegible]	*m*	м	m
ṣādhē	*č*	[illegible]	[illegible]		*č*	ц' ч'	č
Новая монг. буква.		([illegible])	[illegible]		(*ǰ*)	з џ	J
yod	*y*	[illegible]	[illegible]	[illegible]	*y*	j	y
kāph	*k*	[illegible]	[illegible]	[illegible]	*k g*	х ᵏх г г к	g/k
rēš	*r*	[illegible]	[illegible]	[illegible]	*r*	р р р̀ р̀	r
bēth	*β*	[illegible]	[illegible]		*v w*	w	w
Новая монг. буква.		[illegible]	[illegible]		(*h*)	h х	h

From B. Ya. Vladimircov, *Sravnitel'naya grammatika mongol'skogo yazïka i halhaskogo narečiya* (Leningrad, 1929).

from it, the distinction between *o/u* and *ö/ü* is not indicated by the Mongolian letter. In the case of *t/d*, the Mongolian letter is the same, even though *t* is phonematically distinct from *d*. The front and back vowels, however, may be inferred at times from the quality of the velar consonant, if that happens to occur in the word. γ is always used with back vocalic harmony, and g with front.

The transcription of passages from the *Secret History* is the same as that used in various articles published in *HJAS*. It differs somewhat from Haenisch's system of transcription.[17] In the case of some words in the *Secret History*, problems of transcription are still unsolved.

The citations from 'Phags-pa texts are copied just as they are given in Poppe's study on 'Phags-pa inscriptions.[18]

As for the oral transcriptions, the most frequent citations are from Northern and Southern Mongolian. For the latter, in the form of the Ordos dialect, the Reverend Antoine Mostaert's transcription is used. A description of it taken from *Textes oraux ordos* (1937) is in Appendix A. It is based on the Finnish system for transcribing languages and dialects.[19] A modified form of it is also used in Ramstedt's Kalmuk dictionary.[20] Since most of the Northern dialects, particularly Khalkha and Buriat, have been transcribed at one time or another by means of different systems, I have taken the liberty of trying to simplify them by using the Latin alphabet as used by Poppe in his *Khalkha-Mongolische Grammatik*,[21] with the exception of the letter *j*, for which I use *y*. This has entailed some loss in greater phonetic precision, but it suffices for the purposes of this paper, which deals primarily with comparative syntax.

The alphabet used in transcribing these Northern dialects is also used to transcribe mechanically the alphabet now used in Outer Mongolia for the modern literary language. It is given below along with the equivalent Mongolian letters.

TRANSCRIPTION USED FOR THE MODERN KHALKHA MONGOLIAN ALPHABET AND FOR THE NORTHERN DIALECTS

The Mongolian letter equivalents are given in parenthesis. The pronunciation is given primarily as a guide to the reader. For descriptions based on phonetic analysis, one should consult Vladimircov[22] and Poppe.[23]

a (а) *a* in Italian "p*a*dre."

b (б) as in English.[24] *b* is used initially and after *l*, *m*, and *w*.

w (в) voiced bilabial, less energetic than English *w*. This presents an allophone of *b* (б). It is used between vowels, and initially for a few loan-words from Chinese and Russian.

g (г) similar to English g in front vocalic harmony. In back vocalic harmony, it is a velar consonant. As with *b, d, dz, dž,* it is voiceless when initial.

d (д) similar to English, but voiceless.

yö (е) *ö* (see below) preceded by *y*-glide.

yo (ё) *o* (see below) preceded by *y*-glide.

dž (ж) *j* as in "*j*est."

dz (з) *dz* as in "a*dz*e."

i (и) *i* as in "p*i*n."

i (й) *i* as in Italian "ma*i*" (i.e., a *y*-glide after any vowel).

k (к) similar to English and used only for loan-words.

l (л) similar to English.

m (м) similar to English.

n (н) as in English. When final it represents a sound similar to -*ng* of "si*ng*," but unreleased.

o (о) mid-back-round more or less like *o* in "d*o*or" pronounced quickly.

ö (ө) *eu* in French "p*eu*." In Khalkha and Buriat Mongolian, it represents a sound similar to the *u* in the South Swedish pronunciation of "l*u*nd." Cf. *u* in English "p*u*t."

p (п) like English initial *p*.

r (р) trilled alveolar *r*. When final it represents the unvoiced allophone.

s (с) *s* in "*s*ing."

t (т) voiceless and aspirated as in English initial *t*.

u (у) back-sound articulated deep in the oral cavity with the larynx lowered. This gives an acoustic impression of a dull sound between English *oo* in "d*oo*r" and *oo* in "f*oo*t."

ü (ү) *u* in French "l*u*ne." In Khalkha Mongolian, it is a high-mixed-narrow-round sound similar to the Norwegian *u* in "h*u*s" (i.e., the lips are rounded but not protruded). N.B. *ö* has more lip-rounding than *ü*.

f (ф) same as in English, used to spell some foreign loan-words.

x (х) strongly aspirated *h* (English). With back vowels it has a strong velar quality. In Ordos, it corresponds to an aspirated *k* sound when initial and with front vowels.

ts (ц) like *ts* in "ha*ts*."

tš (ч) like *ch* in "*ch*in."

š (ш) like *sh* in "*sh*in."

ъ (ъ) used in spelling some Russian words.

əi (ы) neutral vowel ending in *y*-glide. This is an allophone of *ii* (i.e., "long" *i*). It occurs in the Genitive and Accusative suffix after back vowel harmony.[25]

(ь) short unaccented *i*, usually final. The preceding consonant is palatalized. In inflexions, /'/ (ь) > /i/ (и).

e (э) like *e* in "s*e*t."

yu/yü (ю) *u* or *ü* preceded by *y*-glide.

ya (я) *a* (see above) preceded by *y*-glide.[26]

Long Vowels and Diphtongs

aa (аа) *a* in "f*a*r."

oo (оо) *o* in "d*o*le."

uu (уу) *u* in "r*u*le."

ee (ээ) *e* in "*e*r*e*."

öö (өө) *ö* in German "H*öh*le."

üü (үү) *ü* in German "k*üh*n."

ii (ий) *i* in "mach*i*ne."

ai (ай) *ai* in "*ai*sle."

oi (ой) *oy* in "b*oy*."

əi (эй) *ey* in "ob*ey*." Also without *y*-glide.

The type of long vowel represented above is usually not indicated in the traditional Mongolian alphabet, except where the long vowel stands for the "vowel + γ/g + vowel" of the older language. This situation is discussed below.

The modern alphabet observes a phonetic principle which is shown in the diagram on the next page. The vowels to the right of the first column are the only possible short vowels to be found in that sequence.

Initial Syllable

a, aa, u, uu	(may be followed by)	a (short)	or i
e, ee, ü, üü	..	e ..	or i
o, oo	..	o ..	or i
ö, öö	..	ö ..	or i
i, ii	..	a, e, or i (short)	

A word in Mongolian includes two features which serve as a convenient basis for definition, namely, vocalic harmony and initial stress accent. A word with or without derivational and/or inflexional suffixes has only one of the vowel combinations. Back vowels are *a, o,* and *u*; front vowels are *e, ö,* and *ü*. In the modern dialects *i* is neutral and is found with either series. Spelling variations in old texts indicate that *i* was at one time *i* or **ï*. This may be seen from such examples as *saqiqu* "to watch" and *sakiqu*.[27] This vocalic situation is also reflected in the spelling of certain consonants; *q* and γ are always associated with back vowels, *g* and *k* with front vowels.

In Khalkha speech, the accent is strongly expiratory on the first syllable of a word.[28] There is often a secondary musical accent on the final syllable of a word accompanied by lengthening of the final vowel or the addition of a long vowel. This seems to be associated with the expression of various moods, interrogative, imperative, expression of doubt, surprise, irony, and so forth. It is not to be confused with the lengthening and accenting of final syllables in the reading of a text, which is the result of training. In a phrase such as *ta sainúu*? "are you well?", the answer may be *bi sain baináa* "I am well." The *baináa* of the answer may also be *báina* (or even shorter, *bain*) and would be so usually, if it were not for the secondary accent in the question. In any case, the final *-áa* of *bainaa* is a lengthening of a vowel which is usually short. The proper name *Širwa* (Širab) becomes *Širwáa* in the Vocative. The same principle may be observed in the alternation of such pronunciations as *sáixan* "nice" and *saixáan* "how nice!" Poppe, in his *Khalkha-Mongolische Grammatik* (1951), states that the accent, which is strongly articulated, falls always on the first syllable of words whose following syllables are short. In those words having a short first syllable followed by a long vowel in the second or third syllable, the accent falls on the first long syllable. This is true also of words whose first two syllables are short followed by one or more long syllables. In words whose first and second (also third) syllables are long, the

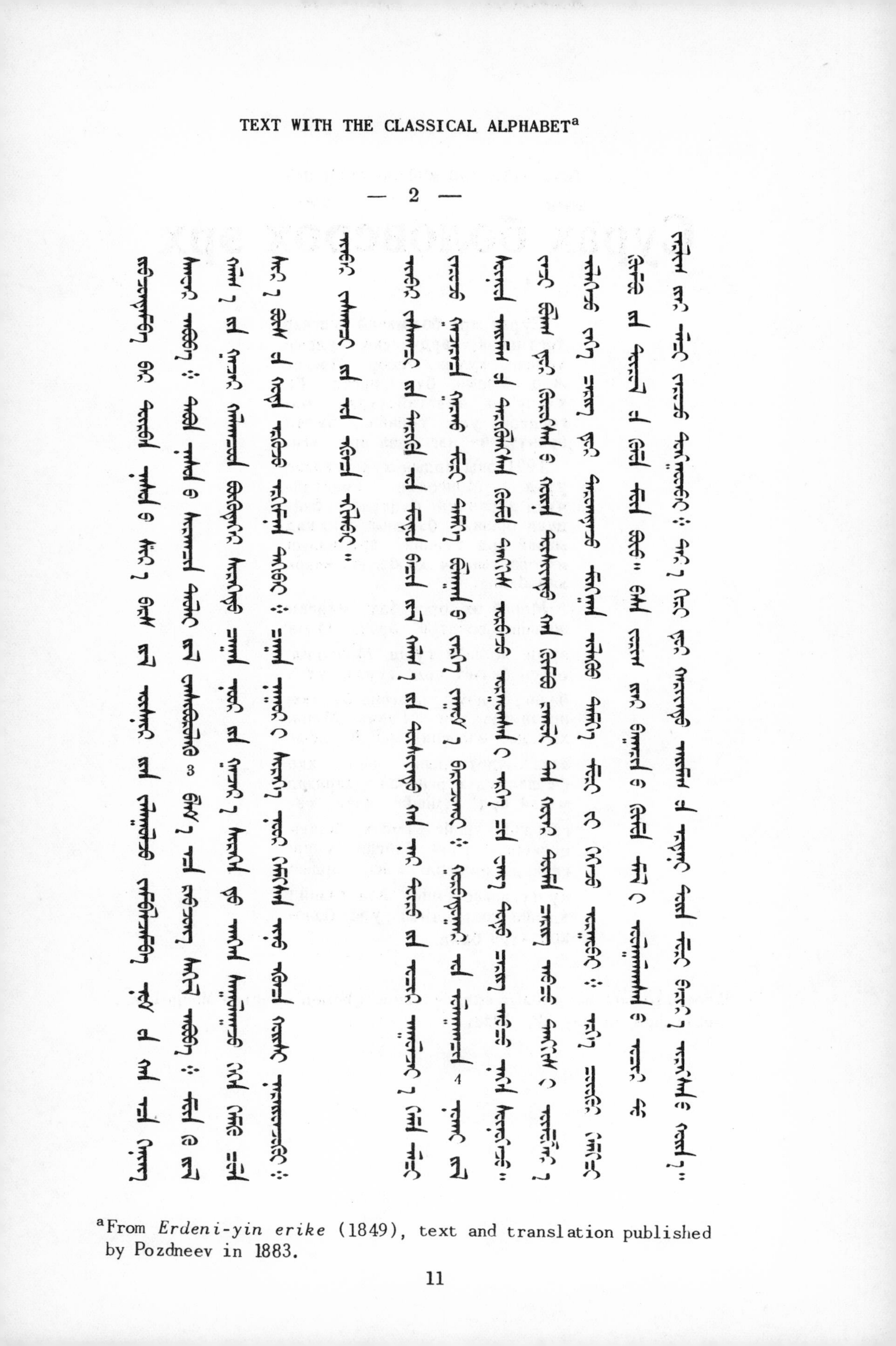

TEXT WITH THE CLASSICAL ALPHABET[a]

— 2 —

[illegible]
[illegible]
[illegible]
[illegible]
[illegible]
[illegible]
[illegible]
[illegible]

[illegible]
[illegible]
[illegible]
[illegible]
[illegible]

[a]From *Erdeni-yin erike* (1849), text and translation published by Pozdneev in 1883.

TEXT WITH THE MODERN ALPHABET[a]

Сурах боловсрох эрх

Сурах эрх бол манай тусгаар тогтносон ардчилсан улсын үндсэн хууль ёсоор Монгол Ард Улсын бүх иргэд ба түүнчлэн эмэгтэйчүүдэд олгогдсон улс төрийн бусад эрхнүүдийн нэг адил эрх юм.

1921 оны ардын хувьсгалаас урьд Монголын эмэгтэйчүүд харанхуй бүдүүлэг байдалд оршиж байсныг санахад манай ард түмний ардчиллын их ололтын ач холбогдол илэрхий байна.

Манай эх орон бол мянган жилийн соёлтой орон. Олон зуун жилийн турш Монголын оюун билэгт ард түмэн, утга бичиг, эрдэм, урлагийг бүтээж ирсэн түүхтэй. Гэвч Манж хятадын эзлэгчид манай улсыг эзэлж дотоодын шар хар феодалууд харгислан дарлаад манай ард түмнийг соёл гэгээрлийн үрийг эмсэх бололцооноос салгаж байсан учир, гадаад Монгол Улс, ардын хувьсгалаас өмнө Ази тэзийн адгийн хоцрогдмол улс болоход хүрч байв.

[a]From *Tšölööt mongoləin emegteitšüüd* [Women of Free Mongolia], published on May 22, 1948.

first takes the accent. Since the old diphthongs function the same as the long vowels, all of the preceding applies to them. Grønbech[29] has also observed, in the case of Chahar speech, that long vowels arising from the loss of intervocalic γ/g may be long or short. He cites as an example *sanaa* / *sana* < *sanaγa* "thought."

In Ordos speech, the accent is regularly on the first syllable, but it is less strong than in the other southern dialects or in Khalkha.[30] This fits in well with the fact that the non-initial short vowels have preserved their original quantity and quality better than in other dialects.

The following is a transcription of the first four lines (from left to right and top to bottom) of the *Text with the Classical Alphabet.*

(1) *J̌ibǰundamba ber dörben nasun-u šir-a bars ǰil üsnir-iyen ǰalaγulǰu J̌ambalǰamba nom-un qan-ača gening* (2) *sanwar abuba* ·:· *tabun nasun-u širaγčin taulai ǰil Wansibürülegü blam-a-ača rabǰung sakil abuba* ·:· *mön kü ǰil* (3) *Qalq-a-yin γaǰar Qalqačud bügüdeger Siregetü Čaγan Nuur-yin γaǰar-a siregen-dü angqa saγulaγǰu* [= *saγulγaǰu*] *Gegen kemekü čola* (4) *sir-a bös-ün qota ergüǰü erkimnen takibai* ·:· *Čaγan Naγur-i Sirege Nuur kemegsen inu egünče qoyisi nereyìdǰüküi* ·:·

Capital letters are used for proper names, but there is no orthographic distinction in the original text. /-/ is used to indicate a break in the writing of a word. This occurs usually in connection with inflected endings.

The following is a transcription of the first two paragraphs of the *Text with the Modern Khalkha Mongolian Alphabet.*

Surax erx bol manai tusgaar togtnoson ardtšilsan ulsəin ündsen xuul' yosoor Mongol Ard Ulsəin büx irged ba tüüntšlen emegteitšüüded olgogdson uls töriin busad erxnüüdiin neg adil erx yum.

1921 onəi ardəin xuw'sgalaas ur'd Mongoləin emegteitšüüd xaranxui büdüüleg baidald oršidž baisnəig sanaxad manai ard tümnii ardtšilləin ix ololtəin atš xolbogdol ilerxii baina.

COMPARATIVE PHONOLOGY

In an article published in *Journal asiatique* for April-June of 1925, P. Pelliot[31] reviews some features of Turco-Mongolian phonology. Particular attention is paid to an initial **p-* of Altaic origin whose history may be traced in Turkish, Mongolian, and Manchu. Its general development is diagrammed as follows:

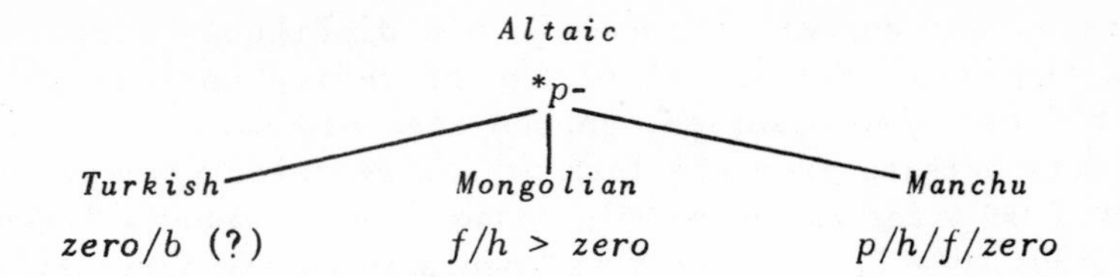

The initial *h-* in Mongolian is found in the transcription of the *Secret History*, in the 'Phags-pa inscriptions, and in Chinese and Moslem sources. It is represented by an initial *h* in the Dagur dialect and by an initial *f-* in Monguor.[32]

Examples

Mongolian	*Turkish*
hači > *ači* < **hati̇̈* "son-in-law"	*ati̇̈* (Orkhon)
hula'an > *ulaγan* "red"	*bulan* "élan"
hon > *on* "year"	

Manchu	*Monguor*
fulgiyan "red"	*fulan* "red"
fon "season"	*fän* "year"

With regard to the historical significance of the Monguor dialect, the Reverend Antoine Mostaert has the following to say. "Like the other dialects of Kansu, this one [i.e., Monguor – F.H.B.] is characterized by archaism of the greatest interest, as much from the point of view of phonetics as from that of morphology and of vocabulary. By virtue of this archaism it stands near, on the one hand, to the dialect of the Moghols of Afghanistan and especially to certain Dahur dialects, and, on the other hand – and this is its most interesting aspect – to ancient Mongolian as it has been handed down to us, principally in the Western sources (Moslems and others) of the 13th and 14th centuries, the inscriptions in 'Phags-pa script, which date from the Yüan and especially the Chinese transcriptions dating from the Yüan and the Ming. The [87] latter are principally Sino-Mongolian vocabularies, such as the *Chih-Yüan-i-yü* [至元譯語– F.H.B.], the *Hua-i-i-yü* [華夷譯語– F.H.B.] (1st part), the *I-yü* [譯語 – F.H.B.], [inserted in chapter 22 of the *Teng-t'an-pi-chiu* 登壇必究– F.H.B.], or coherent texts such as the *Yüan-ch'ao-pi-shih* [元朝秘史– F.H.B.] and the *Hua-i-i-yü* (second part). All these monuments of ancient Mongolian (we have mentioned only the principal ones) are particularly important because of the fact that since they are preserved in a script other than the so imperfect Uiguro-mongol script, they permit us to penetrate deeper into the phonetics of the spoken Mongolian of the 13th and 14th centuries. In these phonetics, one of the striking facts is the presence of an initial *h* in words which (as we have already said) have since lost it in all the known dialects, with the exception of some Dahur dialects and those of Kansu, in which dialects it survives under the form of some consonant derived from it: *χ*, *f*, *s*, etc. In these phonetics as they are revealed to us by these inscriptions and transcriptions, one still sees, in a number of words, a consonantism different from that of the written Mongolian and of the living dialects. Seeing this difference, one asks sometimes if it is not a matter of faulty notation or of a mistake of copyist, but often the Monguor form confirms the reading that one had suspected of being erroneous and one comes to realize that it is an ancient form which has disappeared from modern dialects and which is ignored in the written language, but which has survived in Kansu Mongolian: e.g. *Hua-i-i-yü: küče'e* 'turtle-dove',: written Mongolian: *kütege*, Monguor: *k'uDžiē* 'id.': *Yüan-ch'ao-pi-shih: gödöl-* 'to move (intr.)', written Mongolian: *ködel-*, Ordos: *k'öDöl-*, Monguor: *GuDoli-* 'id.'"[33]

Another feature of Altaic comparative phonology is the corresponding *β > Mongolian γ = Turkish *p (b)* of the type Mongolian *qaγalγa* < **qaβalγa* "gate" = Turkish *qapïγ* "gate."[34] A considerable amount of material of this nature has been studied, but further discussion of it here is not pertinent to the general subject under consideration.

A comparison between modern Mongolian dialects and the traditional written language reveals a very striking difference, namely, that the written "vowel + γ/g + vowel" corresponds to long (i.e., double) vowels in modern speech. The *Secret History* shows the transitional stage of this development by transcribing these combinations as "vowel + hiatus + vowel." This indicated pronunciation is one which also describes the modern Dagur dialect with regard to the words under discussion.

Examples

Written Language	*Secret History*	*Khalkha*
baγatur "hero"	*ba'atur*	*baatər*
ködege "steppe"	*köde'e*	*xödöö*
toγa "number"	*to'o*	*too*
aγula "mountain"	*a'ula*	*uulə*

In Dagur, the word for mountain is *aŭl* / *aŭlă*, a transitional stage between the *Secret History* *a'ula* and the *uulə* of other dialects. This intervocalic consonant began to disappear in the thirteenth century, as may be seen from the transcription of Mongolian words in the medieval Armenian works of Kirakos of Gandjak and of Grigor of Akanc'.[35]

Although this particular correspondence holds good for most words, there are exceptions, some of which have not been satisfactorily explained. In one group of the exceptions, the second vowel of the combination "vowel + γ/g + vowel" is long. The written language gives the form *čaγan* "white." In Khalkha it is pronounced *tsagaan,* with the second vowel long. The *Secret History* has the form *čaγa'an / čaγan,* seeming to indicate that the second vowel is itself a development from "vowel + γ/g + vowel."

There is a large number of words which fall easily into semantic groups and which also have "vowel + γ/g + vowel" in the modern dialects. Since the traditional written language made no distinction between this γ/g and the one which disappeared, no phonematic or phonetic explanation can be based on it, nor is the history of accent sufficiently well known to determine the part it may have played. Grønbech considered the original accent to be free in the Turco-Mongolian languages, and that any discussion of stress accent with regard to phonology was meaningless.[36] The semantic grouping mentioned above is outlined by Vladimircov as follows: words indicating (1) blood relationships and social relationships, (2) animals, plants, minerals, and metals, (3) parts of the body, (4) utensils, tools, clothing, harness. In some cases, the loss of the first vowel of the group "vowel + γ/g + vowel" may account for the survival of the γ/g in the spoken dialects.[37] This in conjunction with the type of metathesis found in modern Khalkha[38] or the appearance of new "glide-vowels" suggest possible approaches to the study of the "vowel + γ/g + vowel" group in these words. In any case, the history of intervocalic consonants of this type (i.e., also intervocalic *b,* β, and *m*) and the history of long vowels still require further research.

Examples

Written Language	*Khalkha*
ečige "father"	*etsəg/etsəgə*
noγosu(n) "duck"	*nogos*
egem "collar-bone"	*egem*
qundaγa "goblet"	*xundəg*

There are also spoken language alternations, such as, Khalkha *sugə / suu* for *suγu* "arm-pit," which is found as *su'u* in the *Secret History.*

The following list gives the principal old and modern orthographical parallels.[39] It also illustrates some phonological developments other than those described above.

OLD AND MODERN ORTHOGRAPHICAL PARALLELS (KHALKHA)

Comment	*Former*	*Modern*
1) *e* (first syllable) > *e*,	almost always:	
	ende "here"	*end*
e (first syllable) > *ö*,	before syllable with *ö*:	
	ebesün "hay"	*öwsön*
	edür "day"	*ödör*
2) *i* > *i* before *e* or *ʼ*:		
	šine "new"	*šine*
	kili "boundary"	*xilʼ*
	kičiyel "zeal"	*xitšeel*
	irekü "to come"	*irex*
	bariqu "to seize"	*barix*
i > *ʼ* after palatalized consonants, at the end of a syllable, or before the "Set of Nine" (see below):		
	qoγsil "property"	*xogšil*
	adali "like"	*adil*
	qari "foreign"	*xarʼ*
	urid(a) "before"	*urʼd*
	toli-dur "in the mirror"	*tolʼd*
	mori(n) "horse"	*morʼ*
i > *ya* as a result of regressive assimilation:		
	minγa(n) "thousand"	*myanga(n)*
	kiraγu(n) "hoarfrost"	*xyaruu*
i > *a, o, ö, u, ü, e* as the result of regressive assimilation:		
	miqa(n) "meat"	*max(an)*
	siγum "line"	*šugam*
	čimüge "marrow"	*tšömög*
i > *ya, yo* when initial by regressive assimilation:		
	ilalta "victory"	*yalalt*
	ilγaqu "to distinguish"	*yalgax*
	iruγal "bottom"	*yorool*
3) *iγa/iya* > *ia, io:*		
	qariγad "returned"	*xariad*
	ǰokiyal "composition"	*dzoxiol*
	tariya(n) "grain"	*taria(n)*
	qiya "adjutant"	*xia*

Comment	*Former*	*Modern*
iγa > *aa, oo:*		
	siγaqu "to beat"	*šaax*
	qoriya(n) "office"	*xoroo*
4) *ige/iye* > *ee, öö:*		
	ergiged "turned"	*ergeed*
	kögǰiged "flourished"	*xögdžööd*
	üliyekü "to blow"	*üleex*
5) *iγu* > *iu:*		
	qariγu "answer"	*xariu*
	qaliγun "otter"	*xaliun*
iγu > *uu* after sibilants:		
	γasiγun "bitter"	*gašuun*
6) *igü* > *üü:*		
	deligün "spleen"	*delüün*
	kögǰigülkü "to develop"	*xögdžüülex*
7) *aγa* > *aa* in the first syllable:		
	daγaqu "to bear"	*daax*
aγa > *aa, oo* in non-initial syllable:		
	daraγa "afterwards"	*daraa*
	on-daγan "other"	*ondoo*
8) *ege* > *ee* in first syllable:		
	deger-e "above"	*deer*
ege > *ee, öö* in non-initial syllable in accordance with vowel harmony:		
	töb-tegen "center" (dat.)	*töwtöö*
	ködege "steppe"	*xödöö*
9) *aγu/uγu* > *uu:*		
	aγula "mountain"	*uul*
	qaraγul "guard"	*xaruul*
10) *egü/ügü* > *üü*		
	küǰügü(n) "neck"	*xüdzüü(n)*
	degüü "younger brother"	*düü*
	tügükei "raw"	*tüüxii*
11) *uγa* > *aa, oo* depending on vowel of first syllable:[40]		
	doluγa(n) "seven"	*doloo(n)*
	yabuγa "going"	*yawaa*

Comment	*Former*	*Modern*
12) *üge* > *ee*, *ȫȫ* depending on vowel of first syllable:[40]		
	dörüge "stirrup"	*dörȫȫ*
	irelüge "has come"	*irlee*
13) *oγa* > *oo* in the first syllable:		
	toγa "number"	*too*
	toγarai "poplar"	*tooroi*
14) *öge* > *ȫȫ*:		
	böger-e "kidney"	*bȫȫr*
	ögede "above"	*ȫȫd*
15) *oγu* > *oo*:		
	oγusur "string"	*oosor*
	toγuna "smoke-hole"	*toono*
16) *ögü* > *ȫȫ*:		
	čögüken "few"	*tsȫȫxön*
17) *eyi* > *ii*:		
	eyimü "thus"	*iim*
	deyilkü "to conquer"	*diilex*
18) *ayi* > *ai*:		
	ayimaγ "aimak"	*aimag*
19) *oyi* > *oi*:		
	oyilγaqu "to understand"	*oilgox*
20) *uyi* > *ui*:		
	uyilaqu "to weep"	*uilax*
21) *sq/sk* > *sg*:		
	asqaqu "to pour"	*asgax*
	öskekü "to raise" (cattle)	*ösgöx*
22) *dq/dk* > *tg*:		
	udqa "gist"	*utga*
	yekedkekü "to enlarge"	*ixtgex*
23) *ng* > g before *-n*:		
	angnaqu "to hunt"	*agnax*
	šangnaqu "to reward"	*šagnax*
ng > *n(g)* when final:		
	tong "very"	*ton(g)*
	sang "treasury"	*san(g)*

Comment	*Former*	*Modern*
24) *b* > *b* when initial or after *l, m, w:*		
	bal "honey"	*bal*
	abubasu "if one takes"	*awbal*
	bolbasu "if so"	*bolbol*
	Damba (a name)	*Damba*
b > *w* in all other cases:		
	töb "center"	*töw*
	yabuba "went"	*yawaw*
25) *lγa* > *laga, logo* by metathesis:		
	bodulγa "policy"	*bodlogo*
	ǰarulγa "courier"	*dzarlaga*
	daγudalγa "calling"	*duudlaga*
lγa > *lga, lgo:*		
	ǰorilγa "intention"	*dzorilgo*
	idqalγa "agitation"	*yatgalga*
26) *lge* > *lge, lgö:*		
	medegülgekü "cause to inform"	*medüülgex*
lge > *leg, lög:*		
	demǰilge "help"	*demdžleg*
	külge "packing"	*xüleg*
27) *rγa, rγu* > *raga, rogo:*		
	siduryu "straight"	*šudraga*
rγa, rγu > *rga, rgo:*		
	tataγurγa "drawer"	*tatuurga*
28) *rge* > *reg, rög:*		
	kögerge "snuff-box"	*xöörög*
	egürge "burden"	*üüreg*
	ǰerge "order"	*dzereg*
29) *γ, g* > *g:*		
	γar "hand"	*gar*
	ger "house"	*ger*
30) *ǰ* > *dž* before *i* and before a "vowel < *i*":		
	ǰil "year"	*džil*
ǰ > *dz* except as above:		
	ǰam "road"	*dzam*
31) *č* > *tš* before *i* and before a "vowel < *i*":		
	či "thou"	*tši*

Comment	Former	Modern
č > ts except as above:		
	času(n) "snow"	*tsas(an)*
32) *q, k > x:*		
	qara "black"	*xar*
	ken "who"	*xen*

ORTHOGRAPHIC RULES

Aside from recognizing the loss of γ/g between vowels in the modern dialects, the new orthography takes into consideration the reduction or loss of non-initial short vowels by classifying consonant and vowel combinations. The result is a series of rules concerning two sets of consonants which may be stated as follows:[41]

1) *Set of Seven Consonants.* Any one of the following consonants, *b, w, g, l, m, n, r,* "includes" for orthographical purposes a short vowel element before or after it. Examples: *öwgön (< öwögön)* "old man," *emgen (< emegen)* "old woman," *er (< ere)* "man."

2) *Set of Nine Consonants.*

a) A short vowel is written before or after any of the following: *d, dž, s, t, x, tš, ts,* or *š.* Examples: *xatadž* "drying up," *modod* "trees," *ulsad* "to people," *etsedž* "being tired."

Exceptions:

b) when this class of consonant is preceded by any of the Set of Seven Consonants. Examples: *ordž (< orodž)* "entering," *mald* "to the cattle."

c) If one of the Set of Nine Consonants occurs between two consonants of the Set of Seven, then the vowel distribution will be one short vowel preceding the three consonants and one following. Examples: *üildwer* "production," *dawtdag* "habitually repeating."

3) No consonant of the *Set of Seven Consonants* has a short vowel before and after it at the same time.

4) The general exceptions to the above are as follows: the form of the verb known as the *Nomen Futuri* always consists of a suffixed *short vowel plus -x.* Final -*g* and final -*n* may have a following short vowel in order to preserve phonematic distinctions in such words as *en* "width" and *ene* "this." Final -*g* and -*d* represent unvoiced consonants. Example: *orox* "to enter, entering."

SHORT VOWELS

According to Poppe,[42] there are only three non-initial short vowels in modern Khalkha, *ă*, *ĕ*, and *ĭ*. These short vowels are pronounced quickly and indistinctly. When final, they alternate with zero. The Mongolian word *quda* "relative by marriage" has three spoken forms, *xudă* / *xudŭ* / *xud*. The -*ŭ* or *xudŭ* is a sound assimilated to the -*u* of the first syllable.

As for *ĭ*, a consonant preceding it is fronted but not palatalized. A vowel in the preceding syllable is also slightly fronted.

amă = mouth	*ȧmĭ* = life
allă = kill!	*ȧllĭ* = which?

Back vowels precede *ă*; front vowels precede *ĕ*. Short *ĭ* accompanies either back or front vowel harmony. When the preceding syllable contains a short *ŭ*, the following short vowel is *ă* with a slight *ŭ* quality.

The intervocalic consonant -*l*- in the second set of examples above is geminated in Khalkha speech, as are some other consonants under the same conditions. Ramstedt[43] states that the gemination is most pronounced when the consonant is between two short vowels of which the first is accented. When the second vowel is long, the gemination is weakened. The consonants geminated under these conditions are *x*, *t*, *ts*, *tš*, *d*, *dz*, *dž*, *y*, *l*, *s*, and *š*.

These reduced vowels are also connected with alternations in the syllabic structure of words. In the examples given here, the form at the left is more frequent in Khalkha than the form at the right.

ta / *mix* "tobacco"	or	*tam* / *xi*
a / *rag* "method"	or	*ar* / *ga*
xaa / *lag* "gate"	or	*xaal* / *ga*

The forms at the right are the ones found in traditional script and in early writings. The consonants used and the possible combinations are as follows: (*v* = short vowel).

r *v* g	or	r g *v*
l *v* g	or	l g *v*
m *v* g	or	m g *v*
r *v* x	or	r x *v*
r *v* b	or	r b *v*
s *v* x	or	s x *v*

ORDOS DIALECT

Some examples cited in the section on "postpositions" are taken from the transcriptions of Ordos speech made by the Reverend Father

Mostaert. The Ordos Mongols form part of the group of Mongols living in the area known as Inner Mongolia, which includes the Chinese provinces of Ninghsia, Suiyuan, Chahar, Jehol, and in Manchuria, Liaoning, Kirin, and Heilungchiang. The Ordos themselves settled within the big bend, called *boro* ᴅoχ̂̄ "the Grey Bend" in Ordos, of the Yellow River during the second half of the fifteenth century and acquired the name Ordos from the name of the "eight white tents of Činggis-qan," which were called *ordu,* and which were brought to that area, forming one of the three *tümen* (= ten thousand) of the empire of Dayan-qan. In 1649 they were organized into six banners, which later became seven. Together they constitute the Confederation of the Great Temple *(Yeke J̌uu-yin Čiγulγan).*[44]

The language of the Ordos region has certain features which should be mentioned. Among the most conspicuous is the de-aspiration of initial stops and affricates by dissimilation under conditions which are regular. The situation may be stated as follows:

In polysyllabic words whose first syllable has a short vowel, an initial voiceless aspirated stop or affricate has become an unaspirated lenis consonant if the short vowel is followed by a voiceless aspirated stop or affricate (or a non-nasal consonant plus a voiceless aspirated stop or affricate).[45]

Examples

tobči "button"	ᴅoʙ'*tš*'*i*
qasiqu "to surround"	*Ģaši-*
kebtekü "to recline"	ɢeʙ'*t*'*e-*
čokiqu "to hit"	ᴅ*žo*'ᵏχ*i-*

The unaspirated lenis consonants are as in other dialects.

dotora "within"	ᴅo'*t*'*oro*
γaqai "pig"	*Ģaχā̂*
ǰokistai "suitable"	ᴅ*žo*'ᵏχ*ist*'̂̄

The Ordos dialect preserves also certain archaic features which have disappeared in other dialects. They may be summarized as follows:

1) The non-initial short vowels, described above, are articulated more clearly, with less reduction of quantity than in Khalkha.

2) The original *č* [tʃ] and *ǰ* [dʒ] sounds remain in Ordos, whereas in Khalkha *č* > *ts* and *ǰ* > *dz* except when followed by *i* or a vowel which has replaced an original *i*.

3) The Ordos dialect has a more clearly articulated *k* as an initial in words with front vocalic harmony. In Khalkha the original *k* > *x* with frontal articulation.

4) The distinction between final *-n* and final *-ng* [ŋ] is kept in Ordos.

5) Words of the type *čilaγun* resist regressive assimilation in Ordos. Cf. Ord. *tš'ilų̄* "stone," Kh. *tšuluu*.

6) When initial *u* in Ordos is represented by *o* in other dialects it is the result of regressive assimilation from an original *u* in the second syllable. Cf. Ord. *mųDų*, Kh. *moDDŏ*.[46] < Mo. *modun* "wood."

II

PARTS OF SPEECH

The "parts of speech" of Mongolian, as in the case of many other languages, have presented problems from the beginning of the study of Mongolian. Since the time of Šmidt's grammar[47] in 1832 up to the present, at one time or another, the parts of speech in Mongolian have been numbered anywhere from three to eight. Notions of grammar, based on the study of European languages, have always influenced the analysis to a greater or lesser degree. However, purely formal features of Mongolian have also always been noted.

The eight parts of speech discussed by Šmidt are *noun, adjective, pronoun, verb, postposition (poslerečie), adverb,* and *conjunction.* These are essentially the same elements discussed by Poppe in his article on parts of speech.[48] However, Poppe classifies the parts of speech on the basis of the morphology and syntax of Mongolian. Both Kowalewski[49] and Popov[50] followed more or less the analysis inaugurated by Šmidt. Rudnev[51] reduced these to three basic parts of speech: *verb, adverb,* and *noun.* The noun, however, was subdivided into adjective, pronoun, and numeral.

This difference of viewpoint seems to be the result of a difference of emphasis, rather than a fundamental disagreement on the part of various grammarians. The grammar written by De Smedt and A. Mostaert on the *Monguor* dialect[52] also reduces the language to three fundamental parts of speech: *noun, verb,* and *particle.* This is in line with Jespersen's analysis of English in his *The Philosophy of Grammar,*[53] where he gives as grammatically distinct parts of speech the following arrangement:

1) Substantives (including proper names).

2) Adjectives. In some respects (1) and (2) may be classed together as *nouns.*

3) Pronouns (including numerals and pronominal adverbs).

4) Verbs.

5) *Particles* (comprising what are generally called *adverbs, prepositions,* and *conjunctions*). This fifth class actually comprises all those words which do not fit into the first four classes.

Jespersen, thus puts into one group (5) elements which have often been treated as separate parts of speech. The reason given is that they are not on a par with the first four classes, and that, as regards form, they are invariable. Their "evident similarities" may be great, but their linguistic counterpart in various languages is very complicated. In contrast to nouns and verbs, the so-called "particles" are often treated with less satisfactory results in both historical and descriptive grammar. This applies particularly to prepositions and their equivalent in Mongolian, namely, postpositions.

The form in which the Mongolian noun appears as subject of the verb and the form in which the verb is used as a simple command are designated here as the ***stem***. The stem may also be the root element itself. It is, therefore, a minimal form within the framework of syntax. The identification of parts of speech by means of morphology does not proceed on the basis of minimal forms as may be seen from the following:

γar "hand" (nominative).
γar "go out!" (imperative).

The morphological test refers to the type of suffixes which may be used with a given minimal form. This analysis results in the distinction of two classes of words which correspond to nouns and verbs in European languages.

γar-un "of the hand," in which *-un* is a noun suffix.
γar-ba "he went out," in which *-ba* is a verb suffix.

Homophonous minimal forms of verbs and nouns such as the examples just cited are rare. Since the minimal form of words (not verbs, however) appear with other syntactical functions in a Mongolian sentence, it is necessary to study features of arrangement, which reveal other tests for the classification of "parts of speech."

Below are given the general features of the different parts of speech in Mongolian. The comments and examples are taken from Poppe's article on parts of speech and from his Khalkha grammar.[54] Aside from the seven regular inflexional suffixes for nouns, there are also about thirty derivational suffixes which are used with verbal or nominal stems in the formation of new nouns. The verbs, on the other hand, have about thirty inflexional suffixes; there are also about sixty derivational suffixes which are used with verbal or nominal stems in the formation of new verbs.[55] The derivational suffixes are not treated here. Only the declensions of nouns and pronouns are important for the present study because of their morphology in postpositional phrases.

1) *Noun*. The noun is distinguished morphologically by the fact that it is declined, forms a plural, and takes possessive suffixes. Syntactically it functions as subject, predicate, object, and attribute. As attribute, it is an adjectival noun, but as such it may not be modified by an adverb.

γar "hand."
γar-un "of the hand."
γar-iyan "one's hand" (acc.).
degüü inu "his younger brother."

2) *Verb.* The verb is distinguished morphologically by the fact that it is conjugated for tense and aspect. The verb stem does not take any of the noun stem suffixes. Syntactically the verb is the final element in the predicate. Some forms may be preceded by the negative particles *ese* and *ülü* "not."

ire "come!"
ire-be "he came."

In Buriat there are predicate suffixes such as, *axab* < *aqa bi* "I am the elder." One also finds in Kalmuk, *irsm-b* < *iregsen bi* "I came," where the verb has acquired a personal suffix.

There are a few surviving stems which may be either verbal or nominal. Cf. *adqu* "handful," *adqu* "clutch with the hand!" Cf. also *γar* above. Otherwise, the differentiation between noun and verb is complete.

3) *Numerals.* Numerals may be considered a subdivision of nouns, having, however, a certain number of suffixes which nouns in general do not have. The following are a few of them.

γurba-duγar "third."
γurba-γula "by threes."
γurba-γad "three each."

The suffixes *-duγar, -γula,* and *-γad* are confined to numerals and a few words used like numerals. Cf. *angqa-duγar* "first" < *angqa* "beginning."

4) *Pronouns.* Pronouns are distinguished morphologically by the fact that they are declined, either by adding suffixes to a different stem, or, in some cases, by adding suffixes to a stem only slightly altered from the one used in the nominative case.

bi "I."
min-u "my."
tere "that."
tegün-ü "of that."

N.B. *ternii* "of that" is a colloquial alternate form with the same stem as the nominative *tere*.

The genitive case of the pronouns usually follows the noun they modify. Cf. *aqa minu* "my elder brother," but *modun-u nabči* "leaves of the tree." The forms *inu* and *anu* originally meant "his" and "their," but they are used frequently now as enclitics merely to make the reference to the noun more definite. Pronouns may combine with the particle *ba* to form indefinite pronouns. Cf. *ali* "which," *ali ba* "any." In all cases, the same declensional suffixes are used with noun or pronoun stems, singular or plural.

5) *Adjective.* The adjective is distinguished morphologically by the fact that it takes no plural suffix, nor is it declined. Substantival adjectives, however, do take a plural suffix and are declined. Adjectives may be used as attributes or predicates, and they may be used as adverbs of manner. Many of them may be modified by such particles as *masi* "very." In his article on parts of speech, Poppe treats nouns as falling into two categories, one of which he calls "object-nouns," and the other "quality-nouns." Here, we have set up the two classes, *noun* (= "object-noun") and *adjective* (= "quality-noun"). The treatment is the same, and these two parts of speech cannot be identified by the types of features which are common to most European languages. According to morphology and/or syntax, adjectives may be identified as follows:

a) Attributive position (preceding the noun).

> *urta modo* "tall tree."
> *γar buu* "revolver" (lit., "hand-gun").

b) Attributive position and retention of *-n* of "*-n* stem." (See below.)

> *modon ger* "wooden house."

c) Predicate position (following the noun).

> *modo urta (baina)* "the tree is tall."

d) Use of intensives with adjectives only.

> *masi sain* "very good."
> *neng sečen* "exceedingly wise."
> *ülemǰi yeke* "exceedingly big."

e) As verb object, never in *casus indefinitus*.

> *maγui-yi alamui* "he kills *the evil* one."
> But, *maγu ungsimui* "he reads *poorly*."
> And, *nom ungsimui* "he reads *books*."
> *tere kümün-ü sayin-i γayiqamui* "I am surprised at the *goodness* of that person."

In other words, the form of the adjective without the accusative suffix and preceding the verb serves as a modifier of the verb, and not as its object.

6) *Adverbs.* Adverbs are distinguishable from nouns in that they have a limited number of case suffixes, if any. They have no plural. Adverbs indicating location may take dative and/or

ablative suffixes. Adverbs indicating time may take the genitive suffix and sometimes the instrumental. These features are also common to postpositions (see below). Adverbs are found with two suffixes which do not occur with ordinary nouns, namely, *-si/-γsi* (called *Lativform* by Poppe) and *-γur* (called *prolatif* by A. Mostaert).

a) Place:

ende "here."
qamiγa "where?"
ende-eče "from here."
qamiγa-si "whither?"

b) Time:

edüge "now."
tuγar "just now."

With the noun inflexional suffixes these words are indistinguishable from ordinary nouns.

The comparison of the minimal forms of these adverbs reveals roots which no longer have an independent existence. The non-root elements usually turn out to be fossilized dative-locatives. Most of these "suffixes" are no longer productive.

en-de "here."
čaγa-si "in that direction."
čaγa-γur "along that side."
dege-re "on."
dege-gsi "upwards."
dege-gür "along the top."
uri-da "formerly."

These words, whether treated as adverbs, nouns, or postpositions, are not very homogeneous with regard to their form when viewed either descriptively or historically.[56]

7) *Postpositions*. Postpositions are auxiliary words which perform the same function as prepositions in European languages. Most postpositions are of nominal origin, but a few are derived from verbal forms. Some adverbs may also be used as postpositions ("adverb-postpositions"). Postpositions govern the stem, the indefinite case, the genitive case, the dative-locative case, the ablative or the comitative cases. They may take reflexive or personal possessive suffixes. The examples given below apply to the Khalkha dialect.[57]

a) The following postpositions govern the plain stem (in the case of *-n* stems, the *-n* is retained); *deere* "on," *doro* "under," *teeši* "in the direction of," *dotoro* "in," etc.

šireen deere "on the table."

tüün deere "on it."
usan dotoro "in the water."
ger teeši "to the house."

b) The following postpositions take the indefinite case: *öödö* "up towards," *xürtel* "up to," *ruu* "(down) towards."

ara öödö "towards the north."
usa xürtel "up to the water."
usa ruu "down the stream."

c) The following postpositions take the genitive case: *tula* "because of," *tölöö* "for the sake of, in exchange for," *tuxai* "concerning," *dunda* "in the middle of," *gadaa* "outside of," *xoino* "behind," *naana* "this side of."

tüünii tula "because of that."
dalain dunda "in the middle of the sea."
geriin gadaa "outside the house."

d) The following postpositions take the ablative case: *gadana* "aside from," *xoiši* "after."

tüünees gadana "aside from that."
tüünees xoiši "after that."

e) The following postpositions take the comitative case: *tsug* "together with," *xamta* "together with."

tšamtai tsug "together with you."
nöxörtee xamta "together with friends."

f) Some postpositions take various cases.

tüünii dzüg "in his direction."
ger dzüg "to the house."
gol xürtel "up to the river."
ulaan baatarta xürtel "as far as Ulan Bator."

Although these examples have been taken from the Khalkha dialect, the situation is much the same in the other dialects. One of the purposes of this study is to list corresponding examples in different dialects and the written language in order to show the specific differences in postpositional constructions.

There are phrases whose function is the same as that of postpositional phrases, but whose construction is that of a noun in an oblique case (usually, dative-locative or ablative).

šireen deerees "from the table(-top)."
usan dotoroos "from (in) the water."
uuliin xadžuu-da "near the mountain (lit., 'at the side of the mountain')."
tšinii oron-do "in place of you."

The simplest postpositional phrase, which is morphologically distinct from other constructions, is one whose final member, the postposition itself, while governing the preceding elements, is in its minimal form and is neither the subject nor object of a verb. It may be identified internally by the phrasal construction and externally by its position in the syntactical arrangement of the sentence. There are, however, many modifying phrases in Mongolian, whose function is similar to the above, but whose construction falls also within other categories. Cf. *ulaan baatar-ta xürtel* "as far as Ulan Bator." The form *xürtel* "as far as" is constructed normally from *xür-* "to reach" by means of the suffix *-tvl* which is applicable to all verbs. In this type of construction, grammarians have usually called *xürtel* a postposition. The suffix *-tvl* belongs to a class of suffixes called *converba*, of which it is the *converbum terminale*. The *converba* modify the main verb in much the same way as postpositional phrases modify verbs. According to Ramstedt,[58] the *converba* seem to be fossil noun forms (i.e., from verbal nouns) with fossilized case endings. This places them etymologically with those postpositions whose form is also the result of fossilized case endings. Hence, it is logical to place such a word as *xürtel* among postpositions. However, in the examples I have listed, I have kept converbal expressions separate from the basic postpositional phrases.

8) *Conjunction.* Conjunctions, like particles, are few in number, and they do not fall readily into other classifications. Nouns and verbal nouns may be connected by the conjunction *ba* "and." The conjunction *bögööd* "and" is of converbal origin and its suffix *-ööd* is productive as a regular verbal ending called the *converbum perfecti*. It may be used to connect sentences whose predicates are verbal nouns.

9) *Particles.* Particles are dependent words, syllables, and at times endings lacking any syllabic value. They add certain meanings to the words they modify. Most of them follow the word they modify and differ from postpositions in that they do not indicate syntactical relationships, and they do not govern the words they follow. They express negation, sanction, emphasis, etc.

a) Preceding:

es irewel "if he does *not* come."

b) Following:

xetsüü daa "it is *indeed* hard."

10) *Interjection.* The situation concerning interjections is the same as in other languages. Whether they should be considered a separate part of speech or not depends largely upon the type of

analysis preferred by the grammarian. At any rate, they are easily identifiable by their invariability and their independence.

ää bagši "oh, teacher!"
xüi "stop! watch out!"

Summary. In accordance with the description given above, the parts of speech may be listed as follows:

1) Noun ("object-noun"): *širege* "table."
2) Adjective ("quality-noun"): *sayin* "good."
3) Numeral: *qoyar* "two."
4) Pronoun: *bi* "I."
5) Verb: *yabu-qu* "to go, going."
6) Adverb (including the "adverb-postposition" as a transitional category): *masi* "very," *dotora* "within."
7) Postposition: *tula* "because of."
8) Conjunction: *büged* "and."
9) Particle: *ese* "not," *ču* "indeed."
10) Interjection: *aa* (an exclamation used to call someone's attention).

III

NOUNS

DECLENSIONS

The declensional suffixes of nouns, although they fulfill functions similar to some postpositions, differ from them in that (1) they never have an existence independent of a noun or pronoun; (2) they are always subjected to vocalic harmony; and (3) they never have an initial accent. Any word having a full set of declensional suffixes is a noun.

In the written language, by the time the earliest documents make their appearance, these declensional suffixes have already undergone a certain amount of phonetic modification in adapting themselves to different noun stems. These same suffixes lingered on in written language long after their forms had undergone further modification in the spoken dialects.

As in Turkish, the plain noun stem serves as both nominative case and indefinite case.[59] The history of the noun stem is complicated by the fact that the written language and modern dialects have evolved separate paradigms with regard to a class of nouns called *-n* stems. Although the *-n* is historically not part of any suffix but belongs to the noun stem, for the sake of contrasting the nominative case with other case forms, the *-n* is included with the case suffix in the diagram given below.

In Khalkha, if the nominative case is taken as the base, then any one of the following suffixes may appear. A final short vowel of the nominative case is reduced or lost before the genitive and accusative, and lost before the ablative and instrumental. */v/* = vowel.

Nominative	-Ø.
Genitive	*(-g-)*[a] *-iin* / *-n* / *-ii*[b] / *-nii.*[c]
Dative-locative	*-dv* / *-tv* / *-ndv.*[c]
Accusative	*-g* / *(-g-)*[a] *-iig.*
Indefinite	-Ø.
Ablative	*(-g-)*[a] *-vvs* / *-nvvs.*[c]
Instrumental	*(-g-)*[a] *-vvr* / *-vvr.*

[a]*Consonne de liaison* used after stems ending in a long vowel or diphthong and followed by a long vowel or diphthong of a suffix. This *(-g-)* also follows stems ending in -ŋ < *-ng*. Only the latter type of word has *-giig* in the accusative case.

[b]Preceded by *-n*, which is the final constant consonant of an "absolute *-n* stem." When final in the nominative, it has the sound of [ŋ] (< [n]) in Khalkha but [n] in Ordos.

[c] "*-n* stem suffixes," which appear in the genitive, dative, and ablative cases of certain nouns whose nominative case ends in a short or long vowel. If the *-n* does appear in the instrumental case, it usually has a secondary meaning.

Cf. *utaagaar* "by means of smoke."
utaanaar "together with smoke."[60]

It is worth noting that the genitive case in Khalkha always has an *n* accompanied by a long vowel (or diphthong) either before or after it or both. This is important because it is in contrast to the situation in Ordos, where in two of the declensions (numbers five and six in A. Mostaert's Ordos grammar[61]) the *n* is accompanied by a short vowel under certain conditions. Moreover, the *-n* stem genitive is the *-n* stem, and the adjectival form of *-n* stem nouns have fallen together in Ordos.

1) Ordos: nom. *mu̯Du̯* "wood."
gen. *mu̯Du̯n DerɢeDe* "near the wood."
dat. *mu̯Du̯n-Du̯* "to the wood."
adj. *mu̯Dũ̯ Ger* "wooden house."

2) Khalkha: nom. *modo* "wood."
gen. *modonii gergede* "near the wood."
dat. *modon-do* "to the wood."
adj. *modon ger* "wooden house."

Since in Ordos *Gerĩĩ DerɢeDe* is "near the house," and in Khalkha *geriin dergede* means the same thing, it is clear that *dergede* governs the genitive case in both dialects. Hence, in *mu̯Du̯n DerɢeDe* / *mu̯Du̯ni DerɢeDe* (*TOO* XXIX) in Ordos, *mu̯Du̯n* is also in the genitive case although its suffix differs from that of the Khalkha form (*modonii*), and although it resembles the adjective (or *-n* stem) form which is found in *mu̯Dũ̯ Ger* "wooden house" (Khalkha, *modon ger*).

"-*N* STEMS"

Kotwicz, in a study on intercalary sounds in Turco-Mongolian,[62] discusses the role of *n* as an intercalary element in Turkish and

Mongolian languages. That the situation in Turkish resembles somewhat that in Mongolian may be observed also in A. von Gabain's *Alttürkische Grammatik.*[63] It should be pointed out here that *-n* stems are not to be confused with nouns having a final *-n* as a constant element. Except in the genitive, these nouns are declined like other consonant stem nouns. They might be called "absolute *-n* stems" to distinguish them from the "conditional *-n* stems" mentioned in note (c) above. The latter we shall continue to call "*-n* stems" for short. The history of the use of these *-n* stems varies with each dialect and has its own tradition in the written language. Below are given three paradigms of an *-n* stem noun, one from the written language, one from the Mogol dialect (its nearest counterpart in this instance), and one from Khalkha.

	Written Language	*Mogol*[64]	*Khalkha*
Nom.	*morin / mori*	*morin*	*mori*
Gen.	*morin-u (= *morin-ï)*[65]	*morinii*	*morinii*
Dat.	*morin-dur / morin-du*	*morindu*	*morindo*
Acc.	*morin-i*	*morinii*	*moriig*
Indef.	*mori*		*mori*
Abl.	*morin-ača / morin-ča*	*morinaasa*	*morinoos*
Instr.	*morin-iyar*	*morinaar*	*mor'oor*
Com. I	*mori-tai*		*moritee*
Com. II	*morin-luγa*	*morinlei*	

As may be seen from the above, the written language may retain the *-n* in all of its forms except the comitative in *-tvi*. Cf. *Buriat* below. In the nominative and the accusative, the *-n* appears or is omitted rather irregularly in the artificial "classical written language," but its use in these cases is more regular in the earlier written language of the thirteenth and fourteenth centuries. It is omitted in the indefinite case, leaving a vowel stem which spread eventually to the nominative case, as may be seen in several modern dialects.[66] In fact, the modern dialects may be arranged within two groups, one group retaining *n* in the nominative case, and the other omitting it. Aside from the nominative and accusative, the *n* has also disappeared from the instrumental case. Following is a summary of the situation in some of the major dialects.

Cases in which the -n stem appears:

1) *-n stem nominative group.*

a) *Written language; all cases* except the comitative in *-tvi* or *-tu*. It may be omitted in the nominative and accusative.

b) *Mogol; all cases.*

c) *Kalmuk; nominative,* genitive, dative, ablative, and comitative in -*lvv*.

d) *Buriat* (except Tsongol and Sartul); *nominative,* genitive, dative, ablative, "second instrumental," and comitative. Cf. (*BMS*, p. 795) *modon-toi*.

2) *Vowel stem nominative group:*

a) *Khalkha;* genitive, dative, ablative, and "second instrumental."

b) *Ordos;* genitive, dative, ablative, and comitative in -*lvv*.

c) *Monguor;* genitive and accusative (there are also alternate forms without the *n*).

d) *Dagur; n* generally omitted in all cases.

All the dialects, except Dagur, retain *n* in certain oblique cases: the genitive, dative, ablative, and comitative in -*lvv*. They omit *n* in other cases: accusative (except written Mongolian, Mogol, and Monguor), instrumental (except written Mongolian, Mogol, and those dialects having a "second instrumental"), and the comitative in -*tvi* (except Buriat). The Kalmuk directive case in -*uur* retains the *n*. Its counterpart in Khalkha and Buriat, -*ruu,* omits *n*. Compare the following forms in Buriat:

1) First instrumental.

modoor "by means of wood."

2) Second instrumental.

modnoor "together with wood."

These alternations, then, have a morphological function. The following examples show the same type of development:

1) Indefinite case.

Buriat, *uha ügei* "dépourvu d'eau."
Kalmuk, *mod čoluuγaar* "avec du bois et de la pierre."

2) Nominative case.

Buriat, *uhan ügei* "il n'y a pas d'eau."

3) Adjectival form.

Kalmuk, *modn̥ ger* "maison en bois."

In the modern dialects (except Mogol) the -*n* stem nouns have now become nouns with two stems, one with and the other without the *n* element. Their subsequent development has to be studied in each individual dialect, where the usage is more or less consistent within any one of them. They have not all survived alike in all dialects. The effect of analogical formation has created new *-n* stems of this type in some dialects, and destroyed old ones in others. In some instances, a noun used as an *-n* stem means one thing, and as a vowel stem means another.

Cf. Ordos *Go't'on-Du* "in the enclosure."
Go't'o-Du "in the town."

The following nouns illustrate the adjectival form of the *-n* stem itself (i.e., as attribute before another noun).

nogoon "green."	Cf. *nogoo* "vegetable."
möngön "of silver."	Cf. *möngö* "silver."
modon "wooden."	Cf. *modo* "tree."
altan "golden."	Cf. *alta* "gold."
yuun "what kind of?"	Cf. *yuu* "what?"

Cf. (*SH* § 255)[67] *Ogödei ya'u ke'emü*? "Was sagt Ogodai?"
(*SH* § 156) *či ya'un gü'ün bui*? "What person art thou?"

Also, by analogy, the Tibetan loan-word *sirü* "coral" becomes *šüren* as an adjective in Khalkha. Cf. *šüren xaalga* "coral gates." The numerals, except *xoyor* "two," have a final *-n* when used attributively before a noun.

gurwan džil "three years." Cf. *bide gurwa* "we three."

Aside from the appearance of the *-n* stem in the oblique cases mentioned above, *it is also used with certain postpositions,* such as *deere, doro, teeši,* and *dotoro* (Khalkha).

usan deer "on the water."
ayagan dotor "in the cup."

As for the "absolute *-n* stems," in Khalkha they belong to the regular consonant stems, with the *n* appearing in all cases. In Ordos, the genitive suffix is short: Ordos, *-ni,* cf. Khalkha, *-nii.* These nouns ending in absolute *n* are common everyday words for the most part. Vladimircov classifies them as follows:[68] (1) nouns referring to reasoning beings, (2) loan-words from other languages, (3) words having derivational suffixes ending in *-n*, and (4) a certain number of unclassified common words of everyday usage.

öxin "girl," *edzen* "master," *byarman* "Brahman," *öwgön* "old man," *oyuu-tan* "student," *xün* "person," *xen* "who?", *irgen* "people," *dzun* "summer," *mörön* "river," *oron* "place" (but, *oro* "bed," which is a conditional *-n* stem). Since final *-n* has become a velar nasal in Khalkha, these endings have the same sound as words ending in an original velar *n*. In Ordos, however, the final *-n* of absolute *-n* stems has remained alveolar.

Written language *ǰobalang* "suffering" > Kh., *dzowolon(g)*.

In Rudnev's *Hori-buryatskiĭ govor,*[69] the noun paradigms include a case called the *inessive* which is not in the paradigms of other Mongolian dialects. It is added to the *n* of *-n* stems; cf. *modon-soo* "in the forest, into the forest." The suffix *-soo* does not follow the vocalic harmony of the word to which it is attached. In a letter to Rudnev, Ramstedt explained the form as follows: cf. Manchu *do* "interior," Mong. *doto-na*; **dotšo* > Buriat **dosoo* (Mongolian *č* > *s* in Buriat) > *soo*.[70] This suffix is not to be confused with another suffix *-soo* (also, *-saa* / *-see*, etc.) which does follow vocalic harmony and which corresponds to *-tš'ē* / *-tš'ȫ* in Ordos meaning "up to the height of." It is called the *limitatif* in the Ordos grammar.[71] In his discussion of the dative case, Rudnev also includes the postpositions *deere* and *doro* as forming related "cases." In keeping with the overall treatment of postpositions in this study, I have placed these Buriat examples along with the other examples of postpositional phrases. The suffix *-soo,* however, seems to be less independent syntactically than postpositions in general. Since there are other types of transitional cases, this might also be included among them. The only other possible designation for *-soo* would be that of declensional suffix, as Rudnev indicated. It does exhibit a peculiarity which some postpositions do have in Buriat, namely, its association with oblique pronoun stems.

Cf. (*WY*, p. 98, l. 13) *tegün degere* "on it."
(*HB*, p. XLVI) *nam-soo* "in me."

The use of the oblique pronoun stems and the general use of the *n* of *-n* stem nouns with postpositions whose initial is a dental seems to indicate that these high frequency postpositions (*deere, doro, dotoro,* and *teeši*) tend to be treated as case suffixes. Indeed, in Ordos *deere* often loses its basic vowel quality and tends to be assimilated to the vowel of the preceding word.

Cf. (*TOO*, p. XLI) *t'anǟᴅār* "chez vous."
(*TOO*, p. 32) *nege ǟlᴅār* "chez une famille."

With regard to the appearance of *n* in the conditional *-n* stems before the postpositions with an initial dental consonant which govern the indefinite case, that the *n* element contrasts with other syntactical constructions is clear from the following examples.

1) With the *n*.

(*TOO*, p. 61) *t'ere ųsųnᴅār i'tš'ēt* "entrés dans cette eau."
(*TOO*, p. 152) *t'ogǫō̄ ᴅo't'oro* "dans la marmite."
(*DO*, p. 473a) *t'ogō̄ mųᴅų* "tuyau de pipe à tabac."

2) Without the *n*.

(TOO, p. 503) *šine emtš'ēs širgēsen ųsų* ᴅēre "de l'eau bouillie vaut mieux qu'un médecin novice." Here *ųsų* "water" is subject, and ᴅēre "is better" is predicate.

(*TOO*, p. 164) *nege t'ogǭ ųsų* "une chaudière d'eau." The function of *t'ogǭ* "marmite" in this phrase is quite different from that found in the third phrase of (1).

That these postpositions govern the indefinite case (= the stem) may be seen from the following examples.

(*TOO*, p. 26) *ɢ̡ä ɢ̡aᴅžar* ᴅ*orǟs, ɢ̡alų̄ ųsųn* ᴅ*o't'orǟs* "un malheur sort de dessous terre, une oie sort de dessous l'eau."

(*DzDz*, p. 122) *bulag deer* "at the spring."

(Kh, p. 141) *dalai dotor* "in the sea."

(*Kh*, p. 74) *gadzar doro* "unter der Erde."

In summary, then, we may say that the *n* element discussed in this chapter falls into at least four different categories, namely, (1) phonetic, (2) morphological, (3) syntactical, and (4) analogical (see below). That they may be associated with nouns called *-n* stems collectively is justified by the fact that, irrespective of the function, only certain nouns exhibit these features, and if they exhibit one of them, they also *usually* exhibit the others.

Within number (4) above, I have included those forms which are in free alternation (i.e., with no change of meaning).

Cf. (*TOO*, p. XXX) D.-Loc. *k'īn*ᴅɯ / *k'ī*ᴅɯ "in the air."
Abl. *noχ⁻nǟs / noχ⁻gǟs* "from the dog."
Abl. *t'ɯrīnēs / t'ɯrīgēs* "from the bootleg."
Com. *tš'ǟnlā / tš'ǟlā* "with tea."

In a letter of July 23, 1951, Mr. William Austin has given me some information about the Chahar dialect. He summarizes the *-n* stems as follows: "I think I can state categorically that when a noun precedes another it takes the attributive *-n* ending if it is an *-n*-stem. Thus we have *šireen deer, araban hün, cagaan bicig*. If it is not an *-n*-stem there is no *-n* attributive, as *ger deer, har hün*, etc.

"My informant says *šireen deer* but *šireegiin, šireegees*, etc. The whole *-n*-stem business is breaking up in spoken Mongol, and the informant is never quite certain about it. Nouns ending in double vowels are generally *-n*-stems, but *ögl̈öö* isn't, and *širee* is only partially."

In comparison with the examples I have been able to obtain from the written language and from colloquial transcriptions, the irregularity of *širee*, mentioned in Mr. Austin's letter, differs from them in that the appearance of *n* before *deer* makes it practically certain that it appears with the dative-locative suffix, i.e., *šireende* and not *šireede*. However, since another Mongolian dialect, namely Dagur, has no *-n* stem forms whatsoever, it seems quite reasonable to suppose that in some areas the *-n* stems are still being modified in one way or another, in this case, by progressive disappearance.

SYNTAX

Noun declensions are important in the study of postpositional phrases because the postpositions themselves govern different cases (see pages 29-31), primarily the indefinite, genitive, dative-locative, and ablative, as well as the conditional *-n* stem. The comparison of different texts old and modern reveals that some postpositions are found in all of them, while others belong to a certain period or a certain dialect. The same may be said of the *cases* governed by postpositions. The following are a few examples of the postposition *adali* "like, as" in phrases taken from varied texts. The early examples all seem to agree in using this postposition with the dative-locative case.

(*SH* § 155) *Yesügen-qatun-u üge-tür adali* "conforme à ce qu'en avait dit (m. à m. 'aux paroles de') Yesügen-qatun."[72]

(*1338*, l. 34) *uqaγan bilig-tür inu adali* "in a manner becoming his understanding and wisdom."

(*SK*, p. 78) *nadur adali* "gleich mir."

In the later language, there is a preference for the comitative case in conjunction with *adali*. The Kalmuk dialect is an exception in that the dative is used as an alternate construction.

(*SS*, p. 284, l. 9) *ötele kümün-lüge adali* "like a common man."
(*TOO*, p. 231) *eme k'ɯnlē aᴅali* "semblable à une femme."
(*Kh*, p. 149) *idžiitee adilxan* "like the mother."
(*N*) *nadtai adil* "like myself."
(*KD*, p. 21) *nandᴰtɛ̄ (nandᴰ / namlā̈) ädḽ* "wie ich, mir ähnlich."

As between Khalkha and Ordos, the latter prefers the comitative in *-lvv*, while the former uses the comitative in *-tvi*.

Sometimes within the same dialect, the postposition governs one case with nouns and another with pronouns.

Khalkha indefinite case *ger dzüg* "to the house."
Khalkha genitive case *tüünii dzüg* "in his direction."

Since the term "nominative case" is used when the noun stem is subject of the verb, the term "indefinite case" may be used to include other uses. In the expression *ene edür* "today" < "this day," which may be used adverbially, the word *edür* is in its minimal form, the same form it has as subject of a verb. By a reverse process, some adverbs and postpositions may appear as subjects of verbs, or as predicate nouns.

Cf. (*SH* § 68) *dotora* *minu ma'ui bui* "in meinem Innern ist mir schlecht."

(*CIN*) *učir ni . . . dayisun baraγun Ewöröpe-eče bosuγsan-u tula bolai* "the reason is because an enemy . . . has arisen in Western Europe."

(*TOO*, p. 152) *t'ogǭǭ Do't'or wī* "il (i.e., le manger) est dans la marmite."

This would be confusing, were it not for the fact that the words in question deviate from ordinary nouns by their lack of complete declensional inflexion and by their position in the syntax of a sentence. As far as their minimal form is concerned, they are not different from ordinary noun-stems, as may be seen from the following list of concrete nouns whose final syllables duplicate those of words used as postpositions.

Final Syllable of Postpositions Compared with Those of Nouns

a/e.	*tala* "steppe," *ǰula* "lamp," *kele* "tongue," *ǰige / ǰege* "grandson through daughter."
da/de.	*ǰida* "lance," *γangda* "drought," *ide* "skill," *tede* "they," *činda* "solid," *quda* "relative," *neyite* "common."
du/dü.	*amidu* "living creature," *kürdü(n)* "wheel," *kündü* "weight."
γa/ge.	*ǰiluγa* "reins," *qayaγa* "horizon," *taγa* "desire," *serege* "fork," *baraγa* "goods," *medege* "knowledge."
si.[a]	*idesi* "food," *tülesi* "fuel."
γu/gü.	*biraγu* "one year old calf," *qataγu* "hard."
γur/gür.	*naγur* "lake," *elgügür* "hanger," *selbigür* "oar," *iǰaγur* "origin."
i.	*aγali* "character," *qauli* "law," *qočurli* "remainder," *soγtanggi* "drunk," *ǰali* "flame," *qarsi* "court."
na/ne.	*qana* "wall," *bataγana* "fly," *quluγana* "mouse," *kögelǰirgene* "pigeon."
ra/re.	*qura* "rain," *ikere* "twins," *üre* "seed," *sira* "white," *qara* "black," *nemüre* "addition." *(SH) odora* "arrow."
tu/tü.	*sutu* "fortunate," *nasutu* "old man," *šatu* "stairs," *mori-tu* "having a horse."

[a]N.B. words ending in *-γsi / -gsi* belong to only one class, namely that of adverbs (of direction). They may be used as postpositions, and, as such, govern the ablative.

The simple Mongolian sentence usually observes the following word order.

1) Expressions (including postpositional phrases) answering the question *where, how,* and *when.*

2) Subject modifier (if any), plus subject, plus pronoun modifiers (if any) such as *minu* "my," etc., *bügüde* "all," *büri* "each," etc.

3) Object of verb (with modifiers if any).

4) Verb (with modifiers if any).

There are exceptions in colloquial speech where the verb-object sometimes follows the verb for the sake of emphasis. In any case, the key word is likely to be last, whether within a phrase, or within the entire sentence. As a result, words indicating *time, place,* and *manner* appear so frequently in a fixed word order, that they have always been identified as adverbs by Mongolianists. Many of these adverbs serve easily in postpositional phrases, which, in turn, are often adverbial modifiers themselves.

In other words, a Mongolian word (but not a verb) appearing in its minimal form may be a noun, an adjective (but -*n* stems retain their *n*), or an adverb, its formal identification being dependent upon its position in a sentence. Only a few words appear only as postpositions. Most of the others, aside from appearing as post-postions, may also be used in other constructions, where they might be classified as nouns, adjectives, or adverbs. That adverbs are closely related to nouns is illustrated by the fact that they may be modified by personal pronouns and other nouns.

Cf. *dotora minu* "within me."
minii tende "there where I live" (= "my there").

The indefinite case.[73] The indefinite case always has the same form as the nominative case of substantives (except in those dialects mentioned on pages 35 and 36). It is used in place of the accusative whenever the reference is indefinite. We have seen that adjectives are never in the indefinite case as verb-object (see page 28). It is found in situations such as the following.

1) *Mass-words,* objects which are not precisely delimited and which are not completely acted upon by the verb.

maxa idexe "to eat (some) meat."
tsai uuxa "to drink (some) tea."

2) *Creation,* the designation of objects which are created in the course of the action of the verb.

ger barixa "to build a house."

3) *Conventional expressions*, composed of words closely associated in one idea.

nom un(g)šixa "to read a book."
bitšig bitšixe "to write a letter."
maani un(g)šixa "to say a prayer."
xele surxa "to learn a language."
mori unaxa "to ride a horse."
ünee saaxa "to milk a cow."
yasa barixa "to set a bone."
aduu aduulxa "to pasture the horses."
mal xar'uulxa "to drive cattle."
oros xele surxa "to learn the Russian language."

4) *Specification*, answering the question "in what respect?"

xöl nütsegen xün "a bare-footed person."

5) *Location*, in answer to the question "where?"

ene gadzar suudži baina "lives in this region."

6) *Direction*, answering the question "to what place?"

ta xoto ornuu "are you going to town?"

7) *Designation of change of status*.

tüüniig said songowo "they elected him minister."

8) *Time*, as duration or point of time.

gurwan sara yawadzää "traveled for three months."
xoito džil irene "comes next year."

9) *Complement*, with verbs which are otherwise intransitive.

usa garxa "to cross over the water."
dawaa dawaxa "to cross over a pass."

10) *Iteration*, in answer to the question "how many times?"

gurwa xonoson "spent the night three times (= spent three nights)."

11) *Co-ordination*, in which the indefinite case appears in all co-ordinated members except the last, which may be in any case.

modo tšuluugaar barisan baišin "a structure built of wood and stone."

12) *Postpositional object*, in connection with many postpositions.

ulaan baatar xürtel "as far as Ulan Bator."

IV

PRONOUNS

DECLENSIONS

Written language, medieval, and Khalkha pronoun-declensions. Since the pattern of declension is typical for the other personal and demonstrative pronouns, only the following two have been selected here; *bi* "I," *tere* "that, he, she, it."

	Written Language		*Khalkha*	
Nom.	*bi*		*bi*	
Gen.	*minu*		*minii*	
Dat.	*nadur*	*nama-du*	*nadada*	*nada*
	nada			
Acc.	*namayi*	*nama* (*SH* § 179)	*namaig(i)*	
Abl.	*nadača*	*nama-ača*	*nadaas*	
	nada-ača			
Instr.	*nada-bar*	*namabar*[74]	*nadaar*	
		nama'ar (*SH* § 53)		
Com.	*nada-luγa*	*nama-luγa*	*nadatai*	
Nom.	*tere*		*tere*	
Gen.	*tegün-ü*		*tüünii*	*terüünii*
Dat.	*tegün-dü(r)*	*tegün-e*	*tüünde*	*terüünde*
Acc.	*tegün-i*		*tüüniig(i)*	*terüüniig(i)*
Abl.	*tegün-če*	*tegün-eče*	*tüünees*	*terüünees*
Instr.	*tegün-iyer*	*tegü-ber*	*tüügeer*	*terüügeer*
Com.	*tegün-lüge*		*tüüntei*	*terüüntei*

The Khalkha dialect has also another stem for the oblique cases of *tere:* gen. *ternii,* acc. *terniig,* abl. *ternees.*

The declensional suffixes of pronouns are the same as those for nouns, and they exist under the same circumstances (such as vocalic harmony, etc.). Personal and demonstrative pronouns have two or more stems. An indefinite case is not used, except possibly in the form *nama* "me" which occurs a few times in the *Secret History* (see below). Since a number of oblique stems occur in the declensions of demonstrative pronouns, it has been considered convenient to call the nominative form "the nominative stem." In some dialects the latter is one of the stems used in forming the oblique cases. Cf. Chahar acc. *teriig* "him" < *tere* "he."

Aside from Khalkha, other Mongolian dialects have a number of oblique stems in the various pronominal cases. The dialect development is more varied than in the case of nouns.

	Secret History		*Mukaddimat al-Adab*	
Nom.	*tere*	*ene* "this"	*tere*	*ene* "this"
Gen.	*te'ün-ü*		*tüüni*	
Dat.	*te'ün-tür*		*tüündü(r)*	
Acc.		*e'üni*	*tüüni*	*eneni*
Abl.		*e'ün-eče*	*tüüneese*	*üüneese*
Instr.	*te'ü-ber*			
Com.			*tüünlee*	

	Ordos		*Buriat*
Nom.	*t'ere*	*t'ere*	*tere*
Gen.	*t'ɯ̄n(i)*	*t'erɯ̄n(i)*	*tere(e)nei*
Dat.	*t'ɯ̄nᴅɯ*	*t'erɯ̄nᴅɯ*	*tere(e)nde*
Acc.	*t'ɯ̄nī(ɡ)*	*t'erɯ̄nī(ɡ)*	*tere(e)nii(ye)*
Abl.	*t'ɯ̄nēs*	*t'erɯ̄nēs*	*tere(e)nhee*
Instr.	*t'ɯŋɡēr*	*t'erɯŋɡēr*	*tereegeer*
Com.	*t'ɯ̄nt'ī*	*t'erɯ̄nt'ī*	*tere(e)ntei*
Soc.	*t'ɯ̄nle*	*t'erɯ̄nlē*	
Dir.	*t'ɯ̄nlɯ̄*	*t'erɯ̄nlɯ̄*	*tere(e)ruu*

In those dialects where the element *-ruu* "towards," which is sometimes called the directive case, does not follow vocalic harmony (as in the case of Buriat), it is just as easily classified as a postposition rather than as a declensional suffix. Ordos also has acc. *t'ɯ̄n* / *t'erɯ̄n*, instr. *t'erɯ'ᵏχēr*, dir. *t'enlɯ̄* / *t'erelɯ̄*.

	Kalmuk		*Chahar*
Nom.	*tere*	*tere*	*ter*
Gen.	*tüünee*	*terüünee*	*ternei*
Dat.	*tüünde*	*terüünde*	*terüünd*
Acc.	*tüüg*	*terüüg*	*teriig*
Abl.	*tüünees*	*terüünees*	*ternees*
Instr.	*tüügeer*	*terüügeer*	*terneer*
Com.	*tüütee*	*terüütee*	*terüüntei*
Soc.	*tüünlee*	*terüünlee*	
Dir.	*tüünüür*	*terüünüür*	

	Dagur	*Monguor*	*Mogol*
Nom.	т̔ε̊рε̊	*t'ie*	*te*
Gen.	т̔ε̊рī́	*t'ie(ni)*	*tenni*
Dat.	т̔ε̊рε̊нд̬ε̆	*t'iänDu*	*tendɯ*
Acc.	т̔ε̊рī́	*t'ie(ni)*	*tenni*
Abl.	т̔ε̊рε̊̄с(ε̆)	*t'iänDza*	*tenaasa*
Instr.	т̔ε̊рε̊̄гε̊̄р	*t'iera*	*tenaγaar*
Com.	т̔ε̊рε̆н т̔ᵉī	*t'iela*	
Loc.		*t'iera*	

The oblique stems found in the above dialects are: *tüü(n)-* (< *tegün-*), *terüü(n)-*, *tere(n)-*, and *te(n)-*. *Tüün-* is found in the Written Language, Khalkha, Buriat, Ordos, and Kalmuk. *Terüü(n)-* is found in Khalkha, Buriat, Ordos, Kalmuk, and Chahar. *Tere(n)-* is found in Buriat and Dagur. *Te(n)-* is found in Monguor and Mogol.

	Ordos	*Buriat*	*Kalmuk*
Nom.	*Bi*	*bi*	*bi*
Gen.	*mini*	*minii*	*mini*
Dat.	*naDa*	*namda*	*nanda*
Acc.	*namā̈(g)*	*namää(yi)*	*namää(g)*
Abl.	*naDās*	*namhaa*	*nanaas*
Instr.	*naDār*	*namaar*	*nanaar*
Com.	*naDa't'ā̈*	*namtää*	*nantää*
Soc.	*naDalā*		
Dir.	*naDalų̄*		*nanuur*

	Chahar	*Dagur*	*Monguor*
Nom.	*bi*	бî	*Bu*
Gen.	*minii*	мíнī́	*muni*
Dat.	*nad(ad)*	намă̆дă̆	*nDā*
Acc.	*namaig*	намᵃī̌	*nDā* (< dative)
Abl.	*nadaas*	намāс	*nDāDza*
Instr.	*nadaar*	намāр	*nDāra*
Com.	*nadtai*	нам т̔ᵃī	*nDāla*
Loc.			*munire*

In Mogol the pronoun *tši* "thou" has the following forms: gen. and acc. *tšinei* / *tšamei*, abl. *tšinaasa*, instr. *tšinaar*, and com.

tšinalee. Cf. also Mogol dat. _nanda_ "to me." The following alternate forms occur: Ordos gen. _minī,_ dat. _namǟᴅų,_ instr. _namǟǫār,_ soc. _namǟlā,_ dir. _naᴅarų̄;_ Buriat dat. _nadada;_ Dagur dat. намдă̌ / надда̌; Kalmuk gen. _minee._

In his article on pronouns,[75] Ramstedt points out that the form _nadur_ "to me" is derived from _*nan-dur._ The _*nan-_ itself goes back to _nama-_ < _*nima-_ < _*mima-._ Cf. Bur. _namada,_ Kalm. _nanda_ < _*namda,_ and Sel. _naada_ < _*nanda._ In Khalkha _nada_ < _*nanda_ forms a new stem and a new dative _nada-da._ The new Khalkha stem _nada-_ is used with all the oblique case endings except in the genitive and accusative.

Ramstedt's comparative study leads to the supposition that, along with the stem _min-_ (in the gen. _minu_) and _*tin-_ (in the gen. _*tinu;_ note also _man-u, tan-u, man-dur,_ etc.), there are also original stems _*mima-_ and _*tima-._ The latter occur primarily in the accusative, written _namayi, čimayi_ with corresponding forms in the later dialects. The extent of the usage of _nama-_ as an oblique case stem may be seen from the paradigms given above. The pronominal stems, on the whole, show a great amount of analogical re-formation. The stem _*nan-_ in _*nandur_ is also a development which goes back to _nama-_ (i.e., instead of _*min-dur_ or _*min-da;_ cf. Turk. loc. _men-de_).

As in the case of _nama-_ where there appears a _nan-_ / _nana-,_ so in the case of _čima-_ we have _čin-_ / _čina-_ which is attested in the glossary of _Ibn-Muhanna_ in the forms of gen. _čini,_ dat. _čina-dur,_ acc. _činai,_ and abl. _činaača._[76] Cf. also Mogol gen. _tšinei,_ abl. _tšinaasa,_ instr. _tšinaar,_ and com. _tšinalee._ Ramstedt was inclined to believe that _nama_ and _čima_ were originally used as accusatives and that later they became stems for other cases through a process of analogical development. In Mogol, where accusative and genitive have acquired the same form, the accusative _namɛi_ is also a genitive; cf. _namɛi köɯn_ = _köɯ-mi_ "my son."

With regard to the possible accusative origin of the stems _nama_ and _čima,_ mentioned above, it is worth while noting the following passages from the _Secret History,_ where _nama_ is used as an accusative form:

(_SH_ § 130) _Qoriǰin-qatun Qu'určin-qatun ǰirin nama ülü teri'ülen Ebegei-yi teri'ülen ker tüsürüyü_ "Comment verse-t-on en ne commençant pas par moi, mais en commençant par Ebegei?"[77]

(_SH_ § 177) _Qan ečige minu ya'un čimar-tur nama ayu'ulba či_ "Mon père qan, à cause de quel grief m'as-tu effrayé?"[78]

(_SH_ § 181) _nama naidaǰu hüldebe-ǰe či_ "par jalousie tu m'as chassé."

(*SH* § 207) *ǰöng ǰöb bolu'asu tenggeri-de sedkil-tür gürgegde'esü nama γučin emestü bolγa ke'ele'e či* "Thou didst say, 'If the prophecy be fulfilled and if thanks to Heaven (thy) desires be realized, let me have thirty women.'"[79]

Nama occurs once in the *Hua-i i-yü* (IIa 20r), and Lewicki identifies it as a dative-locative on page 125 of his grammar.[80]

It is worth noting that the stem of the Ordos forms *namāDu*, *namāgār*, *namālā* are derived from a regular accusative *namā* < *namayi*, an alternate form of *namāg*.

In the light of the above, one is tempted to look for such forms as **čima* or **čina* used under similar circumstances. These forms are not attested as yet. However, Poppe mentions the use of *ima* as an accusative form attested in the *Siddhikür* published by Jülg.[81] Whatever the etymological origin of these forms may be, their later usage is quite clear. In the first place, they are stems used with declensional suffixes to form oblique cases. In the second place, they are pronominal equivalents of the suffixless noun forms used before certain postpositions. Cf. *ger deere* "to the yurt," *nama deere / nada deere* "to me." The oblique stem of demonstrative pronouns also alternates with the "nominative stem" in conjunction with this type of postposition. Cf. *tere deere* = *tüün deere* "on it."

As for the demonstrative pronouns, if the forms in which the old written language stems *egün-* and *tegün-* exist in the modern dialects are examined, it is found that they regularly become *üün-* and *tüün-*. Note for example the Buriat gen. *üünii* "of this," and *tüünii* "of that." In Kalmuk and particularly in Khalkha *üün-* has given way to the analogical formation *enüün-*, since the former was possibly too little differentiated from *tüün-* and its connection with *ene* might not have been sufficiently felt. After the appearance of *enüün-* and in Kalmuk *ünüün-*, Khalkha also developed a *terüün-* and Kalmuk *terüün-*, *türüün-*, and *tünüün-*. Cf. Khalkha Urga gen. *enüünii*, *terüünii*; Kalmuk acc. *ünüüg*, *tünüüg*[75] (note also *üüg* and *tüüg*).

Aside from the Monguor *t'ie* and the Mogol *te* "that" as possible original stems, one should note the form *te-li* "that" (*SH* § 246; *1362*, l. 53).

The oblique stems of the demonstrative pronouns *tere* and *ene* exhibit a characteristic which is common to *-n* stem nouns as described in chapter three, namely a stem contrast between the ablative and instrumental cases. Cf. Kh. abl. *morinoos* "from the horse," instr. *mor'or* "by the horse"; *galuunaas* "from the wild goose," *galuugaar* "by the wild goose." The pronoun *tere* shows the following forms: (ablative) written language *tegün-eče*, Kh.

and Kalm. *tüünees / terüünees*, Ord. *t'ūnēs / t'erūnēs*, Bur. *tere(e)nhee*, Chahar *ternees*, Monguor *t'iänDza*, Mogol *tenaasa*. The instrumental cases are as follows: written language *tegü-ber*, Kh. and Kalm. *tüügeer / terüügeer*, Ord. *t'erɯ'ᵏχēr*, Bur. *tereegeer*, and Monguor *t'iera*.

The *-n* stem instrumental is found in the following: written language *tegün-iyer*, Ord. *t'ūŋgēr / t'erɯŋgēr*, Chahar *terneer*, and Mogol *tenaγaar*.

Whether this persistent feature of stem distinction originated with pronouns or nouns is not clear. In any case, the pronominal feature places pronouns closer in morphology to *-n* stem nouns. As with the latter, the common postpositions with an initial dental are preceded by the *-n* stem form. Cf. *tüün deere* "on it," *morin deere* "on the horse."

The archaic pronouns **i-* "he, she, it," and **a-* "they" are attested only as roots of oblique stems. The later written language makes frequent use of the genitive forms *inu* and *anu* as enclitic pronouns, sometimes in their possessive meaning and sometimes as a sort of definite article. They have become one form in the modern dialects, i.e., *-(v)n*, with no distinction between singular and plural. The attested forms found in old texts are as follows:

	Singular	*Plural*
Gen.	*inu*	*anu*
Dat.	*imadur*	*andur* (*SH* § 165)
	imada	*ana* (*1291*, l. 10)
Acc.	*imayi*	*ani* (*SH* § 84)
	ima (see note 81)	
Instr.	*ima'ari* (*SH* § 167)	
Abl.	*imadača* (*1338*, l. 22)	
Com.	*imaluγ-a* (*1335*, l. 14)	

Concerning *ima* Ramstedt has the following to say:

"Ein meines wissens nur von Jülg in seiner verdienstvollen ausgabe des Siddhikūr vorgeführtes wort ist sing. *ima* 'er' (auch *ima γurban* 'sie drei' eig. 'er drei' wie *tere γurban* 'die drei'), das von keinem anderen forscher bisher weder gefunden noch angenommen zu sein scheint. Ich habe für meine person keinen grund die richtigkeit seiner lesart zu bezweifeln, obwohl auch ich das wort in keiner mundart kenne. Das wort *ima* ist seiner bildung nach mit dem stamme *nama* und *čima* zu vergleichen und gehört als nom. akk. zu dem stamme **in-* gen. *inu* 'ejus,' vgl. mandsch. *i* 'is,' gen. *ini* 'ejus,' akk. *imbe* 'eum.' Es bleibt nur die frage zu beantworten, woher hat der kalmückische übersetzer oder besser transskriptor des Siddhikūr dieses wort *ima* genommen, aus einem west- oder einem ostmongolischen dialekte?"[75]

In a letter to me dated 13 June 1951 Professor Poppe pointed out that in Kalmuk they say *man dörwlääge* < **man dörbegüle-yi* "us four together." This is similar to the phrase *ima γurban* "sie drei" from the Siddhikūr text cited above.

In the modern dialects, **i-* and **a-* pronouns have all disappeared with the exception of the enclitic form *-(v)n* "his, her, its, their, the" < *inu / anu*. In the old language *inu* and *anu* could be governed by postpositions. Cf. (*Ölǰeitü*, l. 30) *anu degere* "against (= on) them." The modern language has *deeren* < *degere inu* (or *anu*) "on him, her, it, them."

ENCLITIC PRONOUNS

The genitive form of the personal pronouns may be used as unaccented endings to nouns, adjectives, nomina verbalia, and converba. In Khalkha they are as follows:

	Singular	*Plural*
1)	*-min* "my"	*-man* "our"
2)	*-tšin* "thy"	*-tan* "your"
3)	*-n* "his, her, its; the"	*-n* "their; the"

axamin "my elder brother," *axatšin* "thy elder brother," *axaman* "our elder brother," *axatan* "your elder brother," *axan* "his, her, or their elder brother; the elder brother."

The endings *-man* and *-tan* do not follow vocalic harmony.

When the word ends in a consonant the third person suffix *-n* acquires a glide-vowel: *geren* "his yurt," *garan* "his hand."

These possessive endings are added to the case suffixes in oblique cases: *axadan* "to his elder brother," *gereesmin* "out of my yurt."

Adverbs of place may also take these possessive endings. *Deere* as an adverb means "above" and as a postposition "on." Syntactically it is still an adverb when it has a possessive ending, but its use is similar to that of a postposition following a pronoun: *nama deere* = *deeremin* "on me." The selection of one or the other phrase is idiomatic and indicates primarily a shift of emphasis.

It follows that many common postpositional words also occur as adverbs with these possessive endings.

(*Kh*, p. 153) *tsaanatšin* "that side of thee."

(*Kh*, p. 57) *deeremin* "on me," *deeretšin* "on thee," *deeren* "on him, her, it, or them," *deereman* "on us," *deeretan* "on you."

(*SH* § 174) *de'ere inu* "sur lui."

(*BE*, p. 52) *dergede anu* "[kam] zu ihm."

(*SH* § 173) *doro inu* "sous lui."

(*Kh*, p. 142) *dotortšin* "in thee."
(*Kh*, p. 143) *dotoron* "in it."
(*MKB*, p. 65) *dundani* "in the middle of it."
(*BE*, p. 52) *emüne anu* "davor."
(*Kh*, p. 110) *xoorondoon* "untereinander."
(*SH* § 177) *esergü činu* "à ta rencontre."

Nomina verbalia having possessive endings always function as nouns: *yawadag* "one who habitually goes," *yawadagan* "his frequent going."

With converbs the possessive endings indicate the actor: *yawaxlaar* "as soon as [one] goes," *yawaxlaaran* "as soon as *he* goes," *irtel* "until [one] comes," *iretelen* "until *he* comes."

Nominative forms of pronouns are used as suffixes in Buriat and Kalmuk: Bur. *axab* < *aqa bi* "I am the elder," Kalm. *irsm-b* < *iregsen bi* "I came."

The accented and unaccented forms of the pronouns such as *minii* ~ *-min*, *tanii* ~ *-tan* may be compared with accented and unaccented Latin *me* as it survives in modern French, *moi* ~ *me*.

SYNTAX

The syntax of postpositional phrases where the postposition governs a noun has been discussed in the section on syntax, chapter three. For the most part, the cases governed by postpositions are the same for both nouns and pronouns. Cf. Kh. *aawiin dergede* "in the presence of the father" and *tüünii dergede* "near him." The genitive case is used with *dergede* whether the postpositional object is a noun or a pronoun.

However, in the case of certain common postpositions indicating locality or direction and governing the stem directly, the existence of at least two pronoun stems has led to the use of either, with slight semantic differentiations, in most dialects. Cf. *tere deere* / *tüün deere* "on it." That the oblique stem *tüün* used with these postpositions may have been reduced from a genitive and that its present form may also have been influenced by analogy with the dative stem as in *tüün-de* "to him" are factors which should be considered. The postpositions under discussion are *degere, doora, dotora,* and *tegesi*. In written language texts the use of the genitive with these postpositions is more frequent than in spoken language texts, but on the whole, even in written language texts, the stem as object is more frequent. That the genitive may have been an older usage is possible in view of the following phenomena:

1) Whereas modern dialects agree in the construction of phrases like *morin deere* "on the horse," and *usun deere* "on the water," old colloquial forms may be observed in the *Mukaddimat al-Adab* such as

(*MSM*, p. 148b) *morini deere* and (*MSM*, p. 369b) *usuni deere* where the postposition governs the genitive. However, it should be pointed out that the *Mukaddimat al-Adab* shows an alternation of *-u* and *-i* for the genitive suffix; hence, (*MSM*, p. 71) *toγaanu* / *toγaani* "of the caldron," (*MSM*, p. 238) *morinu* / *morini* "of the horse." Cf. also the accusative forms (*MSM*, p. 72) *γali* "fire," *γaǰari* "land," *usuni* "water," and *miqani* "meat." The accusative and the genitive have the same form in Mogol, Dagur, and Monguor. The genitive is used with *deere* in Dagur and Monguor: (*Dagur*) *aŭl'ī dḗr* "on the mountain," (*Monguor*, p. 17) *śirie(ni)* Dẹ̌re "on the table." The following construction is used in Mogol: (*Mogholica*, p. 4) *morin deerȧ* "auf das pferd," but the genitive and accusative forms of *morin* are both *morinii*. In Khalkha the possessive suffixes (non-reflexive) have caused a "falling together" of the genitive and accusative forms; cf. gen. *geriin* (with velar *-n*) and acc. *geriig* "house."

a) With *inu*.

Gen. and acc. *geriin* < *ger-ün inu* (gen.) / *ger-i inu* (acc.)

The final *-n* is alveolar.

b) With *minu*.

Gen. and acc. *geriimin* < *ger-ün minu* (gen.) / *ger-i minu* (acc.)

The final *-n* is alveolar.

The genitive form of *-n* stems in Ordos is the *-n* stem itself which alternates occasionally with *-ni*. Cf. *muDun* / *muDuni* "of the tree." The adjective form in *-n* and the genitive have merged into one form. Cf. *muDũ* Ger "a wooden house" (adjective form), *muDũ* Gö̌sɯ̄ "a branch of a tree" (genitive form; i.e., not "a wooden branch"). It is therefore difficult to say whether the *tüün* of *tüün deere* is a genitive form or the stem in Ordos. If *muDun* Dēre < **muDuni* Dēre, the same development might have produced *tüün deere* (< **tüüni deere*). However, in Khalkha the genitive forms are distinct from the adjective forms and the pronominal stem: *morin* and *tüün* are stems; *morinii* and *tüünii* are genitives. Another test of postpositional government is the use of the postposition with non-*n* stems. Since the constructions in use are Kh. *gadzar deere* and *gadzar dotor*, it is clear that the stem alone is used. The genitive of *gadzar* "earth" is *gadzariin*. The development may have been from an earlier use of the genitive case before these postpositions to the modern use of the stem before them. It has also been suggested that the written language constructions of *degere* with the genitive, such as *usun-u degere* "over the water," have been orthographically patterned by analogy with such postpositions as *tula* "on account of" which always require the genitive. It should be noted that the postpositions preceded by the stem are also used alone as adverbs. Cf. *naran deger-e amui* "the sun is above." *Tula* is never used alone as an adverb.[82]

2) The pronouns of the first and second persons are *still* usually in the genitive case before the "dative-locative" postpositions (but this is not true of the demonstrative pronouns as pointed out above). Cf. (*SH* § 205) *minu de'ere* "on me," Ord. *mini* *Dēre* "on me," Kh. *minii dotor* "in me," *minii teeši* "towards me" (also *nada teeši* with the oblique stem). The forms of the demonstrative pronoun used with *deere* are *tere deere, teren deere, terüün deere,* and *tüün deere,* i.e., the genitive *tüünii* is not used. The first and second person pronouns are also found with the oblique stem: cf. Ord. *naDaDār* "on me," Bur. *nama-soo* "in me," Kh. *nama teeši.* Contrast this situation with such phrases as *bi metü / minu metü* "like me," *tere metu* "like that," where the oblique pronominal stems are not used before *metü.*

3) The tendency to use oblique stems of pronouns with these postpositions seems to be connected with the association of the dative-locative stem with "dative-locative" postpositions (*deere, dotor, doro,* and *teeši*).

4) The modern dialects retain a genitive usage for *dotor* with the meaning of "among." Cf. *uls ündestnii dotor* "among the nations"; also *tüünii dotor* "among them," where *tüünii* is used as a collective singular pronoun. Cf. *tüün dotor* "in it."

5) The postposition *ǰüg* "in the direction of" governs the stem or the genitive, preferring the latter with pronouns. Cf. Kh. *ger dzüg* "towards the yurt," *tüünii dzüg* "towards him."

There is further the adverbial usage of these words in such combinations as *deeremin* "on me," *deeren (= degere inu)* "on it." The semantic distinctions in Ordos are described in a letter to me dated 9 September 1951 from the Reverend Antoine Mostaert:

"Pour ce qui concerne *Dēren (< degere inu), t'ere Dēre, t'erɯ̄ɯ̄̃ Dēre,* je pense que les deux dernières expressions veulent dire 'sur cela,' tandis que *Dēren* veut dire simplement 'sur ce dont il est question.' L'usage du pronom démonstratif indique l'objet d'une façon beaucoup plus précise; mais je dois ajouter, pour ce qui regarde *t'erɯ̄ɯ̄̃ Dēre,* si l'on n'appuie pas sur *t'erɯ̄ɯ̄̃,* l'expression *t'erɯ̄ɯ̄̃ Dēre* se rapproche sémantiquement de très près de *Dēren,* parce que *t'ere,* outre qu'il est pronom démonstratif, peut aussi avoir le sens du pronom personnel 'il.'"

Below is given a table of certain postpositions with the types of government which show differences and similarities as between nouns and pronouns. The examples from which the data is taken may be found in chapter six on postpositional phrases. Since the material is far from complete, conclusions should not be hastily drawn. The table is merely suggestive as regards the subject-matter, and further research is needed to obtain more complete data.

1) Postpositions which may use the oblique stem of pronouns in postpositional phrases: *degere* "on," *doora* "under," *dotora* "in," *qoγorundu* "among," *singgi* "like," *tegesi* "towards," *uruγu* "down." The nominative stem refers to demonstrative pronouns, and the oblique stem refers to first and second personal pronouns or to demonstrative pronouns.

	With Nouns	*With Pronouns*
degere	(*-n*) stem genitive ablative "better than"	nominative stem oblique stem genitive ablative
doora	(*-n*) stem genitive ablative "worse than"	nominative stem oblique stem genitive ablative
dotora	(*-n*) stem genitive	nominative stem oblique stem genitive
qoγorundu	stem (nom. fut.) genitive	nominative stem oblique stem (Bur.)
singgi	stem	nominative stem oblique stem (Bur.)
tegesi	(*-n*) stem genitive (Bur.)	nominative stem oblique stem genitive
uruγu	stem (*-n*) stem (*SH*) genitive (Bur.)	nominative stem oblique stem

Examples

a) With nouns.

(*degere*) *mör* <u>*degere*</u> "on the way."
aya<u>n</u> <u>*degere*</u> "on [military] campaigns."
γaǰar-<u>un</u> <u>*degere*</u> "over the earth."
taqimdaγu bolqui-<u>ača</u> <u>*deger-e*</u> "above the fact of being filial."

(*doora*) *gadzar doro* "under the earth."
šireen doro "under the table."
tegri-yin doora "under heaven."
čimača doora "after thee (i.e., after thy time)."

(*dotora*) *ger dotora* "in the yurt."
tergen dotora "in the wagon."
irgen-ü dotora "among the people."

(*qoγorundu*) *tanai irex xoorond* "until you come."
tegexiin xoorond "while that was going on."
olon ulsəin xoorond "among nations."

(*singgi*) (Ord.) *mori šiŋ^{k}χ^{u}ī* "like a horse."

(*tegesi*) *ger teeši* "to the yurt."
oron tesi (= tēši) "to the place."
(Bur.) *galiin teeši / gal teeši* "towards the fire."

(*uruγu*) (Ord.) *ɢol urū* "down the river."
(*SH*) *usun huru'u* "downstream."

b) With pronouns.

(*degere*) *tere deere* "on it, on him, on her; on that."
nad deere "on me."
(Ord.) *t'ani Dēre* "on you."
nadaas deer "better than I."

(*doora*) *tere doro* "under it."
tüün doro "under it."
minii doro "under me."
nadaas dor "worse than I am."

(*dotora*) *tere dotora* "in it; among them."
tüün dotor "in it."
minii dotor "in me."

(*qoγorundu*) *tere xoorondo* "meanwhile."
tegün qoγordumda "meanwhile."

(*singgi*) (Ord.) *t'ere šiŋgɯ* "like those."
(Bur.) *šama-šinyi* "like thee."

(*tegesi*) *biden tiiš* "towards us."
nada teeši "towards me."
tüün teeši "towards it."
minii teeši "towards me."

(*uruγu*) (Bur.) *teree ruu* "towards that."
(Ord.) *ene urū* "vers l'est d'ici."
nama ruu "towards me."

2) Other postpositions which show a contrast between nominal and pronominal usage: *darui* "following," *ǰabsar* "between," *ǰüg* "toward," *ögede* "up," *qoyina* "after," *siγ* "like" (a postposition?), *šitü* "like," *tege* "in the region of," *tuqai* "concerning," *tus* "facing," *ügei* "without," *urida* "before."

	With Nouns	*With Pronouns*
darui	stem (nom. perf.) ablative	nominative stem ablative
ǰabsar	genitive	nominative stem
ǰüg	stem genitive	genitive
ögede	(*-n*) stem (Ord.) stem	nominative stem genitive (Ord.)
qoyina	stem (nom. perf.) genitive ablative	nominative stem (Ord.) genitive ablative
siγ	stem	oblique stem (Kh.)
šitü	stem	nominative stem (Ord.)
tuqai	stem (Bur.) genitive	nominative stem oblique stem genitive
tus	stem genitive	oblique stem (Bur.)
ügei	(*-n*) stem (Kh.)	oblique stem (Bur.) (< nominative stem)
urida	stem "previous to" genitive ablative	nominative stem genitive ablative

Examples

a) With nouns.

(*darui*) (Ord.) *ųnt'asan* Darᵘī "as soon as he was asleep."
tegünče darui "right after that."

(*ǰabsar*) *aγula talayin ǰabsar* "between the mountain and the plain."

(*ǰüg*) *ger ǰüg qariǰu* "returning towards the yurt."
gindan-u ger-ün ǰüg güyüldükü "to run toward the prison."

(*ögede*) (Ord.) *ųsųn* ȫDö *jawų-* "to go against the current."
(Ord.) *ger* ȫDö *jawų-* "to go towards the yurt."

(*qoyina*) *arban ilegüü qonuγsan qoyina* "after more than ten days."
yawasan xoino "after [he] went."
kedün ödür-ün qoyina "after several days."
geriin xoino "behind the yurt."
(Mong.) *ɢor uDurDza χuɐno* "after two days."

(*siγ*) *xün-šig* "like a man."
modo-šig "like a tree."

(*šitü*) *oyir-a sitü* "as if [he were] near [him]."
(Ord.) *χoni šint'ī* "like a sheep."

(*tuqai*) (Bur.) *asuudal tuxai* "concerning the question."
maləin tuxai "concerning cattle."

(*tus*) *ene burqan-u terigün tus* "facing the head of this Buddha."
qubisqal-un tus "concerning the revolution."

(*ügei*) (Kh.) *usan güi* "without water."
edür söni ügei "day and night."

(*urida*) *arwan džil ur'd* "ten years ago."
xotonii urda "before the city."
xuw'sgalaas ur'd "before the revolution."

b) With pronouns.

(*darui*) *ter darui* "at that moment."
tegünče darui "immediately after that."

(*ǰabsar*) *ene dzabsar* "during this period."

(*ǰüg*) *tüünii dzüg* "towards him."

(*ögede*) (Ord.) *t'ereDɯ* < *tere ögede* "towards that."
(*SH*) *tere ö'ede* "up that [valley]."
(Ord.) *mani öDö* "towards us."

(*qoyina*) (Ord.) *ene χöɢno* "east of here."
tegün-ü qoyina "after that."
(Bur.) *tegünče qoyina* "after that."

(*siγ*) (Kh.) *nama-šig* "like me."
(Kh.) *nada-šig* "like me."

(*šitü*) (Ord.) *Bi šint'ī* "like me."
(Ord.) *ene šint'ī* "like these."

(*tuqai*) *ene tuxai* "concerning this."
tüün tuxai "concerning that, him, etc."
tüünii tuxai "concerning that, him, etc."

(*tus*) (Bur.) *tegün tus* "with regard to that."

(*ügei*) (Bur.) *eneen güi* "without this."

(*urida*) *ene urd* "south of here."
(Ord.) *t'ere urDa* "formerly."
üünii ur'd "before this."
üünees ur'd "before this."

The use of the stems of nouns, on the one hand, and the use of the genitive of pronouns, on the other, in connection with postpositions is also found in Turkish, as may be seen from the following:

(stem) *demir-ile* "with iron."
(gen.) *benim-ile* "with me."
(stem) *su gibi* "like water."
(gen.) *onun gibi* "like him."
(stem) *mekteb-için* "for the school."
(gen.) *senin için* "for thee."

3) The government of pronouns by the many remaining postpositions is the same as that for nouns. The lists and classification of these postpositions are given in chapters five and six.

The examples cited in this chapter, together with additional material, should be helpful in the study of the historical development of syntax in Mongolian. The patterns of development in postpositional phrases vary somewhat from dialect to dialect. Within a given dialect the leveling effect of analogy is observable when comparisons are made with other dialects. The distinctive syntactic features of a given dialect are as characteristic of that dialect as are its phonological features. In the study of the latter it is generally accepted that when one speech sound is substituted for another, it is applied systematically throughout the dialect without exceptions, provided the change is original in the dialect and not borrowed from another tongue. Professor Whatmough has applied the term *selective variation* to the combination of changes observed in the history of a language. He states:

> Changes in inflection, in syntax, in meaning - these, too, are commonly regular and systematic. Once a change disturbs the established pattern of a language, selection sets to work and eventually creates a new pattern.[83]

Both selection and variation may be observed in the comparison of Mongolian dialects, where the patterns for *-n* stem nouns and oblique stem forms of pronouns are consistent within any one dialect but differ from one dialect to another. Independent patterns of development in the syntax of postpositional phrases illustrate the same principles at work.

V

POSTPOSITIONAL PHRASES

ADVERBS

As pointed out in chapter two on parts of speech, many linguists have preferred to set up only three parts of speech in Mongolian, namely, noun, verb, and particle. However, nouns and particles can be broken down into sub-categories on the basis of morphological and syntactical characteristics (see chapter three on nouns).

The form of adverbs is undifferentiated from that of nouns (except in such cases as that of the adverbial suffix *-γsi*, etc.). They are identified for the most part by their position in the sentence. A few "adverbial" suffixes may be observed in the modern dialects, such as: Kh. *saitar*, written language *sayitur* "well" from *sayin* "good"; Kh. *dzügeer* from *ǰüg-iyer* "well, fine." The latter word is in an instrumental case form. In the modern language many "adjectives" are converted into adverbs by means of the instrumental case. Cf. *šineer* "newly" from *šine* "new."

Some adverbs whose present form shows no distinctive or productive suffix are composed of elements which may be traced back to original roots (or stems) plus suffixes neither of which exist independently of each other today. Lewicki lists the following: *uma-ra* / *üme-re*, *dege-re*, *doo-ra*, *doto-ra*, *ǰaγu-ra*, *čina-ru*.[84] The Turkic suffixes *-ra (-re)*, *-ru*, *-ri* are taken as variants of the same suffix. As loan suffixes in Mongolian, they have become differentiated by the use of *-ra* / *-re* as a locative suffix and *-ru* as a directive suffix. These same words are also postpositions. Other suffixes which appear with adverbs or postpositions are *-γsi* / *-si* and *-γur* / *-gür*. Cf. *qamiγa* "where?" *qamiγa-si* "whither?" Kh. *tee-ši* "in the direction (of)," *urda* "in front," *urduur* "along the front."

Although the stems of such words no longer exist, they still may account for sub-division. The suffixes *-si* / *-γsi* and *-uur* are not added directly to *tsaana* "on that side," but to its original stem **tsaa*. Cf. *tsaa-g-uur* "along that side," *tsaa-si* "in that direction."

Syntactically adverbs are distinguishable from nouns in that they have a limited number of case suffixes, if any. They have no plural. Adverbs indicating location may take dative and/or ablative suffixes. Adverbs indicating time may take the genitive suffix and sometimes the instrumental. These features are also common to postpositions (see below). Adverbs are found with two suffixes which do not occur with ordinary nouns, namely, *-si* / *-γsi* (called *Lativform* by Poppe) and *-γur* (called *prolatif* by A. Mostaert).

Grammarians dealing with the Mongolian language have shown a great variety of views with regard to non-verb and non-noun elements in the language. Bobrovnikov, Kotvič, and Rudnev[85] tended to group all these elements under the general heading of "particles." Rudnev called adverbs (= particles) "all non-declined and non-conjugated parts of speech, known (in part) as adverbs, conjunctions, prepositions, postpositions, interjections, and particles." Šmidt, Kowalewski, and Popov[86] preferred to group the "particles" or "adverbs" into three parts of speech: adverbs, postpositions, and conjunctions.

Among the adverbs which are listed by Šmidt are such expressions as *ali nigen čaγ-tur* "at any time," *tere kürtele* "until then," *tegun-dür* "thither," and *ene edür* "today." The first three are usually identified by their suffixes as either nouns or verbs. The last one presents a curious problem. Cf. the following:

(*SH* § 200) *ken-ü kö'üd ene üdür (= ene edür) uγulǰa alaǰu eyin idemüi* "Les fils de qui aujourd'hui ayant tué (m. à m: 'tuant') un mouflon mangent ainsi [comme vous le faites]?"[87]

The expression *ene edür* "today" is used adverbially in the same sense that *tere degere* "thereon" < "on it" is used. The difference is that *degere* may be preceded by *tegün* instead of *tere* and that *degere* "governs" the preceding word as a postposition. In Khalkha *ene edür* becomes one word *önöödör* "today." What the two have in common is their status as adverbial phrases, but the syntactical functions of *edür* and *degere* are different. As adverbial phrases, *ene edür* refers to time and *tere degere* refers to place; both modify the action of the verb.

In an article on parts of speech in Mongolian,[88] Poppe notes the following characteristics of adverbs.

There are a certain number of circumstantial words which may be used independently as adverbs or may modify nouns. Some of them with their adverbial meanings are the following: *erte* "formerly," *öni* "long ago," *edüge* "now," *qola* "far," *oyira* "near," *lab* "truly," *maγad* "definitely," etc. These words are also found as modifiers of object-nouns. Cf. *erte čaγ* "former time," *öni čaγ* "ancient times," *qola γaǰar* "distant place," *maγad ünen* "exact truth." When used thus, they are not adverbs. Moreover, they are partially inflected after the fashion of regular nouns. Cf. *qolayi ülü bodoγči* "short-sighted" < "one who does not consider the distant [in time]." These words are no different from quality-nouns such as *sayin* "good," which may also be used with a verb in the sense of "well." The fact that these words are usually only partially declined means that some quality-nouns have "defective declensions."

Once this group of words is sifted out from the general category of adverbs, there remain five sub-categories which may be described as follows:

1) *Circumstantial (obstoyatel'stvennïe) words which are found in the predicate.* They are not governed by other words in the sentence, nor do they modify nouns. They are never used as post-positions, but they are always associated with verbs (including *nomina verbalia* and *converba*). Cf. *qamiγa* "where?"

2) *Circumstantial words which are not found in the predicate.* They are not governed by other words in the sentence. They do not modify object-nouns. They are never used as postpositions, but they are associated with verbs (including *nomina verbalia* and *converba*). Cf. *uγuγata* "completely," *sayitur* "comme il faut," *arai* "hardly," *ker* "how?" *oγtu* "completely," etc.

3) *Circumstantial words which are not found in the predicate, but which differ from (2) in that they may modify not only action (the verb) but also property or quality (quality-nouns).* Cf. *masi* "very," *masi sayin* "very good," *masi bayasuba* "he rejoiced greatly."

4) *Circumstantial words of a type similar to those indicated in (2) and (3), which differ from them in that they modify quality-nouns but do not modify verbs.* Cf. *tong* "very," *asuru* "very," *ülemǰi* "remarkably," etc.

5) *Circumstantial words, sometimes used in the predicate, which are not used to modify object-nouns. What distinguishes them from (1) is the fact that they may be used as postpositions.* Cf. *dotora* "in, inside," *γadana* "out, outside," *doora* "under, underneath." Some words such as *adali* "like," *degere* "above," *alus* "across, beyond," and *orčin* "near" may be used attributively. This whole group might well be called "adverb-postpositions."

There is a sixth group of "adverbs" which function only as *postpositions* (cf. *tula* "because of," *tölöge* "for the sake of"). As lexical elements they may be designated as postpositions only, but the phrases in which they are found are adverbial, as is the case with most postpositional phrases (see below).

Todaev's classification of adverbs[89] is drawn up somewhat differently. He places them into two fundamental groups: (1) Basic Adverbs, and (2) Derivative Adverbs. The forms given are Khalkha.

1) Basic Adverbs remain undeclined for the most part and have no productive suffixes; cf. *naaš* "hither," *arai* "hardly," *oroi* "late," *ürgeldž* "continuously," *xaayaa* "somewhere, sometime," *ert* "early," *büren* "completely," *but* "in pieces," *tsöm* "together," *odoo* "now," etc.

(*SMY*, p. 154) *bi odoo surguul' deeree adžiltai yumsan* "I *now* have work at my school."

(*SMY*, p. 154) *ta tür amartš bai* "you rest *a little*."

2) Derivative Adverbs are derived from nouns, adjectives, pronouns, verbs and other parts of speech usually by means of suffixes added to their base.

a) From nouns.

Instr. *xawraar* "in spring."
namraar "in autumn."
mongoloor "in [the] Mongolian [language]."

Whether the word is an adverb or a noun in the instrumental case is determined by the context (Todaev).

b) From adjectives.

1. Adverbs from quality-nouns: *sain* "well," *muu* "poor(ly)," *tšanga* "solid(ly)," *bat* "firm(ly)," *türgen* "quick(ly)," *xurdan* "quick(ly)," *šingen* "thin(ly)," *ariun* "pure(ly)," *tsewer* "pure(ly)," *baga* "a little," *tegš* "equal(ly)," *sul* "loose(ly)," *nimgen* "thin(ly)."

2. The same words with the instrumental suffix: *sainaar, muugaar, tsangaar, bagaar, nimgeer, tsewreer, xurdaar, sulaar, dzudzaanaar* "thickly," *šineer* "newly," *örgönöör* "broadly," *manaigaar* "according to our custom," *bügdeer* "all," etc.

(*SMY*, p. 154) *türgen otšood ir'ye* "I'll be *right* back."

(*SMY*, p. 155) *ter adžil sainaar yawna* "this work is going *well*."

(*SMY*, p. 155) *ert yaw* "go early"; *erteer yaw* "go earlier"; *tšangaar bar'* "hold it *tighter*." The last two sentences show the tendency to contrast the minimal form with the instrumental form by differentiating them semantically, the instrumental becoming the comparative expression.

c) Adverbs which are inseparable from verbs: *mult, but, xamx, xuga, suga, xaga,* etc., all of which mean more or less "thoroughly, entirely, in pieces."

(*SMY*, p. 156) *mult tatax / suga tatax* "to pull out."

(*SMY*, p. 156) *but nirgex* "to destroy completely."

(*SMY*, p. 156) *xamx tsoxix* "to break to pieces."

(Poppe classifies the above elements with the "left-overs" under the heading of particles).

Note also verb forms derived from these words: *multlax, sugalax* "to pull out," *xamxlax* "to smash," etc.

Some converbs are used like adverbs (Todaev). The usual suffixes are *-n* and *-dž*. Cf. *ürgeldž* "continuously" < *ürgelex* "to continue."

Todaev also classifies adverbs according to their general categories of meaning.

1) Place: *dotor* "inside," *dor* "underneath," *deer* "thereon," *oir* "near," *tsaiš* "in that direction," *ömnö* "before," *gadna* "outside," *xoino* "behind," *xoorond* "in the middle," *dund* "in the middle," *naaš* "towards this direction, hither," *end* "here," *tend* "there," *xoloor* "by far," etc.

2) Time: *odoo* "now," *oroi* "late," *üdeš* "in the evening," *ert* "early," *ur'd* "before, formerly," *xoiš* "backwards, northwards, in the future," *daraa* "afterwards," *ürgeldž* "continuously," *darui* "immediately," *xaayaa* "sometime," etc.

3) Manner: *ulam* "even more, by far," *but* "in pieces," *tsöm* "together," *sem* "quietly, secretly," *xaga* "in pieces," *yaaruu* "hurriedly," *genet* "suddenly," *xeterxii* "too much," *newt* "right through," *xalt-mult* "superficially," *tus-tus* "separately," *daxin-daxin* "again," *suga* "thoroughly," *büren* "entirely," *sain* "well," *tsewer* "purely," *tšangaar* "solidly," etc.

4) Measure and degree: *maš* "very," *nen* "very," *tun* "completely," *baga* "a little," *bas* "also," *tsöön* "a little, not much," *arai* "barely," *olon* "much," etc.

Todaev lists as adverb-postpositions the following words: *ömnö* "before," *xoiš* "to the rear," *deer* "on," *dor* "under," *dotor* "in," *xoino* "after," *ur'd* "before," and *dund* "in the middle." Whether they are adverbs or postpositions is determined by the context (Todaev).

It should be noted that Todaev's classification of adverbs relies very heavily on Russian grammar.

When adverbs appear with regular case suffixes, they are indistinguishable from ordinary nouns. *Ende-eče* "from here" is grammatically the same as *ger-eče* "from the yurt," the chief difference being that *ende* uses no other case suffix. Kh. *xedzee* "when?" is found with the genitive and the ablative cases; *xedzeenii* "since long ago" and *xedzeenees* "since when?" It might be objected that the "meaning" of these words limits the probability of a full declension. However, the concept of "of here" has a special adjectival suffix reserved only for adverbs, *-ki*. Cf. *ende-ki* "of here," Kh. *endexi*. Many adverbs, especially those expressing spatial concepts, are found with reflexive-possessive suffixes. Cf. *tende-ben* "there [where he is], at his place." In Buriat a personal pronoun suffix may be used: *endeb* < *ende bi* "I am here." Some temporal words are found with the instrumental suffix. Cf. *odoogoor* "around now."

Many common postpositions take a limited number of declensional suffixes much the same as adverbs do and under the same conditions. Since most postpositional phrases are adverbial, their syntactical relationship to the sentence as a whole is the same as that of adverbs. In a sense, one could call such a postpositional phrase a "complex adverb" which consists of two parts, (1) a postposition and (2) its object.

MINIMAL FORM POSTPOSITIONS

In chapter two it was noted that *the simplest postpositional phrase, which is morphologically distinct from other constructions, is one whose final member, the postposition itself, while governing the preceding elements, is in its minimal form and is neither the subject nor the object of a verb.* This definition places in a separate group those postpositions whose form is minimal, in contradistinction to those postpositions having productive suffixes, whether nominal or verbal (see pages 29 through 31). Non-productive suffixes may be extracted from some of these postpositions by analysis. These postpositions, for the most part, may also be adverbs by themselves. The following list separates the root from the suffix:

1) *čaγa-da, čaγa-du, čaγa-na, čaγa-si; čina-du, čina-na.*
2) *dege-gsi, dege-gür, dege-re.*
3) *derge-de, derge-de-gür.*
4) *doγo-γsi, doγo-γur; doo-ra*[90] / *do-ra, do-ro-γsi, do-ro-na.*
5) *doto-γur, doto-ra.*
6) *dumda, dumda-γur.*
7) *γada-γa, γada-γsi, γada-γur, γada-na.*
8) *ina-du, ina-γsi, ina-ru; naγa-γur, naγa-na, naγa-si.*
9) *qoγorun-du, qoγorun-du-γur.*
10) *qoyi-γur, qoyi-na, qoyi-na-γsi, qoyi-si.*
11) *te-düi, te-n-de, te-isi (= teyisi).*
12) *uru-γsi, uru-γu.*

This analysis is based primarily on inspection and not on historical principles. It leaves us with the following final elements: *-γur* / *-gür*, *-γsi* / *-gsi* / *-si*, *-da* / *-de*, *-du*, *-ra* / *-re*, *-ru*, *-na*, *-γa*, *-γu*. These final elements are also found in ordinary nouns (except for the suffix *-γsi* / *-gsi*).

In the *Secret History* there are also examples of the postpositional root elements with the suffix *-γun* / *-gün*. These are both adverbs and postpositions. Cf. *čina'un, dege'ün, ǰaγa'un, qoyina'un, urida'un, γada'un, dotora'un*, etc.

(*SH* § 199) *müren-ü čina'un möseldükün ta* "au delà des fleuves vous vous séparerez."[91]

(*SH* § 229) *kebte'ül-ün dege'ün ken ber bu yabutuγai* "no one is to pass beyond the guards (= between the guards and the tent)."

(*SH* § 244) *qoyar ebüdüg dege'ün bisari'ulǰu* "auf die beiden Kniee hinbreitend."

(*SH* § 278) *kebte'ül-ün ǰaγa'un bu yabutuγai* "there shall be no passing between the guards."

(*SH* § 278) *ordo-yin qoyina'un urida'un kebte'ül muquritu γai* "the guards are to patrol in the front and in the rear of the palace-yurt."

(*SH* § 145) *dayin dotora'un güyüǰü* "rushing into [the camp of] the enemy."

In a letter written to me and dated 13 June 1951, Professor Poppe has the following to say about the suffix *-γun* / *-gün:*

"The suffix *-γun* in adverbs is rare, but not unknown. It is the same as in Written Mongolian *inaγuki* (with the adjectival suffix *-ki*) 'der diesseitige.' You find it also with other meanings in Kowalewski (dictionary p. 275; it is misspelled there. *inaγunki*). Kowalewski has also *inaγun* 'exterior, outside, the visible, vanity, etc.' Here it is a substantive (like *degere* or any adverb which can act as a substantive). Its use is so different in various sources that it is difficult to decide what it was primarily. I believe it was used mainly in the function of a *lative* (direction), e.g., *dayin dotora'un güyüǰü* (*SH* paragraph 145) 'he rushed into (the camp of) the enemy.' Only single forms occur in Written Mongolian, e.g., *inaγun, dotoraγun, γadaγun* (in old documents)."

Another suffix found with these postpositional root elements survives in the Ordos dialect, i.e., **-tai* / **-tei*. Cf. Ord. ᴅē'*t'ī* < **dege-tei, u̯rt'ä̈* < **uri-tai, χȯǫ̈'t'ɔ̄ *qoyi-tai, tš'ā't'ä̈* < **čaγa-tai*, etc. For semantic reasons these have been listed in chapter six under *degere, urida, qoyina,* and *čaγana.*

(*TOO*, p. 65) ʙ*alǥu̯su̯n* ṻᴅ*en* ᴅē'*t'ī* "au dessus de la porte de la ville."

(*TOO*, p. 202) *mini u̯rt'ä̈* "avant moi."

(*TOO*, p. 38) *jawu̯sã χȯǫ̈'t'*^ "après [ton] départ."

(*DO*, p. 697a) *k'e*ᴅɯ*n* ɯᴅɯ*rĩī tš'ā't'ä̈* "après quelques jours."

The Reverend Antoine Mostaert discusses them as follows:

"Ces formes [ᴅē'*t'ī, u̯rt'ä̈*, etc.], je ne les ai entendues qu'en ordos, mais il est possible qu'on les retrouve aussi dans d'autres dialectes, une fois qu'on aura examiné un plus grand nombre de parlers. Les Ordos n'écrivent pas ces formes. Celles-ci appartiennent exclusivement à la langue parlée. Quant au suffixe *-t'ä̈*, il sort de **-tai, *-tei*. Ce suffixe *-t'ä̈, -t'ī* a dans ces divers adverbes une signification locative (localization dans l'espace ou dans le temps), la même qu'il a par exemple dans *loŋχo't'*^, *χū̯'t'ä̈* des expressions *loŋχo't'ᵔ ari'ᵏχi* 'l'eau-de-vie qui est dans la bouteille,' *χṳ't'ä tš'ä* 'le thé que est dans le pot.' Ceci est vrai pour les adv. *De't'ī, Dō't'ᵔ, ṷrt'ä, χȯǫ't'ᵔ, tš'ä't'ä, nā't'ä* mais pas pour le mot *šint'ī*. Je tiens pour très probable que dans ce dernier mot *-t'ī* est aussi < **-tei*. Quant à *šin-*, cf. *šitü* du mongol médiéval, mo. *sitü*, ord. *šiŋgɯ, šiŋᵏχɯ*, etc. *Šin-* doit avoir le sens de 'comme, égal à, etc.' et j'incline à croire qu'il faut rapprocher le *-t'ī* de *šint'ī* du *-t'ä* qu'on entend dans le mot ordos *aDilt'ä* 'égal, ressemblant à.'"[92]

Monguor, like other Mongolian dialects, has a limited number of postpositions. Most of these also serve as adverbs. Cf. *Dęre* = *degere*, *Dōro* = *doora*, *χuęno* = *qoyina*, etc. Curiously enough some Monguor postpositions are loan-words from Tibetan; cf. *sDār* < Tib. *ltar* "according to," *męnDi* < Tib. *min-pa* "aside from," and *śDźī* < *dkyil* "middle."

(*DM*, p. 333) *muni sDār* "selon moi, à mon avis."

(*DM*, p. 333) *mōr sDār yṳ* "marcher en suivant le chemin."

(*DM*, p. 235) *nDāDza męnDi k'uŋGe Dṳ̌Da* "appelle quelqu'un d'autre que moi."

(*DM*, p. 235) *nie GerDza męnDi sę̄n Ger uGuā* "excepté cette maison-ci, il n'y en a pas de bonnes."

(*DM*, p. 419) *muni t'iGī Bayān* "aussi riche que moi."

In his Buriat grammar, Poppe discusses the Buriat postpositions *soo, ruu, xudruu, tee,* and *šingi*.[93]

1) The postposition *soo* (Tsong. *tsoo*, other dialects *soo*) is used in answer to the question "in what?" "within what?" "into what?" It may take the prolative case, the ablative case, or the adjectival suffix *-xi* (written language *-ki*). It may take the personal and reflexive possessive suffixes. (N.B. Ts. = Tsongol, Barg. = Barguzin, Al. = Alar, Ag. = Aga, Hori = Hori-Buriat, = all Buriat dialects).

Literary *ger soo* "in the yurt."
Ts. *ger tsoo* "in the yurt."
Al. *ger soogɒhoo* "from the yurt."
Al. *uhɒŋsooguur* "downstream in the water."
Ts. *ger tsoogoos* "from the yurt."
Ag. *uhɒŋ soox'ɒ* "being in the water."
Al. *ger soos'ɒ* "being in the yurt."
Al. *ger soom* "inside my yurt."
Hori *ger soogoo* "inside one's yurt."

Cf. Ramstedt's letter to Rudnev on the origin of *soo*;[94] i.e., Manchu *do* "interior," Mong. *doto-na*; **dotšo* > Buriat **dosoo* (Mongolian *č* < *s* in Buriat) > *soo*.

2) The postposition *ruu* is used in answer to the question "on what side?", "in what direction?" The final *-n* of the base of a preceding *-n* stem is dropped. This postposition takes the personal and reflexive possessive suffixes, but it takes no other formative elements.

Literary *uha ruu* "along the water, towards the water."
Hori *modɒ ruu* "in the direction of the woods."
Al. *enee ruu* "in this direction."
Hori *tarx'ɒ ruum* "in the direction of my head."
Al. *uhɒ ruugaa* "in the direction of one's water."

If the preceding word ends in *-r*, then the *r-* of the postposition is dissimilated and is changed into *l-*. Cf. *mor'ɒ luu* "in the direction of the horse."

3) In the Aga, Hori, Barguzin, and Tsongol dialects, the postposition *xudruu* or *xudɒr* is used in answer to the question "on what side?", "in what direction?" The final *-n* of preceding *-n* stems falls.

Hori *modɒ xudɒr* "to the woods."
Hori *xada xudɒr* "to the cliff."

4) The postposition *tee* is used in all the Buriat dialects with the meaning of "on the side."

baran tee "on the right side."
züün tee "on the left side."

This postposition may take the prolative, ablative, or adjectival suffixes. It may take the personal and reflexive possessive suffixes.

ger teehee "from beside the yurt."
Al. *barɒŋ teehee* "from the right."
Al. *züün tees'* "being on the left."
Al. *züün teegüür* "along the left side."
Al. *züün teegee* "on one's left."
Al. *züün teeni* "on his left."

The postposition *tee* with the suffix *-še* is used in answer to the question "in what direction?" In the orthography of the Buriat-Mongolian literary language, the incorrect form *tiiše* "in that direction" has become habitual in place of *teeše* "in the direction (of)," with the result they have both become graphically the same. This *teeše* takes the personal and reflexive possessive suffixes.

ger teeše "towards the yurt."
züg teešee "in one's direction."
niutag teešee "in the direction of one's homeland."
Al. *uhɒŋ teešee* "in the direction of one's water."

5) The postposition *šingi* (Ag., Hori, and Barg. *šiŋg'ə*, Ts. *šin'd'ə*, Al. *šeyə*) is used in comparisons.

Literary *xün šingi* "like a man."
Hori *deerhee buuhɒŋ šiŋg'ə* "as though descending from above."
Al. *tömör šeye* "like iron."
Hori *šamɒ šiŋg'ə* "like thee."

This postposition does not take possessive endings. Occasionally one finds the instrumental suffix.

tömör šin'yeer "in an iron-like manner."

Todaev makes the following summary of postpositions for Khalkha:[95]

The most commonly used postpositions in Khalkha are the following: *xamt* "together (with)," *xoiš* "since," *xoino* "after," *xürtel* "up to," *xoorond* "between," *ömnö* "before," *ur'd* "before," *dor* "under," *dotor* "in," *deer* "on," *tuxai* "concerning," *met* "like," *dund* "in the middle," *tölöö* "for the sake of, in order to, in place of," *turš* "during," *tul* "on account of, for the sake of."

Classification according to categories of meaning.

1) Place: *deer, dor, dotor, ömnö, xoorond, dund, xürtel.*
2) Time: *xoiš, ömnö, xürtel, dotor, turš, ur'd.*
3) Accompaniment: *xamt.*
4) Comparison: *met.*
5) Purpose: *tölöö, tul.*

The following postpositions are used with the stem: xürtel, deer, dor, dund, met, dotor.[96] *Dotor* is used with the genitive case when it is used to indicate position *inside* something, or when it has the temporal meaning of "during." Postpositions used with the noun stem indicate space and time relationships, as well as comparison or equality. Nouns used with *xürtel, dor, dotor,* or *deer* appear in the sentence as place or time modifiers. *Dotor* may still be used as a noun. Cf. *tüünii malgain dotor xar* "the lining of his hat is black"; but, *gün oin modon dotor* "in the thick forest."

The following postpositions are used with the genitive cases: tuxai (usually), *tul, dotor, xoorond, tölöö, xamt, ömnö, turš, dor. Tuxai* is used with verbs meaning "to talk, think, ask, know, hear." Cf. *uls ündestnii xamtəin adžillagaanəi tuxai xelexdee* "while [they] talked about universal cooperation among nations." It indicates the subject-matter of the opinion, thought, utterance, etc. *Dotor* with the genitive means "during" or "among." Cf. *önöö šöniin dotor* "during that night," *uls ündestnii dotor* "among the nations." Postpositions with the genitive case show space, time, or purpose relationships.

The following postpositions are used with the ablative case: ömnö, xoiš, tsaiši, deeš, naiši, xol, ur'd. Xoiš has a temporal as well as a spatial use. Cf. *ter tsagaas xoiš* "since that time," *xotnoos xoiš* "north of the city."

The postposition *xamt* is used with either the genitive or the comitative case.

(*SMY*, p. 67) *nöxörtei xamt* "together with a companion."

(*SMY*, p. 87) *ter dzaluugiin xamt* "[he went out] with that young man."

The last two examples remind one of the word *čuγ* as an adverb or postposition. In the sentence *bi tšinii axtai tsug otšino* "I'm going together with your elder brother," *tsug* may be considered as a postposition governing the comitative case in the same manner as *xamt* in the sentence above. However, in the Ordos sentence *naDalā tš'ųG̨ irelē*, the meaning is "they all came together with me." The meaning seems to indicate that the comitative case is separate from the adverb *tš'ųG̨*. This situation again seems to reflect the dual nature of postpositions and adverbs and provides us with a transitional case. That *tsug* is following the same pattern as *xamt* may be seen in Buriat, where, like *xamt*, it may take either the comitative or genitive case. Cf. (*BMS*, p. 410) *axataigaa sug* "together with one's brother," and *tedenei sug huuži baina* "he lives together with them."[97] In the last sentence, the genitive must be dependent upon *sug* because Mongolian verbs do not govern the genitive, nor is the genitive ever used alone to express the idea of something being associated or connected with something. It would seem that *tsug* is an adverb-postposition like *deer, doro,* and *dotor,* but, unlike the latter, it does not take personal or possessive reflexive suffixes.

Another set of controversial words is the following: *činegen* "extent," *darui* "at once," *γarui* "more than," *ilegü* "superfluous," and *ülemǰi* "superior."

(*DzDz*, 1. 619) *xoninii tšineen tsagaan tšuluugaar* "with a white stone the size of a sheep."

(*AYM*, 1. 6) *tegünče darui* "right after that."

(*CSN*) *dayisun-u doluγan saya γarui čerig* "more than seven million of the enemy's soldiers."

(*EE*, p. 2) *mingγan ilegüü temege mori-yi gegeǰü* "losing more than one thousand camels and horses."

(*K*, p. 1749) *tegün-eče ülemǰi* "plus que cela, d'autant plus."

What these phrases have in common with postpositional phrases is the close syntactical relationship between the final element and preceding word. The examples with *darui* and *ülemǰi* are actually postpositional phrases since the whole phrase serves as an adverb.

The others, however, obviously modify a following noun. The internal syntax of all these phrases is similar to that found in postpositional phrases. Rightly or wrongly, they have been included in chapter six, which lists postpositional phrases. The chief reason for doing so is (1) their internal syntactical similarity to postpositional phrases and (2) the fact that when the phrase is adverbial it fits the general type of postpositional phrases. These words, like *adali* and *metü*, are used in making comparisons.

Let us examine the words *büri* "each" and *tutum* "each, all." Rinčine gives them in his dictionary as "postpositions," (*R*, p. 216) *tutam*, (*R*, p. 39) *bür*. Following are some examples of their usage:

> (*1338*, l. 4) *nasu büri* "each year."
> (*SH* § 31) *üdür büri* "each day."
> (*KhN*) *ödör tutam* "day by day."
> (*CSN*) *ǰil irekü tutum* "each succeeding year."

These expressions are adverbial and are similar to such expressions as *ene edür* "this day > today." The chief reason why the final word is not a postposition is because it receives the case suffix which the preceding word would have taken if it were used alone; cf. *kümün-dür* "to a man," *kümün büri-dür* "to every person."[98]

That most of the common postpositions in Mongolian survive in the majority of dialects in related forms may be seen from the following:

Written Language	*degere*	*dotora*	*qola*	*emüne*
Secret History	*de'ere*	*dotora*	*qola*	*emüne*
'Phags-pa	*de˙ere*	*dot'ora*		
Mukaddimat al-Adab	*dēre*	*dotara*	*qola*	*emüne*
Ordos	Dēre	Do't'oro	χolo	ömönö
Khalkha	Dērə	Do't'or	χoḻḻɒ̆	v̈man
Buriat	*deer*	*dosoo*	χoḻŏ	
Kalmuk	*dēr*	*dotr̥*	χol^{o}	ömn̥
Monguor	De̜re	*t'uro*	χulo	*mieşe̜*
Dagur	d̬e̊r	Dǫa't'ăr	χoḻ	e̬me̜ḻ

Since most of the postpositions listed in chapter six are also other parts of speech according to the circumstances, a mere listing of postpositions as such is not sufficient. Without the postpositional phrase, a discussion of postpositions is impossible.

An examination of the government of postpositions over the elements preceding them reveals a certain pattern of construction within each dialect, and shows that the various dialects actually have more in common as regards syntactical construction than otherwise. In any case, below is given the type of government associated with the postpositions listed in chapter six. In a number of instances the postposition is preceded by any of two or three cases often with a slight change in meaning or emphasis.

1) Postpositions found with a preceding genitive case: *adali* (Kh.), *alus, aru, čaγada, čaγadu, čaγana, činadu, činana, činegen, čuγ* (Bur.), *daraγa, degegür, degere, dergede, dergedegür, doγoγur, doora, doroγsi* "after," *dorona, dotora, dumda, dumdaγur, ebür / öbür, ečine, emüne, ende, esergü, γadaγa, γadaγsi* (Monguor), *γadaγur, γadana, ǰabsar, ǰaγura, metü* (Monguor), *naγaγur, naγana, oyira, qamtu, qoγorundu, qoγorunduγur, qoyina, tedüi, tegesi* (Bur.), *tende, tölöge, tula, tuqai, tursi, tus, učir, umara / ümere, urida, uruγu* (Bur.).

2) Postpositions found with a preceding word in its stem form. Postpositions preceded by the *-n* of *-n* stems are preceded in this list by *(-n)*: *alus, darui, (-n) degegür, (-n) degere, (-n) doγoγsi, (-n) doγoγur, (-n) doora, (-n) dotoγur, (-n) dotora, (-n) dumda* (Kh.), *γarui, ilegü, ǰaγura, ǰüg, metü, ögede, qoyina* (after nom. perf.), *(-n) selte, siγ, singgi, sitü, tege, tegegür, tegesi, teyisi, tuqai* (Bur.), *tus, učir* (Kh.), *(-n) ügei* (Kh.), *urida, uruγu*.

3) Postpositions found with a preceding ablative case: *čaγasi, činaγsi, darui, degegsi, degere* "better than," *doora* "worse than," *doroγsi, emüne, γadaγsi, γadana, γarui, ilegü, inaγsi, inaru, naγasi, ögere / öbere, qola, qoyiγur, qoyina, ulam, ülemǰi, urida, uruγsi*.

4) Postpositions found with a preceding comitative case: *adali, čuγ, qamtu*.

5) Postpositions found with a preceding dative case: *adali* (in older texts), *dorona, sidar*.

The most frequent postpositional government is that of the genitive. The next in frequency is the stem, the peculiarities of which (i.e., the *-n* stem noun and the oblique stem pronoun) suggest in some cases a development from an earlier use of the genitive. At the same time, the use of the *-n* stems with certain postpositions indicating location is parallel to the use of the same stems in forming the regular dative-locative case. Postpositions ending in *-γsi / -gsi / -si* are characteristically preceded by the ablative case.

Certain postpositions are used in their minimal form with *nomina verbalia*. The latter are derived from verb stems with the addition of aspectual suffixes, the most common of which are the *nomen futuri -qu / -kü* and the *nomen perfecti -γsan / -gsen*. The new nominal form becomes a noun stem to which regular declensional suffixes may be added. These verbal nouns are used with postpositions, but the government sometimes differs from that associated with ordinary nouns or pronouns. Cf. *geriin xoino* "behind the house" with the genitive, and *yawasan xoino* "after he went" with the stem. Cf. *šiidweriig biyelüülexiin tul* "in order to carry out the decision" with the genitive, and *boroo orson tul* "because it was raining" with the stem.

Postpositions commonly used with *nomina verbalia* are the following: *ömnö, tul, tölöö, tuxai, ur'd, utšir, xoin, xoiš*. Their uses in Khalkha are as follows:[99]

Nomina verbalia	*Government*	*Postposition*	*Meaning*
nomen verbale	genitive	*ömnö*	"before"
nomen verbale	nominal stem	*tul*	"because"
nomen futuri	genitive	*tul*	"in order that"
nomen futuri	genitive	*tölöö*	"in order that"
nomen verbale	nominal stem	*tuxai*	"with regard to the fact that"
nomen verbale	ablative	*ur'd*	"before"
nomen verbale	nominal stem	*utšir*	"because"
nomen perfecti	genitive	*xoin*	"after"
nomen perfecti	nominal stem	*xoin*	"after"
nomen perfecti	ablative	*xoiš*	"after"

This postpositional construction with *nomina verbalia* is equivalent to clausal construction in English. Other types of clauses in Mongolian are constructed with the verbal forms known as *converba.*

NOUN POSTPOSITIONS

Up to this point we have been dealing with postpositions whose form is that of a word in its minimal form. Most of these words are nouns or adverbs in other syntactical constructions. Now we come to those words which are reasonably classed as postpositions but which have productive suffixes, nominal or verbal.

The noun-postpositions fall readily into two classes: (1) all the postpositions previously discussed whenever they have any of their limited number of declensional suffixes, such as the ablative form of *degere*, which is *degere-eče* "from above"; (2) other words having full nominal declension, whose nominative form is not used as a postposition. Cf. *uuləin xadžuuda* "near the mountain," where *xadžuu* "side" exists as an independent word and requires the dative-locative suffix in this type of postpositional phrase.

The verb-postpositions fall into the class of verbs otherwise known as converbs, which are used in clausal constructions and are by nature adverbial. Cf. *gol xürtel* "up to the river."

The suffixes *-da* / *-de* and *-du* / *-dü* are dative-locative suffixes in Mongolian. Their appearance in the written language is the result of borrowing from the spoken language; the usual written language suffix is *-dur* / *-dür*. The dental is voiced after vowels, *l, m, n, ng* and voiceless after other consonants (i.e., *-ta* / *-te, -tu* / *-tü*, and *-tur* / *-tür*). The *Secret History* uses the colloquial forms quite freely. Cf. (*SH* § 179) *Jamuγa anda-da ügüle* "dites ceci a l'*anda* Jamuqa." The *Secret History* uses alternately *nada* or *nadur* "to me" and *čimada* or *čimadur* "to thee."

This colloquial suffix *-da* / *-de* is found with a large number of adverbs in both the written language and the dialects. It is found with adverbs (or postpositions) as part of their minimal form; cf. *en-de, ten-de, čaγa-da, öge-de, uri-da, dum-da,* etc. It is added to many adverbs (or postpositions) which retain approximately their same meanings but are no longer in their minimal form. Cf. *degegsi-de, činaγsi-da, inaγsi-da, qamtu-da, qola-da, qoyinaγsi-da, qoyisi-da, tula-da (tul-da), tuqai-da, uruγsi-da,* etc. Following are some examples of these words in postpositional phrases:

(*K*, p. 277) *törügsen-eče inaγsida* "depuis la naissance même."

(*K*, p. 853) *egün-eče qoyinaγsida* "après cela, ensuite."

(*'P*, XIII, l. 5) *alt'an ǰoriq č'i-un tulada* "as a result of his golden steadfastness."

Poppe's dictionary of words in 'Phags-pa script lists *tulada* but not *tula.*[100] The *Mukaddimat al-Adab* gives thirty-six examples of phrases with *tulada* and ten with *tula.* A peculiarity of the latter is the use of *tulada* and *tula* with the preceding word in its stem form. Cf. (*MSM*, p. 223b) *muu üile tulada* "for a bad affair," (*MSM*, p. 383a) *tengri tulada* "for heaven," but (*MSM*, p. 380b) *tengriin tulada* "for heaven."

(*1338*, l. 3) *aγali aburi yabudal inu sayin-u tulada* "because his character and deportment were good."

(*EE*, p. 5) *yal-a küliyeǰü iregsen-ü tulada* "because ye have come, receiving (lit., 'awaiting') punishment."

(*ÜD*, p. 134, l. 1) *γaγčaqan minu tulada* "[do not grieve] for my sake alone."

(*K*, p. 1894) *tegün-ü tulada* "à cause de cela."

(*SK*, p. 3) *nara urtuyin tulada* "weil der Tag lang war."

(*SMY*, p. 140) *maləig üxüülexgüin tuld* "so that [we] will not allow the cattle to die.

(*R*, p. 216) *ter tuxaid* "at that time."

(*BMS*, p. 734) *enüün tuxaida* "concerning this."

(*Monguor*, p. 156) *uDieni t'usDu* "vis à vis de la porte."

Some of the noun-postpositions whose nominative form is not used as a postposition, but which appear as postpositions with the dative-locative suffix in *-da* / *-de* are the following: *alda-da, anggi-da, aru-da, ǰaqa-da, oron-da (oron-du, oron-dur), qaǰaγu-da (qaǰiγu-da, qaǰau-da)*, etc. Some words appear with an old dative-locative suffix *-a* / *-e*, such as *ǰabsar-a, učir-a*, etc. The words with the *-da* / *-de* suffix sometimes appear in the written language with the dative-locative suffix *-dur (-tur)* / *-dür (-tür)*.

(*Kh*, p. 148) *üür tsaixiin aldada* "at [the time of] daybreak."

(*Hy*, IIa, 4v) *tenggiri-yin ǰaya'an-ača angida ken üiledün čidaqu* "who can act without the will of heaven?"

(*SH* § 233) *bidanača anggida* "without us."

(*K*, p. 19) *bi-yi beye-eče anggida üǰekü* "considérer le moi isolé du corps."

(*BMS*, p. 59) *xamagai arada* "behind all."

(*ST*, p. 248, l. 3) *bulaγ-un ǰaqa-da* "am Ufer des Quellbaches."

(*TOO*, p. 116) Dalǟ̃ Džaχaᴅụ "au bord de la mer."

(*WM*, p. 130) *edeger-ün orom-dur (= oron-dur)* "in place of them."

(*R*, p. 159) *tüünii orond* "in place of him."

(*Kh*, p. 75) *tšinii orondo* "an deiner Stelle."

(*BMS*, p. 375) *šinii orondo* "in place of thee."

(*MKB*, p. 43) *nigen yeke usun-u qaǰiγu-dur* "near a large body of water."

(*Kh*, p. 75) *uuləin xadžuuda* "neben dem Berge."

(*Kh*, p. 148) *tergenii xadžuudan* "beside the cart."

Cf. (*TOO*, p. 222) *t'erǖǖ χawirɢanᴅụ* "beside it."

(*R*, p. 95) *ter xoyorəin dzawsart* "between those two."

(*K*, p. 2265) *küriyen-ü ǰabsar ǰabsar-a* "entre les enceintes."

(*1335*, l. 51) *maγun aran samaγuralduγsan učir-tur* "at the time when evil men revolted."

(*TOO*, p. 108) *ėŋᵏχesen ụ'tš'irt'ụ* "parce que tu as agi de la sorte."

That the word *anggi-da* "apart" is treated as an adverb may be seen from an expression found in one of the letters from Idiqut-Schähri[101] where it says *asan-ača ačinegün (= ečinegün) angγidaγun* "aloof and away from Hasan." Here *anggi-da* has the suffix *-γun (-gün)* which is usually affixed to minimal form adverbs or postpositions. Cf. (*SH* § 229) *ordo-yin qoyina'un urida'un* "in the front and in the rear of the palace-yurt."

The words mentioned in (1) and (2) with the suffix *-da* / *-de (-dur* / *-dür*, etc.) avoid the stem form of a preceding noun. Note also that in modern speech the usual dative-locative is *-dv* / *-tv*, the short vowel being colored by the vocalic harmony of the word it goes with. Ordos favors the *-du* / *-dü, -tu* / *-tü* forms; otherwise the *-dur* / *-dür*, *-tur* / *-tür* forms belong only to the written language.

The suffix *-ki*, which is sometimes called the *adjectivum loci*,[102] is usually added to the dative-locative suffix, but it is also added directly to the minimal form of adverbs and postpositions. Cf. *ger-te-ki* "häuslich," *γaǰar-ta-ki* "auf der Erde befindlich," *emüne-de-ki* "frontal," *qola-da-ki* "distant," *qaǰaγu-da-ki* "adjacent"; *degere-ki* "upper," *emüne-ki* "frontal," *ende-ki* "of this place," etc.

Another declensional suffix which minimal form postpositions frequently take is the ablative suffix *-ača* / *-eče*. A postposition with this suffix is indistinguishable from an ordinary noun with the same suffix; cf. *qotan-ača* "from the town," *degere-eče* "from above, from the top." One should distinguish postpositions from nouns governing other nouns and playing a role similar to that of postpositions. Like the words ending in productive *-da* / *-de*, these words might be referred to as noun-postpositions since the phrases in which they occur have the same general function as simple postpositional phrases. Following are some common words of this type: *degere-eče, doora-ča, dotoroča, emüne-eče, γadana-ča, qoyinača, uridača,* etc.

(*SH* § 275) *ayan de'ereče* "vom Feldzug her."

(*SH* § 55) *morin de'ereče* "vom Pferde herunter."

(*BMS*, p. 734) *eneen deerehee* "because of this."

(*BMS*, p. 469) *tereen deerehee* "as a result of that, with regard to that."

(*DO*, p. 154a) *t'ere* ᴅēreš "de là-haut."

(*TOO*, p. 135) *t'erūūū* ᴅorōs "from under it (i.e., the earth)."

(*TOO*, p. 26) *ǥā ǥaᴅžar* ᴅorās, *ǥalų̄ ųsųn* ᴅo*'t'orās* "un malheur sort de dessous terre, une oie sort de dessous l'eau."

(*SH* § 252) *J̌ungdu dotoroča* "aus [der Stadt] Dschung-du."

(*K*, p. 1843) *dalai dotor-ača* "de la mer."

(*BE*, p. 52) *γutul-un dotor-ača* "from inside [his] shoes."

(*SK*, p. 12) *tere dotor-ača* "aus ihrer Mitte."

(*TOO*, p. 61) *t'ere* ᴅo*'t'orās* "au milieu d'elles."

(*K*, p. 216) *niγur-un emüne-eče irekü salkin* "le vent qui souffle en face."

(*SMY*, p. 119) *bidnii ömnöös ugtan irew* "[he] came to meet us."

(*SH* § 102) *Temüǰin-ü qoyina-ča* "in pursuit of Temüǰin."

Mention has already been made of the use of the instrumental case suffix as an adverbial suffix (see page 59). Cf. (*SMY*, p. 155) *ter adžil sainaar yawna* "that work is going *well*." A few nouns in Mongolian with the addition of the instrumental case suffix govern preceding elements in much the same manner as postpositions in postpositional phrases. Cf. *ačibar* "thanks to" < *ači* "profit," *siltaγabar* "by reason of, because of" < *siltaγan* "origin, cause," *talaγar* "in the field of" < *tala* "side, field," *üre-iyer* "as a result of, thanks to" < *üre* "fruit, seed, effect," *yosuγar* "in the manner of, in accordance with, according to," *yosu(n)* "custom, manner, rule, method."

(*K*, p. 118) *tegun-ü ačibar* "grace à lui; à cause de cela."

(*SMY*, p. 162) *üünii atšaar* "as a result of this."

(*R*, p. 394) *atšaar* preceded by the *nomen futuri* in the genitive case means "as a result of the fact that."

(*SH* § 208) *ǰirin ökid-üyen siltaγ-iyar* "um seiner beiden Töchter willen."

(*1362*, l. 11) *ǰrlγ boluγsan-u siltaγabar* "because there was [again] an imperial order."

(*1362*, l. 22) *küčü öggügsen-ü siltaγabar* "because [he] rendered service."

(*1335*, l. 49) *ečige eke-degen taγimdaγu boluγsan-u siltaγabar bolbai ǰ-e* "it is by reason of the fact that [their ancestors], [having in a befitting manner rendered service to the emperor], have been filial to their parents (lit., 'father and mother')."

Cf. (*CSN*) *učir ni bükü kümün törölkiten-dü ayul-yi učiraγuluγči dayisun baraγun Ewöröpe-eče bosuγsan-u tula bolai* "the reason is because an enemy, bringing fear to all mankind, has arisen in (lit., 'from') Western Europe."

(*KhN*) *soyoləin talaar* "in the field of culture."

(*R*, p. 245) *tuslamdžiin atš üreer* "thanks to the help."

(*R*, p. 394) *üreer* preceded by the *nomen perfecti* in the genitive case means "as a result of the fact that."

(*SH* § 278) *ǰarliγ-un yosu'ar* "in accordance with the imperial order."

(*'P*, 1, l. 10) *uridanu ǰarliqun yosu'ar* "in accordance with the former edict."

(*1362*, l. 25) *ner-e yin yosuγar* "in conformity with the title."

(*K*, p. 2382) *tere yosuγar* "ainsi de la sorte."

(*K*, p. 2382) *yambar yosuγar* "de quelle manière?"

(*OS*, p. 321) *tere ǰirum yosuγar* "conformant à cet usage."

(*KhN*) *ündsen xuul' yosoor* "according to the constitution."

(*KhN*) *alban yosoor* "officially."

(*KhN*) *enexüü gereenii yosoor* "according to this contract."

(*SMY*, p. 178) *xelsen yosoor* "in the prescribed manner."

(*BMS*, p. 734) *ene yohoor* "in this manner."

(*TOO*, p. 40) *t'ere ju̯su̯gār* "de cette façon."

ju̯su̯gār is borrowed from the literary language form *yosuγar* with the intervocalic -γ- pronounced; hence, it is in its minimal form in the spoken language. A curious feature about *yosuγar* is that it may govern a noun stem. Cf. *ündsen xuul' yosoor* "according to the constitution."

VERB POSTPOSITIONS

There is a series of suffixes which are used with verb stems forming what are known as *converba.*[102] Todaev notes that some *converba* are used like adverbs; cf. *ürgeldž* "continuously" < *ürgelex* "to continue."[103] According to Ramstedt,[104] the *converba* seem to be fossilized noun forms (i.e., from verbal nouns) with fossilized case endings. This places them etymologically with those postpositions whose form is also the result of fossilized suffixes or case endings. The *converba* modify the main verb in much the same way as postpositional phrases modify verbs. In different periods and in different dialects the selection and frequency of certain *converba* in phrases which are very similar to ordinary postpositional phrases places them in the category of verb-postpositions. Some of these are the following: *atala* "until, as for, meanwhile," *bayitala* "until, in spite of," *boltala* "up to," *ekilen* "beginning with," *ǰorin* "in the direction of," *kürtele* "up to, while, even, including," *orčin* "around, near," *siqan* "near, almost, nearly," *toγorin* "around, about, vicinity," etc. These verbs are no different from ordinary verbs in that they all have a full set of verbal suffixes.

(*SH* § 11) *tedüi atala* "sur ces entrefaites."
(*SH* § 32) *qoram atala* "au bout de peu de temps."
(*K*, p. 2685) *teyin atala* "mais, malgré cela."
(*KhM*, p. 50) *tegedž baital* "unterdessen."
(*TOO*, p. 176) *tš'iɡeᴅži ʙä't'ar* "sur ce."
(*K*, p. 1198) *γulir boltala nidükü* "reduire en poudre."
(*K*, p. 1198) *edür söni boltala časun orobai* "il a neigé le jour et la nuit."
(*EBQ*, l. 439) *uuləg tal boltal* "[sie packten einander], dass der Berg zur Ebene wurde."
(*TOO*, LXI) *k'eᴅɯn aŋɡi ʙolt'ol ᴅžaʙ'tš'i-* "hacher en plusieurs morceaux."
(*CSN*) *namur-ača ekilen* "from autumn on."
(*KhN*) *1921 onoos exlen* "from 1921 on."
(*SH* § 115) *Qorqonaγ-Jubur ǰorin ičuba* "[ils] se retirèrent dans la direction de Qorqonaγ-Jubur."
(*SH* § 86) *iseri-yin doro gürtele* "jusque sous son lit."
(*SH* § 247) *Čabčiyal-a gürtele* "bis zum Čabčiyal Pass."
(*1335*, l. 8) *γurban üyes-tür kürtele* "unto three generations."
(*1362*, l. 7) *eǰiy-e kürtele* "until now."

(*ST*, p. 134, l. 14) *uu bečin ǰil-dür kürtele* "up to the earth-monkey year."

(*Doc. A*, l. 7) *qamǰilγa-dur kürtele* "including the serfs."

(*R*, p. 280) *odoo xürtel* "up to now."

(*R*, p. 282) *Xanga xürtel xetšineen kilometr be* "how many kilometers is it to Xanga?"

(*Kh*, p. 75) *ulaan baatarta xürtel* "bis Ulan Bator."

(*MKB*, p. 99) *ter tsag xürtel* "up to that time."

(*SMY*, p. 160) *bid ögloö xürtel xamt yaw'ya* "let us travel together until morning."

(*SMY*, p. 160) *Erdeniin ügiig sonsood Bat xürtel yum tsugluulax adžlaa dzogsow* "hearing the words of Erdeni, *even* Bata stopped his work of gathering things."

(*Kh*, p. 74) *usa xürtel* "bis zu dem Wasser." When the noun stem alone is used before *kürtele*, *-n* stem nouns do not retain their final *-n* in Khalkha.

(*SH* § 57) *modun horčin* "um den Baum herum."

(*SH* § 229) *kebte'ül süni ordo horčin kebteǰu* "die Wachen lagern zur Nacht um die Palastjurte herum."

(*SH* § 278) *ger-ün horčin* "um die Jurte."

(*K*, p. 468) *γar-un orčin* "autour de la main."

(*K*, p. 468) *balγasun-u orčin* "près de la ville."

(*CSN*) *qota-yin orčin* "near the city."

The curious thing about this converb is its use after the genitive case. Since Mongolian verbs do not govern the genitive case, this word loses its converbial status and becomes a noun-postposition. Cf. (*DO*, p. 522b) *orts'in* "voisinage," *G̨arīn orts'inDų* "à proximite de la main." As in the case of *siqan* / *siqam*, there is an alternate form *orčim* (*R*, p. 160). The *Secret History* verb from which this word comes is *horčiqu* "to wind around, to go around."

(*SH* § 190) *üge-tür šiqan* "im Verlass auf die Worte."

(*SH* § 118) *a'ula šiqan ba'uya* "descendons [de cheval] près de la montagne."

(*SH* § 118) *γol-tur šiqan ba'uya* "descendons [de cheval] près du torrent."

(*KhN*) *naim šaxam* "about eight." Cf. (*R*, p. 314) *šaxam* "nearly, almost." The verb from which this word comes is *siqaqu* "to press on, to lean on; to approach, to be near."

(*MSM*, p. 308b) *quduγiin toorin* "around the well."

(*K*, p. 1813) *ger-ün toγorin* "autour de la maison."

(*K*, p. 1813) *ǰil toγorin* "environ un an."

(*DO*, p. 670b) *Dzil t'ōrim* "pendant toute l'année." This is from the verb *t'ōri- (toγoriqu)* "faire le tour de, être autour."

As in the case of *orčin* / *orčim, siqan* / *siqam, toγorin* alternates with an *-m* ending, *toγorim*. The use of the genitive before *toγorin* places it in the same category as *orčin* under noun-postpositions. Cf. Kh. (*R*, p. 205) *toirin* "around."

The suffix *-n* is used in forming the *converbum modale*, which was originally a deverbal noun. It may be followed by the negative *ügei*, which is used only with the *nomina*. A number of deverbal nouns have this suffix; cf. *singge-n* "fluid" < *singgekü* "to be absorbed"; *orči-n* "environs; around" < *orčiqu* "to turn around."[105] Some words in *-n* are used as adverbs; cf. *γarun* "more than" < *γarqu* "to go out," *qarin* "but" < *qariqu* "to return," *toγorin* "around" < *toγoriqu* "to go around."

The *nomen verbale* in *-m* is productive and is found in a number of deverbal nouns; cf. *ürü-m* "drill" < *ürükü* "to rub," *bari-m* "seizure" < *bariqu* "to seize."[106]

Mongolianists often refer to a number of postpositive words as being "subject particles." The most common of these are the following: *inu, anu, ber, bolbasu, bolbala, bol, bügesü*, and *kemebesü*. The first two *inu* and *anu* are pronouns and have been discussed in the chapter on pronouns. The remaining words are *converba conditionalia* formed from ordinary verbs. They are used to emphasize the subject under discussion. *Inu* and *anu* sometimes serve as a sort of definite article and are used only with *nomina*. The converbal forms are used with nouns or pronouns.

(*WM*, p. 24) *morin ni* "the horse"; Kh. *mori-n* (the final *-n* being alveolar).

(*R*, p. 370) *saixan n'* "beauty," *örgön n'* "width." Here the quality-noun is converted into an object-noun.

(*R*, p. 370) *ax n' bagš, düü n' suragtš* "the elder brother is a teacher, and/but the younger brother is a student."

Yabuγsan anu yasu möljikü, kebtegsen inu kegeli-ben aldaqu "walking one gnaws on a bone; sleeping one destroys one's stomach."[88]

(*WM*, p. 24) *bi ber* "as for me." *Ber* is a literary particle.

(*WM*, p. 24) *baγsi bolbala* "as for the teacher."

(*KhM*, p. 44) *ene wolwol sain, ter wolwol muu* "this is good; that is bad."

(*TOO*, p. 191) *Bī Bolwol* "quant à moi."

(*TOO*, p. LVII) *ene Bolwol* "quant à ceci."

A reduced form of *bolbala* is *bol* / *bel*. The latter, losing its normal accent, tends to be affected by the vocalic harmony of the word to which it is affixed. Its appearance in the written language is the result of borrowing from the spoken language.

(*CSN*) *manu egürge bol* "as for our burden."

(*KhN*) *ene bügd bol* "as for all this."

(*R*, p. 32) *bi bol yawna* "*I* am going."

(*R*, p. 32) *bi yawax bol tanai nom awna* "if I go, I'll take your book."

(*Kh*, p. 99) *ene bol nom* "This [is] a book."

(*KhM*, p. 45) *ügüi-wəl* "if not."

(*KhM*, p. 45) *uul-wɒl* "a mountain for instance."

(*KhM*, p. 45) *uulant-wɒl* "on a mountain for instance."

(*R*, p. 332) *Mongol uls bol mal adž axuin oron yum* "Mongolia is a cattle-raising country."

Cf. (*1362*, l. 12) *totoγ kemebesü ötögüs-ün guiloγu ner-e inu ǰuγu* "As for *totoγ (totoq)*, it is the title *guiloγu (kuo-lao)* of the elders."

(*1362*, l. 11) *γutuγar inu Indu kemebesü bingǰang Oron-u ečige inu aǰuγu* "as for Indu (= Hindu), the third [son], he was the father of Oron, the *bingǰang (p'ing-chang)*."

The expression ". . . *bol* . . . *mön* (or *yum*, etc.)" is the same formula as that used in the written language ". . . *kemebesü* . . . *aǰuγu* (or *bui*, etc.)."

The "subject particles," illustrated in the last set of examples, are not postpositions. They have been mentioned because, like declensional suffixes and postpositions, they have become syntactical markers, even though they originate in other parts of speech.

REMARKS

G. K. Zipf, in his studies on the statistical measurement of speech, notes the following concerning parts of speech:

> The part of speech of a word is derived primarily from its behavior or usage, and not its behavior or usage from its part of speech. The allocation of a word to a part of speech reflects the probabilities of its usage rather than all possibilities of its usage, for one can, for example, use any substantive as a verb, indeed use the word of any part of speech in the manner of another: e.g., (prepositions as substantives) 'the *ins* and the *outs*'; (verbs as prepositions) 'all *except* John,' 'all *save* John.' . . . In utilizing the categories of parts of speech, then, we shall remember that they are not mutually exclusive in their membership and that they reflect likelihoods in the behavior of their individual members and not the limits of possible usages.[107]

The results of our study of postpositional words has left us with the identification of postpositional phrases which contain postpositions as the final elements in the phrases. These postpositions fall into three sub-categories.

1) *Minimal form postpositions*, illustrated in such a phrase as *morin deere* "on the horse."

2) *Noun-postpositions*, illustrated in such a phrase as *uuləin xadžuu-da* "near the mountain."

3) *Verb-postpositions,* illustrated in such a phrase as *ulaan baatar xürtel* "as far as Ulan Bator."

Alphabetized lists of all postpositions occurring in the examples cited in this study are given in appendix D under three sub-category designations. Some of those words listed are transitional cases, and some of them are controversial, but the main purpose of the study has been to clarify the lines of demarcation and to provide some basic material for further study.

On the subject of grammatical frequencies, G. K. Zipf has the following to say:

> One interesting feature of the different parts of speech is the great disparity between them in the number of members and the average relative frequency of their members. For example let us present the evidence of the French- Cater -Koenig investigation of the parts of speech of the 500 telephone conversations in American English:

Occurrences of Parts of Speech in English

	Total	Different	Ratio of Total to Different
Substantives	11,660	1,029	11.3
Adjectives and Adverbs	9,880	634	15.6
Main verbs	12,550	456	27.5
Auxiliary verbs	9,450	37	255.
Pronouns*	17,900	45	398.
Prepositions and Conjunctions*	12,400	36	344.
Articles*	5,550	3	1850.

*Computed from data derived from less than 500 conversations.

> The curious feature about these statistics is that the parts of speech fall into two distinct groups according to the number of different words and the ratio of total words to different words (average relative frequency). In Group I are the substantives, adjectives, adverbs, and main verbs, which have many different words, and a low ratio; in Group II, consisting of auxiliary verbs, pronouns, prepositions, conjunctions, and articles, are parts of speech containing but a few words and a high ratio. The members of the two groups differ, then, decidedly in their average relative frequency of occurrence, and this difference has significant consequences.
>
> The first consequence of this difference in average relative frequency is that the actual words represented by the parts of speech in Group I will on the whole have a higher degree of articulatedness of meaning than those in Group II. That is, the words in Group I will, on the whole, whether in configurations of phrases and sentences or not, contain independent meaning with a higher degree of specificity and precision of reference (e.g., *house, dog, swim, walk, black, faithfully*) than those in Group II (e.g., *he, it, of, for, while, and, the, a*). Though the latter are, strictly speaking, not meaningless, yet the specificity and precision of their reference generally does not appear until they are arranged in larger sequences. Naturally the meaning of every speech-element is modified when arranged with other speech-elements, but the members of Group I preserve an independent meaning in their own right to a greater degree in arrangement than do those of Group II.

The difference in meaning between the members of the two groups becomes more manifest if one views that to which the words of the two groups generally refer. The words of Group I (substantives, main verbs, adjectives, and adverbs) refer on the whole to the world of our perceptions and our inferences about our perceptions; that is, the world of perception and inferences is their frame of reference. In this frame of reference the meaning of each word of Group I is to a very considerable degree stable (e.g., the meanings of *house, dog, swim, walk, black, faithfully*), so stable indeed that at a random occurrence of a word of this group, one is generally in little doubt about its referent. Not so with words of Group II, of which the individual words have meaning because of grammatical habits and the nature of the context in which they occur; their frame of reference is the patterns and content of the stream of speech: pronouns, auxiliaries, prepositions, have meaning in the frame of reference of our perceptions primarily because the stream of speech to which they refer has ultimate reference to our experiences. The meanings of *he, while,* etc., are not stable as are those of *house, dog,* and *swim,* nor can one from a random occurrence of a word of Group II be as certain of its referent as one can of a word of Group I.

But the lack of a stable independent meaning in words of Group II has compensation in a greater stability or determinacy of usage. Indefinite in reference to our world of experiential data, the meanings of the members of Group II are highly stable in their reference to the stream of speech in which they occur.[108]

Although no actual statistical count of parts of speech has been made in the course of this study, it is obvious that such a procedure would reveal additional information on the nature of Mongolian grammar. The relational elements in Mongolian which have the greatest frequency are supposedly declensional and conjugational suffixes. These, however, are not parts of speech. Aside from suffixes, the next most frequent elements in individual occurrence should be postpositions, in the light of the frequency studies mentioned by G. K. Zipf. This may or may not be the case, since no frequency tabulation has been made. However, among the postpositions themselves, certain ones occur far more frequently than do others. One might select *degere, dotora, dora,* and *tula* (*tölöö* in most dialects) as examples of these, particularly *degere.* The latter occurs with such greater relative frequency that its modern usage shows both a semantic and a phonological development, associated with words having "a low degree of articulatedness of meaning and a comparatively high relative frequency." This may best be explained as follows:

In the first place, if the original meaning of *degere* was "on top of, above, on; superior," then its later usage seems to acquire the more general and less intense meaning of "to, at, in." It does not replace the dative-locative suffix, which is considerably reduced in clarity of utterance as compared with its earlier forms, but it is used as a stronger alternate form, particularly when the location indicated is to be emphasized or when the location is one of comparative importance. In these circumstances, *degere* is often used with the meanings of "to; at, in," depending upon whether motion is involved or not. The following are locations mentioned in the examples of postpositional phrases with *degere* in chapter six.

1) *To*; a lamasery, the temple, the yurt, (any person).
2) *At*; the north gate, the factory, the Olympics, that place, the fighting front, the market, the yurt, the spring (of water), airport, school.
3) *In*; the universe, a few years, the great assembly, all branches of work, the Mongolian language.

Whether this usage of *degere* is merely of an idiomatic nature or not, the meaning of *degere* in these phrases is less "articulate." Not only that, but in the speech of some Mongols, notably the Ordos Mongols, the postposition *degere* is undergoing a phonological reduction which is not regular for general Mongolian words, but which must be attributed to the greater frequency of occurrence. The phonological reduction is in the form of loss of independent accent and vocalic harmony and hence greater assimilation to the preceding word. Cf. (*TOO*, p. 159) *t'ere sɯmeDēr* "à ce temple" and (*TOO*, p. 203) *t'ere ɢ̬aDžarDār* "at that place." Here we have a situation where -Dār / -Dēr is more like a declensional suffix than it is like a postpositional word. Furthermore, it is always attached to the same nominal or pronominal stem as the dative-locative. Rudnev, in his noun paradigms, listed *degere* and *dora* as supplementary dative-locative "suffixes," and *soo* (< *dotora*) as an "inessive-illative" suffix. However, he recognized the fact that these forms were different from other declensional suffixes in that they did not conform to the vocalic harmony of the words preceding them.[109]

Degere is not the only word to be affected in this manner in Mongolian. The "subject particle" *bol* (< *bolbala*) and the negative word *ügei* show the same phenomena. Cf. (*KhM*, p. 45) *ügüi-wəl* "if not" and *uul-wɒl* "as for the mountain." Ramstedt gives the following forms for *ügei* in his Kalmuk dictionary: *ügε̄* > *ugε̄* > *ugā̈* / *uγā*.[110] Cf. (*TOO*, p. LII) where the *nomen futuri* in -χu̯ / -ᵏχɯ is followed by *ügei* (ɯgᵘī / ɯgᵘē) > -*k'ᵘī* / -*k'ᵘē*. Cf. also Ord. Barū̯nt'ā < *Barū̯ū̯ t'ē (= *barayun tege*) "au Sud."

G. K. Zipf refers to this phenomenon as coming under the "law of abbreviation." He states it briefly as follows:

> In view of the evidence of the stream of speech we may say that the length of a word tends to bear an inverse relationship (not necessarily proportionate) to its relative frequency: and in view of the influence of high frequency on the shortenings from truncation and from durable

and temporary abbreviatory substitution, it seems a plausable deduction that, as the relative frequency of a word increases, it tends to diminish in magnitude. This tendency of a decreasing magnitude to result from an increase in relative frequency, may be tentatively named the Law of Abbreviation.

The law of abbreviation seems to reflect on the one hand an impulse in language toward the maintenance of an equilibrium between length and frequency, and on the other hand an underlying law of economy as the *causa causans* of this impulse toward equilibrium.[111]

These general remarks are made in passing and are intended more as suggestive of possible avenues of approach rather than as conclusions. The study of postpositions has been limited primarily to the syntax within postpositional phrases themselves. One feature of postpositional classification, not fully presented here, is the dichotomy between those postpositions which may be followed by the possessive-reflexive suffix (equivalent in meaning to Latin *suus*) and those which do not take this suffix. The postposition *degere* may be followed by the possessive-reflexive suffix, and it has this feature in common with ordinary declensional suffixes. Cf. *ger-t-ee(n)* "at one's yurt" and *surguul' deer-ee(n)* "at one's school." This situation is further proof of the fact that the minimal form postpositions are not in the same category as the nominative case forms of nouns, since the latter never appear with the possessive-reflexive suffix.

Additional information is needed concerning the occurrence of verbs with particular postpositions. The verbs in the sentences containing the postpositional phrases have been omitted for the most part, it having been stated that the postpositional phrases selected were adverbial to begin with (i.e., neither the subject nor the object of the main verb of the sentence). However, a beginning could be made in examining the types of verbs occurring with postpositional phrases by re-checking the examples cited here, since the source is given in each case. The chief reason for not including the entire statements in which the postpositional phrases found themselves is that a greater number of examples could be included in less space. By and large, once the postpositional phrase is identified, the major part of the task of analysis lies within the phrase itself, including the postposition involved. Since the elements of utterance are all inter-related it has been necessary to discuss many grammatical features which at first sight do not seem to have much in common with a postpositional phrase in its simplest form.

VI

LEXICON OF MINIMAL FORM POSTPOSITIONS WITH EXAMPLES OF USAGE

For purposes of arrangement, postpositions have been placed in the three following categories: (1) minimal form postpositions, (2) noun-postpositions, and (3) verb-postpositions. This chapter contains examples of minimal form postpositional phrases. Examples of postpositional phrases of categories (2) and (3) are given in chapter five. Lists of all postpositions mentioned in this study are given in appendix D.

The minimal form postpositions are listed below in alphabetic order and are numbered from 1 to 86. The examples of postpositional phrases are arranged under the appropriate postposition as determined by the postposition in the phrase. The examples are taken from texts, both oral and written, of all periods and from as many dialects as were available in published form at the time of writing. Since the postpositional phrases are taken from both historical and dialectal sources, it should be borne in mind that some of the postpositions are now obsolete and that others are confined to one or more dialects. In general, the examples themselves tend to reveal the state of affairs.

In most cases, where a good published translation exists, I have used it, whether the language is English, French, or German. For the *Secret History*, the French translations are by P. Pelliot,[112] unless indicated otherwise in the notes. The German translations of the *Secret History* are by E. Haenisch.[113] The translations of the examples from the Ordos dialect are by the Reverend Antoine Mostaert.[114] German translations published by N. Poppe are usually given in German; his Russian translations, however, are re-translated into English. The English translations of the Mongolian texts of the fourteenth century Sino-Mongolian inscriptions are by Professor F. W. Cleaves. Other translations are by the author of the publications from which the examples are taken. Except for the foregoing and unless otherwise indicated in the notes, the English translations are my own.

The examples under each postposition are listed in more or less historical sequence. The abbreviations indicating the textual sources are explained in the list of abbreviations on page xiii. "Cf." before a cited example indicates that the phrase is not adverbial in its original context.

(A) WITH NOUNS

1) *adali* "same, like, equal; similarly, equally; the same thing."
Cf. (*SH* § 31) *gü'ün ber morin ber činu suraγu-tur adali buyu* "et l'homme et le cheval existent, tels que tu interroges."
Cf. (*SH* § 155) *Yesügen-qatun-u üge-tür adali boldaǰu* "comme elle (= *Yesüi-qatun*) était conforme à ce qu'en avait dit (m. à m. 'aux paroles de') Yesügen-qatun."[115]

(*HsCh* 23b6) *toγaγsan-dur adali* "[it is] like having counted."

(*1338*, l. 34) *uqaγan bilig-tür inu adali* "[he was not employed] . . . in a manner becoming his understanding and wisdom."

(*Hy* IIa 7r) *de'ere tenggiri-yin ǰoriγ-tur adali* "like the will of heaven."

(*MSM*, p. 369b) *usundu adali* "like water."

Cf. (*SME*, l. 9) *mön minu enerin asaraqui ǰoriγ-tur adali bolumui ǰ-e* "[then thy conduct] likewise will be consistent with My loving and affectionate will."

(*SK*, p. 55) *qaγan-dur adali* "gleich einem Könige."

(*SK*, p. 55) *qaγan-luγa nigen adali* "einem Könige ganz gleich."

Cf. (*SK*, p. 13) *ǰireken-dür adali tere nökör* "dieser mein Busenfreund."

Cf. (*ST*, p. 284, l. 9) *ötele kümun-lüge adali busu* "mit keinem gewöhnlichen Menschen zu vergleichen."

(*AYM*, p. 12) *gegegen ariγun oron-luγa nigen adali tengčebei* "it compared with the shining pure place (i.e., with paradise)."

(*QQK*, p. 5) *niγur anu čilaγun adali* "his face [was] like stone."

(*QQK*, p. 9) *qarangγui kösige-yin adali* "like a black curtain."

(*QQK*, p. 13) *subud-un adali* "[tears] like pearls."

Kh. (*Kh*, p. 147) *urdanii adil* "wie früher, auf dieselbe Weise."

(*KhN*) *eregteitšüüdiin adil xödölmörlödž* "[the women] work the same as men."

(*Kh*, p. 149) *idžiitee adilxan* "like the mother."

(*SMY*, p. 164) *aawtaigaa adil* "like my father."

Ord. (*TOO*, p. 231) *eme k'ɯnlē aᴅali* "[pourquoi] semblable à une femme [t'occupes-tu d'idees mesquines]?"

(*TOO*, p. 73) *mini k'ɯ̄lē aᴅali* "à l'égal de mon fils."

Bur. (*BMS*, p. 33) *urdəinxida adli* "as formerly."

(*BMS*, p. 33) *Xolxoondol* (< *Xolxoondo adli*) "like Kohlkhon."

Cf. the Ordos examples of assimilation on page 65.

Mong. (*Monguor*, p. 160) *morila ᴅali ʂɢewa* "c'est aussi grand qu'un cheval."

Nom. Verb. (*EE*, p. 3) *abisig gün nom-ud-i qumqa-yin usun yegüleküü adali büridken abuγad* "having received [from the many sages . . .] ordinations and [communication of] the profound religious doctrines . . . assembling them even as one pours the water of a vessel."
Cf. (*TOO*, p. 210) *tšʿi enᴅēr ɯ ʿkχɯwel ʙi tšʿamā̈ alasan aᴅali* "si tu meurs ici, ce sera comme si moi je t'avais tuée."

(*BMS*, p. 33) *xebtexeteigei adli untašaba* "as soon as [he] lay down, [he] fell asleep."

Adali is used to form a derivative verb in the same manner as nouns or adjectives by means of a suffix. Cf. (*K*, p. 2318) *yekedkü* "s'agrandir" from *yeke* "grand," (*K*, p. 67) *adalidqu* "etre égal" from *adali* "égal."

2) *alus* "across, through, beyond."

(*SH* § 195) *a'ula alus* "beyond the mountain."

(*ST*, p. 74, l. 19) *mören alus* "[campaigning] beyond the river."

(*K*, p. 78) *γurban ger alus üldeged* "après trois maisons, trois maisons de passées."

(*WM*, p. 38) *Yool alus* / *γool-un alus* "uber den Fluss."

(*K*, p. 78) *temegen-ü alus qarayiqu* "sauter par dessus un chameau."

3) *aru* "back; north; after, in back of, following."

(*K*, p. 149) *aγula-yin aru* "derrière la montagne."

4) *čaγada* "beyond; in the vicinity."

(*SH* § 232) *ger ča'ada* "near the yurt."

(*SH* § 278) *e'üten ča'ada* "dicht an der Tür."

(*1335*, l. 35) *degedüs-ün derge čaγada yabuγad* "having been in the service of the Emperor (lit., 'having circulated in the presence and in the vicinity of the Emperor')."

(*1362*, 21) *qoton-u čaγada kürčü* "[they] arrived in the vicinity of the town."
Kh. (*R*, p. 288) *tsaad* = *tsaana*. Cf. *čaγana* below.

5) *čaγadu* "in that direction; beyond."

(*ČQ*, p. 128) *γurban kötel-yin čaγadu* "beyond three passes."
Cf. (*K*, 2081) *čaγa* "au delà de," (*BMS*, p. 392) *saa* "beyond."

6) *čaγana* "further on, beyond, behind, in that direction, on that side."
Kh. (*SMY*, p. 176) *dalain tsaana* "beyond the sea."

(*R*, p. 288) *geriin tsaana* "behind the yurt."

(*Kh*, p. 60) *uuləin tsaana* "jenseits des Berges."

(*MKB*, p. 23) *noməin sangiin tsaana* "behind the library." Also Ord. *tšʿāʿtʿā̈* (< **čaγatai*).[116]

(*DO*, p. 697a) *ɢolīī tš'ā't'ā* "de l'autre côté de la rivière."

(*DO*, p. 697a) *k'eᴅɯn ɯᴅɯrīī tš'ā't'ā* "après quelques jours."

Bur. (*HB*, p. 104) *neg dabaanee saana* "beyond a mountain pass."

(*BMS*, p. 392) *saa* "beyond," cf. (*K*, p. 2081) *čaγa/čege* "au delà de, derrière, après," used for *čaγana*.

7) *čaγasi* "further on, there, in that direction."

Cf. (*K*, p. 2096) *časi/činaγsi* "de côté, un peu plus haut, là."

Cf. (*Geserica*, p. 27) "die Formen *naγasi* und *čaγasi* gehen auf *inaγasi* und **tiγasi* (Primärstamm **ti-*) zürück und kommen in der Schriftsprache als Entlehnung aus der Umgangsprache vor."

Kh. (*Kh*, p. 158) *ternees tsaiši* "beyond that [place]."

Ord. (*DO*, p. 697b) *margā't'ās tš'āši* "après le jour de demain."

Bur. (*BMS*, p. 393) *endehee saaša* "from now on."

8) *činadu* "beyond, on the other side, outside; foreign."

(*K*, p. 2130) *dalai-yin činadu kedülǰü γarqu* "traverser la mer."

(*MKB*, p. 111) *xiliin tšanad baix dzuur* "while being beyond the border."

Cf. the plural noun form *činadus* "enemies, adversaries."

9) *činaγsi* "further on, in the opposite direction; aside from; henceforth, in the future."

(*K*, p. 2131) *tegüneče činaγsi* "plus loin, outre cela."

10) *činana* "beyond."

(*SH* § 142) *te'ün-ü činana* "au delà de celui-là."

11) *činegen* "size, extent, measure; force, power; ability, skill."

(*K*, p. 2134) *kedüi činegen* "combien?"

(*K*, p. 2134) *edüi činegen* "autant, si souvent."

(*K*, p. 2134) *tedüi činegen* "autant."

(*K*, p. 2134) *ker činegen* "combien?"

(*K*, p. 2134) *kedüi činegen qola γaǰar bui* "quelle est la distance du lieu?"

Kh. (*R*, p. 307) *uuləin tšineen* "as large as a mountain."

Cf. (*DzDz*, l. 619) *xoninii tšineen tsagaan tšuluugaar* "with a white stone the size of a sheep."

Cf. (*Kh*, p. 143) *üxeriin tšineen bul xara tšuluugaar* "with a round stone the size of an ox."

Cf. (*Kh*, p. 152) *nege moriin tolgoin tšineen erdeniig* "a jewel the size of a horse's head."

Ord. (*TOO*, p. L) *sųɢā k'ɯni tš'önön* "aussi haut qu'un homme qui est assis."

Cf. (*TOO*, p. 148) *ʙi tš'amaᴅų t'ere šiwųų̄ ᴅö'tš'önoō (< tedüi činegen) maχa öɢöjō* "Je te donnerai une quantité de viande égale au poids de cet oiseau."

Cf. (*TOO*, p. 201) *moŋgol Gerīī Dö'tš'ōnōn eD erDeni owōloDži wān* "[devant le trône] étaient amoncelés des objets précieux [qui formaient un tas] aussi grand qu'une tente mongole."

12) *čuγ* "together, with."
Kh. (*MKB*, p. 38) *ter nöxörtei tsug* "together with that friend."
(*MKB*, p. 38) *bi tšinii axtai tsug otšino* "I'm going together with your elder brother."
(*Kh*, p. 65) *aawatai tsug* "zusammen mit dem Vater."
Bur. (*BMS*, p. 410) *axataigaa sug* "together with one's brother."

13) *daraγa* "after, one after the other, afterwards, following."
Cf. (*K*, p. 1663) *dara (= darā) / daraγa.*
(*OS*, p. 318) *qotala tegüs geyigülügseger iregsen-ü daraγa* "[il]... leur procura un lustre plein et parfait. Plus tard..."
(*K*, p. 1663) *tegün-ü daraγa* "à la suite, après."
Kh. (*KhN*) *ene sanal xuraaltəin daraa* "following this plebiscite."
(*KhN*) *töröxiin ömnö ba törsnii ni daraa* "before and after birth."
(*SMY*, p. 163) *tüünees xoiš neg sar bolsnəi daraa Xišgee xüüxnii xariu dzaxidləig xüleedž awaw* "after that, when a month had passed, [he] received an answer by letter from the girl Khishge."
(*SMY*, p. 66) *tus xurləin daraa n'* "after the meeting."
Cf. (*WY*, p. 98) *tegünü udaγa* "vsled za nimi."

14) *darui* "immediately, at once; following."
(*AYM*, l. 6) *tegünče darui* "right after that."
(*R*, p. 68) *ter darui* "at that moment."
(*TOO*, p. 16) *unt'asan Darᵘī* "dès qu'il fut endormi."

15) *degegsi* "upwards; up towards."
(*K*, p. 1744) *degereče degegsi* "plus haut et plus haut."
(*ÜD*, p. 133) *oγtorγui-dur degegsi üǰeged* "looking up to the sky."
(*OS*, p. 329) *mingγan-ača degegsi erüke* "plus de mille familles."
Kh. (*KhN*) *tawin xuwias deeš* "above fifty per cent."
(*SMY*, p. 88) *dzuugaas deeš* "more than one hundred."
Ord. (*DO*, p. 143) *salᵏχi(n) Deš jawu̯-* "marcher contre le vent."
(*DO*, p. 144a) *miŋgās Deš* "plus de mille."
(*DO*, p. 152) *Doras Dešen* "de bas en haut."
Mong. (*DM*, p. 419) *k'ōrGuoni t'iese t'as īna* "en amont du pont il y a des pierres."

16) *degegür* "along the top of, above; the surface."
(*WM*, p. 134) *Sümbür aγula-yin degegür* "along the top of mount Sumeru."
(*WM*, p. 134) *Aziya tib-ün degegür* "over the Asian continent."
Kh. (*Kh*, p. 74) *usan deegüür* "uber dem Wasser."

(*Kh*, p. 138) *dzaxa dzeeli deegüüren* "along the market-place."
(*SMY*, p. 149) *tsasan deegüür güix* "to run over the snow."
(*SMY*, p. 150) *dzax deegüür* "at the market."
Ord. (*TOO*, p. 155) *k'örgön Degür* "sur le pont."
(*TOO*, p. 332) *mösön Degür* GɯigeG*'tš'i* "[celui] qui a l'habitude de passer en galopant par-dessuss la glace."
(*TOO*, p. 114) *ene suwagii Degür* "[jump] over the ditch."

17) *degere* "on, above, high; besides, aside from; superior, better; supreme."
(*SH* § 89) *γajar de'ere* "auf Erden."
(*SH* § 75) *Onan-u ergi de'ere sa'uju* "sitting on the shore of the Onan [river]."
(*SH* § 194) *ni'ur de'ere anu* "ihnen ins Gesicht."
(*SH* § 146) *daba'an de'ere* "auf dem Bergübergang."
(*SH* § 149) *tergen de'ere* "sur la charrette."
(*HsCh* 7a5) *delekei deger-e* "on earth."
(*HsCh* 6a2) *mölsün deger-e geckikü* "treading on thin ice."
(*1346*, l. 17) *ayan deger-e* "on [military] campaigns."
(*1362*, l. 47) *iren odun yabuqu mör degere* "on the way where one goes to and from [the tomb]."
(*Hy* IIa 26r) *delegei de'ere* "on earth."
(*Hy* IIa 17v) *γajar de'ere* "sur la terre."
(*MSM*, p. 368b) *usun deere* "[the fish came] to the surface of the water."
(*ST*, p. 226, l. 1) *Čabčiyal degere kürcü ireged* "having arrived at Čabčiyal (i.e., 'the pass')."
(*ST*, p. 287, l. 8) *Ordus-un nutuγ Toli kemekü degere* "im Lande der Ordos, in der Gegend Toli genannt."
(*ST*, p. 204) *Qalq-a degere* "[ruling] over the Khalkha."
(*ST*, p. 158, l. 4) *kötel degere* "im Engpasse."
(*ST*, p. 156, l. 9) *ayan degere* "auf [diesem] Feldzuge."
(*ST*, p. 262, l. 5) *siregen degere* "on the throne."
(*ST*, p. 208, l. 18) *Könggei Sabqan degere* "on [mount] Könggei Sabqa."
(*ST*, p. 214, l. 1) *Sira mören degere* "on the Yellow river."
(*OS*, p. 318) *bariγun γurba kemekü ordus tümen degere ejilen saγuju* "devint le seigneur du peuple ordos qu'on appelait 'les trois *tumen* (= 10,000) de droite.'"
(*EE*, p. 7) *Erdeni Juu degere Qalq-a bügüdeger tangsuγ ergüjü* "[having invited the Gegegen] to [the lamasery of] Erdeni Juu and having offered him *tangsuγ*."[117]
(*WY*, p. 107, l. 14) *ürtüsün degere* "on a piece of cloth."
(*CSN*) *yirtinčü degere* "in the universe."
(*CSN*) *Mongγol kele degere-ben* "in our Mongolian language."

(*CSN*) *tayiǰa<u>n</u>* <u>*degere*</u> "on the [theatrical] stage."
Note *tayiǰa(n)* < *t'ai-tzu* 臺子, an *-n* stem by analogical formation.

(*MKB*, p. 140) *man-u ger* <u>*degere*</u> *tabun čaγan čerig ireged* "five white soldiers having come to our yurt."

Gen. (*SH* § 205) *bürin-<u>ü</u>* <u>*de'ere*</u> *sa'uǰu* "occupying [the throne] over all."

(*Hy* IIa 2r) *olon ulus irgen-<u>ü</u>* <u>*de'ere*</u> *qan* "khan over all peoples."

(*MSM*, p. 378a) *ükeer<u>iin</u>* <u>*deere*</u> *qailaqu* "to weep over the corpse."

(*MSM*, p. 369b) *usu<u>ni</u>* <u>*deere*</u> "[grass] on the surface of the water."

(*MSM*, p. 110a) *balγasun ger<u>iin</u>* <u>*deere*</u> "above the palace."

(*MSM*, p. 148b) *mori<u>ni</u>* <u>*deere*</u> "on the horse."

(*SK*, p. 16) *bayising-<u>un</u>* <u>*degere*</u> *γarču* "[sie] stieg auf das Dach der Wohnung."

(*ST*, p. 2, l. 19) *tere usun-<u>u</u>* <u>*degere*</u> "auf der Wasserfläche."

(*WM*, p. 127) *qabtaγai čilaγun-<u>un</u>* <u>*degere*</u> "on top of a flat stone."

(*WM*, p. 134) *γaǰar-<u>un</u>* <u>*degere*</u> "over the earth."

(*WM*, p. 134) *delekei-<u>yin</u>* <u>*degere*</u> "over the world."

Kh. (*SMY*, p. 159) *Galdan sandil* <u>*deer*</u> *otšidž suuw* "Galdan sat down on the chair."

(*KhN*) *xog* <u>*deer*</u> *xayax* "to throw into the rubbish."

(*SMY*, p. 102) *sambar* <u>*deer*</u> "on the blackboard."

(*SMY*, p. 127) *olon xüniig atšaanəi mašin* <u>*deer*</u> *suulgaw* "[they] loaded many people on the truck."

(*Kh*, p. 146) *tolgoi* <u>*deere*</u> "on [his] head."

(*Kh*, p. 159) *uuliin oroi* <u>*deere*</u> "on the mountain top."

(*SMY*, p. 129) *oro<u>n</u>* <u>*deer*</u> "in bed."

(*SMY*, p. 179) *dalnəi yasa<u>n</u>* <u>*deer*</u> "on the shoulder blade."

(*SMY*, p. 160) *tsagaan toso<u>n</u>* <u>*deer*</u> *xaluun tsai daxin xiidž yaaraltaigaar uudž baiw* "pouring hot tea on the cream-butter, [he] drank [it] hurriedly."

(*EBQ*, l. 427) *χar mor!<u>n</u>* <u>*Dēr*</u> "[er sprang] auf das schwarze Ross."

(*Kh*, p. 153) *mörö<u>n</u>* <u>*deere*</u> "on the shoulder."

(*Kh*, p. 156) *usa<u>n</u>* <u>*deere*</u> "on the water."

(*DzDz*, l. 655) *xada<u>n</u>* <u>*deer*</u> "on the cliff."

(*Kh*, p. 74) *širee<u>n</u>* <u>*deere*</u> "auf dem Tisch."

(*Kh*, p. 158) *širee<u>n</u>* <u>*deere*</u> "on the throne."

(*SMY*, p. 52, 95, 166) *širee* <u>*deer*</u> "on the table."

Note (*R*, p. 86) lists this noun as an *-n* stem, *širee<u>n</u>* <u>*deer*</u> "on the table." The Buriat dictionary (*BMS*, p. 718) lists it as a vowel stem, the genitive being *šereegei*. See below (*HB*, p. 114) *širee* <u>*deer*</u> "on the throne." Cf. Mr. Austin's letter on page 39. For morphological alternations, see also pages 37 and 39. Cf. below Ord. *ene širenDēr* "sur ce trône."

(KhN) üildweriin gadzar deer "at the factory."

(KhN) olimpiad deer "at the Olympics."

(KhN) teatrəin tawtsan deer "on the theatrical stage."

(*SMY*, p. 157) *front deer* "at the [fighting] front."

(Kh, p. 139) *xaanii dzaxa deere* "into the presence of the Khan."

(KhN) nisex ongotsnəi buudal deer "at the airport."

(KhN) büx delxii deer "in the whole world."

(KhN) ix xural deer "in the great assembly."

(KhN) tüüxii ed deer adžilladag "[they] work on raw materials."

(Kh, p. 160) *sonin tsetseg deere* "[ran up] to Sonin Tsetseg."

(DzDz, l. 122) *bulag deer* "at the spring."

(*DzDz*, l. 655) *dzam deer* "on the way."

(*SMY*, p. 133) *oros xel deer* "in the Russian language."

Cf. Buriat (*BMS*, p. 237) *buryat xelen deere* "in the Buriat language."

(KhN) adžləin salaa mötšir büxen deer "in all branches of work."

(Kh, p. 152) *xoito xaalgan deere* "at the north gate."

(*Kh*, p. 160) *mangas untaxa-deere* "while the mangus slept."

Gen. *(KhN) ix yadarsnəi deer* "in addition to being very tired."

(KhN) tsaling xölsöö büren awdgiin deer "in addition to receiving all [one's] pay."

(KhN) exlex yostoin deer "aside from the necessity of beginning."

Ord. (*TOO*, p. 98) *t'ere orⁿDār* "sur cette éminence."

(*TOO*, p. 14) *nege tš'agāā t'alaDār* "dans une plaine unie."

(*TOO*, p. 137) *suDurDār* "dans les livres."

(*TOO*, p. 185) *ene širēnDēr* "sur ce trône."

(*TOO*, p. 113) *naB'tš'inDār* "sur les feuilles."

(*TOO*, p. 130) *nėge muDun Dēre* "sur un arbre."

(*TOO*, p. 141) *ūlan Dēr* "sur le mont."

(*TOO*, p. 61) *t'ere usunDār i'tš'ēt* "entrés dans cette eau."

(*TOO*, p. 161) *mini mörönDōr* "sur mes épaules."

Cf. page 38 for remarks on postpositions following vocalic harmony.

(*TOO*, p. 224) *t'ɯlēē Dēre* "sur le [monceau de] bois."

(*TOO*, p. 136) *k'eDɯn DžilDēr* "quelques années après."

(*TOO*, p. 52) *t'ere maŋgusīī GerDēr i'tš'iDži* "[ils] se rendirent à la maison du manghus."

(*TOO*, p. 32) *nėge ālDār i'tš'iDži* "il entra chez une famille."

(*TOO*, p. 113) *χuDugīn amanDār* "dans le voisinage d'un puits."

(*TOO*, p. 159) *t'ere sɯmeDēr* "[il se rendit] à ce temple."

(*TOO*, p. 203) *t'ere GaDžarDār* "at that place."

Cf. (*DO*, p. 140b) *salᵏχin Dēre t'ala* "le côté d'où souffle le vent." Also Ord. *Dē't'ī (< *degetei).*[118]

(*TOO*, p. 104) *t'ere salᵏχin* Dē't'ī "au dessus [de la poussière soulevée par] ce vent."

(*TOO*, p. 65) Balqụsụn ūDen Dē't'ī "au dessus de la porte de la ville."

Bur. (*BMS*, p. 237) *delxii deere* "in the world."

(*HB*, p. 115) *ger deeren* "in his house."

(*BMS*, p. 397) *sambar deere bešexe* "to write on the blackboard."

(*HB*, p. 114) *širee deer* "on the throne."

(*BMS*, p. 665) *stul deer* "on the chair."

(*BMS*, p. 237) *nogoon deere* "on the grass."

(*HB*, p. 12) *šuluun deere* "on the stone."

(*HB*, p. 78) *morin deeree* "on one's horse."

(*BMS*, p. 237) *buryat xelen deere* "in the Buriat language."

Cf. Khalkha (*SMY*, p. 133) *oros xel deer* "in the Russian language."

Kalm. (*KD*, p. 359) *širēn dēr* "auf den stuhl."

(*KD*, p. 91) *mösn dērᵊ* "on the ice."

(*KD*, p. 91) *mörn dērᵊ gạrχɒ* "sich auf das ross setzen."

Dag. (*Dagur*) *aŭlī dēr* "on the mountain."

(*Dagur*, p. 46) *somᵒī dēr* "above the [shot] arrow."

Mong. (*Monguor*, p. 17) *śiriēni* Dẹre / *śiriē* Dẹre "sur la table."

Mog. (*Mogholica*, p. 4) *morin dērä* "auf das pferd."

Abl. (*HsCh* 16a7) *taqimdaγu bolqui-ača deger-e* "above the fact of being filial."

(*R*, p. 86) *nadaas deer* "better than I."

Cf. (*Kh*, p. 82) *xöl xugarsan nere xugarsanaas deere* "besser seine Beine zu brechen, als seinen Namen zu verderben."

(*DO*, p. 140b) *tš'amās* Dēre "meilleur que toi."

Cf. (*TOO*, p. 503) *šine emtš'ēs širgēsen ụsụ* Dēre "de l'eau bouillie vaut mieux qu'un médecin novice."

(*Monguor*, p. 158) *niănDza* Dẹre "outre ceci."

18) *dergede* "near, alongside; in the presence of; at, to."

(*SH* § 90) *ger-ün dergede* "[chevaux . . . qui étaient debout] près des tentes."

(*SH* § 234) *ordo-yin dergede* "near the palace."

(*SH* § 255) *aqa-yu-an dergede* "by the side of my elder brother."

(*HsCh* 6a1) *gün čegel-ün dergede* "on the brink of a deep abyss."

(*SK*, p. 4) *nigen yeke qadan-u dergede* "in der Nähe einer grossen Felswand."

(*SK*, p. 55) *tere qaγan bolun naγaduγči keüken-ü dergede oyira irebesü* "wer diesen den König spielenden Knaben nahe kam."

(*ST*, p. 268, l. 14) *J̌uu Sakyamuni-yin dergede* "in der Nähe des J̌uu Sakyamuni."

(*BE*, p. 89) *ordun-u dergede* "vor das Zelt . . . [gekommen]."

(*ÜD*, p. 132, l. 11) *tere bars-un dergede kürügsen-dür* "when [they] arrived in the vicinity of the tiger."

(*K*, p. 1776) *yasun-u* *dergede* "près de cadavre."
(*K*, p. 2040) *modun-u* *dergede* "auprès d'un arbre."
(*MKB*, p. 31) *tere bayising-un* *dergede* "near that building."
(*MKB*, p. 31) *manu ger-ün* *dergede* "near our yurt."
Kh. (*Kh*, p. 157) *aawiin* *dergede* "in the presence of the father."
(*Kh*, p. 156) *xatan idžiin* *dergede* "in the presence of the queen mother."
Ord. (*TOO*, p. 110) *ŪDenīĩ Baryŭ̃ Ga'tš'aB'tš'inīĩ DergeDe sy̆* "assieds-toi près du jambage droit de la porte."
(*TOO*, p. 49) *Dẹren* *DergeDɯ* "près de l'oreiller."
(*TOO*, p. 102) *nojon* *Derget* *i'tš'ēt* "il se présenta devant le magistrat."
(*TOO*, p. 212) *t'ere mụDụn* *Derget* "près de cet arbre."
(*TOO*, p. 62) *ụsụn* *DergeDɯ* "à proximité de l'eau."
(*TOO*, p. 147) *t'ere jasụn* *Derget* "près de ces ossements."
(*TOO*, p. 159) *jāmụni GaDžarīĩ* *DergeDe* "près d'un tribunal."
Bur. (*BMS*, p. 235) *gerei* *dergede* "near the house."

19) *dergedegür* "along the vicinity of."
(*ČT*, p. 76, l. 2) *süme keyid-ün* *dergedegür* *buu abal-a* "do not hunt in the vicinity of monasteries."
(*TOO*, p. 202) *t'ere Gụ'tš'an* *DergeDɯ̄r* "près de ces béliers."

20) *doγoγsi* "towards the bottom."
(*DO*, p. 154a) *salᵏχi(n)* *Dōš* *jawụ-* "marcher suivant la direction du vent."

21) *doγoγur* "downwards, further down."
Cf. (*K*, p. 1803) *doγuur* "en bas, vers le bas, plus bas."
Kh. (*KhM*, p. 25) *sụgɒn* *Dōgụ̄r* "unter dem arm."
(*NB*, p. 71) *šireen* *dooguur* *ordžee* "he crawled under the table."
Ord. (*TOO*, p. 106) *χāni šaŋgīĩ* *Dōgụ̄r* "sous le palais de l'empereur."

22) *doora / dora* "beneath, under; low place; low; insignificance; on the spot, here."[119]
(*SH* § 194) *tayang Qan-u* *doro* *medegü yeke noyan* "a great prince who commanded under Tayang Qan."
(*SH* § 210) *J̌öči-yin* *doro* *tümen-ü noyan* "myriarch under J̌öči."
(*SH* § 86) *iseri-yin* *doro* *gürtele* "jusque sous son lit."
(*K*, p. 1786) *toγoγan-u* *doora* *yeke γal tülikü* "faire un grand feu sous la chaudière."
(*K*, p. 1786) *burqan-u ömei-yin* *doora* *mörgükü* "se jeter aux pieds de bouddha."
(*WM*, p. 134) *tegri-yin* *doora* "under heaven."
Abl. (*HsCh* 22b1) *bürin-eče* *door-a* *bolbasu* "if he should be lower than all [others]."
(*ST*, p. 130, l. 15) *čimača* *doora* "after you (i.e., after your time)."

Kh. (*Kh*, p. 74) *gadzar doro* "unter der Erde."

(*SMY*, p. 160) *end gadzar dor tšuluun nüürs bii* "coal is found here under the ground."

(*DzDz*, l. 457) *širdeg dooron* "under the mattress."

(*Kh* [Rudnev], p. LXII) *tšuluun door* "under the stone."

(*DzDz*, l. 143) *tulgan door* "under the andiron."

(*NB*, p. 71) *gadasan door arwan alda gadzar* "[having dug up] an area of ten *alda* under the post."

(*R*, p. 71) *šireen dor* "under the table."

(*EBQ*, l. 366) *gedž xelxe-dor* "als [er] so gesprochen."

(*R*, p. 71) *nadaas dor* "worse than I."

(*KhN*) *udirdlagəin dor* "under the leadership [of]."

Ord. (*TOO*, p. 104) *mini Ģar Doro* "sous mes ordres."

(*TOO*, p. 45) *ụrDụ Doro nėge Bụlak̥ Bī* "à l'est il y a une source."

(*DO*, p. 152b) *ene ụrDụ Doro* "à l'est d'ici."

(*TOO*, p. 200) *ūDen Doro* "under the door."

(*TOO*, p. 117) *ene mụDụn Doro* "au bas de cet arbre."

(*TOO*, p. 61) *naran Doro* "sous le soleil."

(*TOO*, p. 84) *t'ogoo Doro* "sous une marmite."

(*DO*, p. 152b) *širee Doro* "sous la table."

(*DO*, p. 152b) *tš'amban Doro* "au pied du mur."

(*DO*, p. 152b) *ụ̄lāe Doro* "au pied de la montagne."

(*DO*, p. 152b) *χụDụgīī Doro* "au fond du puits."

(*DO*, p. 152b) *malās Doro* "pire que les bestiaux."

Bur. (*HB*) *modon-doro* "under the tree."

(*HB*, p. 79) *teren-doro* "under it."

(*BMS*, p. 214) *tahaldaxəin ayuul doro* "under fear of collapse."

(*KD*, p. 95) *gazr dor^o* "unter der erde."

(*KD*, p. 95) *ter^ə dor^o* "da (wo sie waren)."

Mong. (*Monguor*, p. 156) *muni Dōro* "sous moi."

(*DM*, p. 61) *Ger Dōro re* "entre dans la maison."

23) *doroγsi* "downwards."

(*K*, p. 1890) *egün-ü doroγsi* "après, puis."

(*K*, p. 1890) *nayiman nasutu-ača degegsi arban nasutu-ača doroγsi* "depuis huit jusqu'à dix-huit ans."

Kh. (*R*, p. 71) *xoyor saraas dorogš güi* "not less than two months."

24) *dorona* "east; in the east."

(*SH* § 214) *eke-yin ger-tür dorona sa'uǰu büle'e* "[elle] se trouvait assise du côté est dans la tente de [ma] mère."[120]

(*SH* § 177) *Tüngge γoroqan-u dorona ba'uǰu* "étant descendu [de cheval] à l'Est de la rivière Tönggä."

25) *dotoγur* "along the inside; within; secretly."

Cf. (*R*, p. 73) *dotuur* "within; secretly."

Ord. (*DO*, p. 154b) *ɯnisɯn Do'ť'ųr Gar-* "passer entre le monceau de cendres et la maison."
Bur. (*HB*, p. 118) *uhaŋ-sooguur* "in the water."

26) *dotora* "in, inside, into; among, during; the inside."
(*SH* § 16) *ger dotora* "in the yurt."
(*SH* § 145) *sedkil dotora minu* "in my mind."
(*SH* § 101) *ene tergen dotora* "dans cette charrette."
(*SH* § 230) *oron dotora* "in [meinem] Bette."
(*SH* § 86) *nungγasun dotora* "in the wool."
(*'P* XII, l. 6) *gün sudurnu'ud dotora* "in the profound books."
(*'P* XIII, l. 5) *č'abč'a'al dot'ora* "in the pass."
(*1338*, l. 6) *bidan-u ordu dotor-a* "within our *ordu*."
(*MSM*, p. 167a) *setkil dotura* "in [his] mind."
(*ÜD*, p. 134, l. 7) *tere abdar-a dotor-a oroγulǰu* "causing [it] to be put into that box."
(*WY*, p. 80, l. 3) *Qori dotora* "among the Khori."
Gen. (*SH* § 254) *činu kö'üd-ün dotora* "among thy sons."
(*SH* § 6) *irgen-ü dotora* "among the people."
(*HsCh* 16b3) *amitan-u dotor-a* "among all creatures."
(*ST*, p. 124, l. 8) *qota-yin dotora oroǰu* "entering into the city."
(*ST*, p. 160, l. 15) *qoyitu ger-ün dotora* "inside the rear yurt."
(*ST*, p. 264, l. 17) *ulus-un dotora* "unter dem Volke."
(*OS*, p. 326) *tasuldal-ügei iregsen-ü dotor-a* "et pendant qu'elle (i.e., la religion) poursuivait le cours de son développement sans que la (racine) en fut coupée."
(*AYM*, l. 8) *ene süme-yin dotora* "inside this temple."
(*ÜD*, p. 133, l. 9) *nigen oi-yin dotor-a* "im Inneren eines Waldes."
(*EE*, p. 19) *aqa degüü-yin dotora* "in the midst of the younger and elder brothers."
(*EE*, p. 42) *ǰarliγ-un dotora* "inside of a *ǰarliγ*."
(*Doc. C*, l. 9) *iregsen bičig-ün dotora* "within a letter which came."
(*Doc. C*, l. 17) *man-u qosiγun-u dotora* "within our banner."
(*K*, p. 1844) *ger-ün dotora oroqu* "entrer dans la maison."
(*CSN*) *dayin-u γurban ǰil-ün dotora* "during three years of war."
(*CSN*) *ene sumu-yin dotor-a* "within this arrow (i.e., the administrative unit)."
(*CSN*) *mal taγuγčid-un dotora* "among cattle-herders."
(*MKB*, p. 140) *mayiqan-u dotora* "inside the tent."
Kh. (*R*, p. 73) *ger dotor* "in the yurt."
(*MKB*, p. 92) *ene dzoxiol dotor* "in this [literary] work."

(*Kh*, p. 141) *dalai dotor* "in the sea."

(*Kh*, p. 153) *yixe süme dotor suudag imaa* "[he] lives in a large monastery."

(*Kh*, p. 160) *bulgan xöndžil dotor* "in a sable bedspread."

(*SMY*, p. 160) *maixan dotor yamar tš tšimee anirgüi* "not a sound was heard in the tent."

(*SMY*, p. 81) *tüünii baruun garəin algan dotor* "in the palm of his right hand."

(*SMY*, p. 158) *gün oin modon dotor xeden maixan baina* "in the thick forest there are some tents."

(*Kh*, p. 157) *usan dotor* "in the water."

(*Kh*, p. 146) *ayagan dotor* "in the cup."

(*Kh*, p. 185) *tulaman dotor* "im Sack."

(*DzDz*, l. 638) *tere xodoodon dotor* "in his stomach."

(*R*, p. 73) *sarəin dotor* "during the month."

(*SMY*, p. 159) *manai dzaluutšuudəin dotor* "among our young people."

(*KhN*) *uls ündestnii dotor* "among the nations."

(*SMY*, p. 159) *tölöwlögööt tawan dziliin dotor* "during the five-year plan."

(*KhN*) *baga tsagiin dotor* "within a short time."

(*MKB*, p. 115) *arwan xonogiin dotor* "within ten days."

(*Kh*, p. 148) *önöö šöniin dotor* "during that night."

Ord. (*TOO*, p. 73) *G̨ụrwa χonoḳ ᴅo‘t‘oro* "within three days."

(*TOO*, p. 26) *nėg̨e χa͞rtš‘aḳ ᴅo‘t‘or t‘aw^i a͞t* "il [la] (=souris) mit dans une boite."

(*TOO*, p. 133) *t‘ere G̨urwã sara ᴅo‘t‘oro* "pendant ces trois mois."

(*TOO*, p. 105) *χụᴅụḳ ᴅo‘t‘oro* "à l'intérieur du puits."

(*TOO*, p. 60) *t‘ere ʙụ‘t‘a ʙụrg̨asụn ᴅo‘t‘oro* "dans ces broussailles et saules des dunes."

(*TOO*, p. 186) *mụᴅụn ᴅo‘t‘or* "dans la forêt."

(*TOO*, p. 29) *ụsụn ᴅo‘t‘oro* "dans l'eau."

(*TOO*, p. 15) *ᴅeʙšin ᴅo‘t‘oro* "in the plate."

(*TOO*, p. 36) *t‘ere aʙᴅaran ᴅo‘t‘oro* "dans cette caisse."

(*TOO*, p. 152) *t‘og̨o͞o ᴅo‘t‘oro* "dans la marmite."

(*TOO*, p. 113) *ene χụᴅụg̨i͞i ᴅo‘t‘oro* "dans ce puits."

(*TOO*, p. 102) *k‘ɯre͞e ᴅo‘t‘oro* "à l'intérieur de l'enclos."

Bur. (*HB*, p. 123) *ger-soo ordž* "entering the yurt."

Note Manchu *do* "interior," Mong. *doto-na*; **dotšo* > Buriat **dosoo* (Mongolian *č* > *s* in Buriat) > *soo*. See also page 38.

(*HB*, p. 67) *nuur-soo* "to the lake."

(*HB*, p. 61) *ayaga-soo* "in the cup."

(*HB*, p. 106) *xiit-soo* "in the monastery."

(*BMS*, p. 404) *nege minuta soo* "in a minute."

(*BMS*, p. 404) *ambar-soo* "in the warehouse."

(*HB*, p. LX) *uhan-soo* "in the water."

(*HB*, p. LIV) *modon-soo* "into the wood."

(*BMS*, p. 216) *haraɡin dotor* "within the month."

Note *dotor*; a literary loan form? Also (*BMS*, p. 216) *ger dosoo* "inside the yurt." Also (*BMS*, p. 273) *dzosoo = dosoo* "in, into, within."

Kalm. (*KD*, p. 97) *dalā̄ dotr̥* "im meer."

(*KD*, p. 97) *ūlīn dotr̥* "in dem berge."

Mong. (*DM*, p. 434) *amani t'uro* "dans la bouche."

(*DM*, p. 434) Ger *t'uro uro-* "entrer dans la maison."

Dag. (*Dagur*, p. 59) awcªī доа'т'ăр "in the tomb."

(*Dagur*, p. 36) бараӊ хорⁱējī маӊ доа'т'рīн "in our western court." хорⁱējī is in the genitive case.

Misc. (*TOO*, p. 127) Bolχų Do't'oro "néanmoins."

(*MKB*, p. 77) *kereg xeleltsesnii dotor* "while discussing the matter."

27) *dumda* "in the middle; middle; among; while; between, among."

(*SH* § 156) *ǰirin-ü dunda sa'uǰu* "zwischen beiden sitzend."

(*SH* § 244) *kilinglaǰu aqui dunda* "während er zürnte."

(*K*, p. 1864) *usun-u dumda büküi ongγoča* "vaisseau qui se trouve au milieu de la mer."

(*CSN*) *ene yeke nigedül-ün dumda tabun tiib-ün yeke baγa olan ulus orolčaǰai* "all nations great and small of the five continents have entered within this great union."

(*CSN*) *Ladoγa Oneγa qoyar-un dumda* "between lakes Ladoga and Onega."

Kh. (*DzDz*, l. 311) *ödör dunda* "in the middle of the day."

(*EBQ*, l. 516) *t'aɫ DųnDɒn t'àwⁱāt* "[er] lies los [das Ross] mitten in der Ebene."

(*EBQ*, l. 519) *ɢoɫ DųnDɒn ɢow!Dž* "[er] strengte sich an mitten im Flusstal."

(*EBQ*, l. 517) *t'ąegɒ̰ DųnDɒn nisχēt* "[sie] fliegen mitten im Urwald."

(*EBQ*, l. 520) *ɢorⁱχɒ̰ DųnDɒn nisχēt* "[sie] fliegen mitten im Bach."

(*SMY*, p. 177) *dalain dund* "in the middle of the sea."

(*SMY*, p. 160) *ta agaart üülnii dund baildana* "you fight in the air among the clouds."

(*KhM*, p. 47) *àrɪχīẕ DųnDɒ* "inmitten des festes."

(*Kh*, p. 163) *xöl-güi džargalangiin dunda* "midst endless pleasure."

Ord. (*TOO*, p. 188) *t'ere mųDųn DųnDa nėge χoŋχo ɯlgɯDži Bī* "au milieu de cetter forêt pend une clochette."

(*DO*, p. 161b) *k'ɯrēẽ DųnDa* "au milieu de la cour."

(*TOO*, p. 5) *t'ere gerelii DynDa* "au milieu de cette lumière."
(*DO*, p. 161b) *χojor e't'egedii DynDa* "entre deux parties."
(*TOO*, p. 93) *Dajārii DynDa* "devant toute l'assemblée."
(*TOO*, p. 119) *χojor ūlāē DynDa* "entre deux montagnes."
Bur. (*BMS*, p. 471) *tala dunda* "in the middle of the plain."
Kalm. (*KD*, p. 102) *ulᵘsin dundᴰ* "unter dem volke."
Mong. (*Monguor*, p. 156) *śirieni DunDani* "au milieu de la table."
(*DM*, p. 64) *ǵaDźiärni DunDa* "au centre de la terre."

28) *dumdaγur* "along the middle, halfway throughout."
(*KhN*) *dainəi dunduur* "throughout the war."

29) *ebür / öbür* "front, breast; south."
(*SH* § 107) *Burqan Qaldun-u ebür ba'uǰu* "[il] descendit [de cheval] en avant de Burqan-qaldun."

30) *ečine* "behind the back of."
(*SH* § 18) *Alan γo'a-yin ečine ügüleldürün* "[they] spoke to each other behind the back of Alan-γo'a."
(*SH* § 18) *eke-yü'en ečine* "during the absence of their mother."
(*SH* § 224) *nidün-ü ečine ilegü* "to banish from one's eyes."
Cf. the phrase *asan-ača ačinegün (= ečine-gün) angγidaγun* "aloof and away from Hasan" from one of the Idiqut-Schähri letters.[121] Here *ečine* has the adverbial suffix *-γun / -gün*.
Cf. (*SH* § 278) *ordo-yin qoyina'un urida'un* "in the rear and in front of the palace-yurt." The form *ečine'ün* is also in the *Secret History* (§ 244).

31) *emüne* "before, in the presence of; previously; in favor of; front; south; (Ordos) east."
(*SH* § 147) *qahan-u emüne* "vor dem Kaiser, für den Kaiser."
(*1362*, l. 6) *ulus-un emün-e* "[rendered service] to the Empire."
(*1362*, l. 20) *yeke törü-yin emün-e küčü öggün* "rendering service to the Empire (lit., 'before the great law')."
(*ÜD*, p. 132, l. 7) *bars-un emüne* "before the tiger."
(*WY*, p. 133, l. 8) *Bayiqal dalai-yin emüne* "south of Lake Baikal."
(*K*, p. 1301) *qan saγurin-u emüne* "devant le trône du khan."
Kh. (*SMY*, p. 162) *ex ornəi ix dainəi ömnö* "before the great patriotic war."
(*KhN*) *bidnii nüdnii ömnö* "before our eyes."
(*SMY*, p. 52) *geriin ömnö* "in front of the yurt."
(*KhN*) *xorin džiliin ömnö* "twenty years ago."
Abl. (*SMY*) *xuw'sgalaas ömnö* "before the revolution."
(*SMY*) *boroonoos ömnö* "before the rain (i.e., before the rain comes)."

Nom. Verb. (*SMY*, p. 109) *surguul' exlexiin ömnö* "before school opens."

(*SMY*) *öwsiig buxaldaxəin ömnö* "before stacking the hay."

(*KhN*) *Amerikaas garts̆ yawaxəin ömnö* "before [I] left America."

Ord. (*TOO*, p. 69) *mini nɯDɯn ömönö* "sous mes yeux."

(*DO*, p. 399b) *k'ɯni ömönö jawų-* "être au service de quelqu'un en qualité de domestique."

(*TOO*, p. 201) *t'ere s̆irēn ömönö* "devant le trône."

(*TOO*, p. 219) *mini Go't'ōn ömönö* "à l'est de ma ville."

(*TOO*, p. 211) *t'ere χųDųgās Barūn ömönö* "au sud-est de ce puits."

Mong. (*Monguor*, p. 13) *Ger(ni) mieşe* "devant la maison."

Cf. Ord. *ömös̆ön (< *emügsi-ben)*.

(*DM*, p. 237) *noyōni mieşe* "en présence d'un mandarin."

(*DM*, p. 237) *Gųrān uDurDza mieşe* "avant trois jours."

32) *ende* "here, at this place."

(*R*, p. 327) *manai end* "at our place here."

(*TOO*, p. 705) *mani enDe* "ici chez nous."

(*TOO*, p. 222) *ts̆'i mini enDe sų* "reste ici chez moi."

33) *esergü(ü)* "against, facing, opposite, toward."

(*SH* § 245) *Teb-Tengeri Odc̆igin-u esergü ǰaqa bariǰu barilduba* "Tebtenggeri griff nach Ottschigin und fasste seinen Kragen und sie rangen miteinander."

(*SH* § 142) *J̆amuγa-yin esergü inu morilaya* "montons à cheval à la rencontre de J̆amuqa."

Kh. (*R*, p. 330) *ardəin esergüü* "against the people."

(*R*, p. 330) *xuw'sgaləin esergüü* "counter-revolutionary."

(*KhN*) *Yaponəi esreg daineig dzarlaw* "[they] declared war on Japan."

(*KhN*) *s̆as̆nəi esreg* "against religion."

34) *eteged*, cf. number 69 (*tege*).

35) *γadaγa* "outside."

(*Kh*, p. 74) *geriin gadaa* "ausserhalb des Hauses."

(*DO*, p. 284a) *mani GaDā k'ɯni χoni irelē* "des moutons qui ne sont pas à nous sont arrivés à notre porte."

(*BMS*, p. 153) *burtaagai gadzaa xulyeexe* "to wait outside the gate."

(*Monguor*, p. 156) *Ger(ni) GaDa* "en dehors de la maison."

(*DM*, p. 114) *uDieni GaDa* "en dehors de la porte."

36) *γadaγsi* "outwards."

(*K*, p. 993) *qaγalγan-ac̆a γadaγsi buu γarγa* "ne fais pas sortir au delà de la porte."

(*DM*, p. 116) *uDieni ĢaDaşe* BĪ *Ģari* "ne mets pas le pied hors de la porte."

37) *γadaγur* "along the outside."
(*K*, p. 992) *ordu qarsi-yin γadaγur* "hors du palais."
(*BMS*, p. 153) *salin xülhenhöö gaduur* "aside from [one's] pay."

38) *γadana* "outside; besides, except."
(*1338*, l. 10) *anu balγasun-u γadana* "outside of their city."
(*EE*, p. 37) *Čiγulultu Qaγalγan-u γadana* "outside of Čiγulultu Qaγalγan."
(*EE*, p. 39) *J̌ang kiya qau-yin γadana* "outside of J̌ang kiya qau (Chang-chia-k'ou)."
(*K*, p. 989) *arban ǰil-ün γadana arban sara bülüge* "par dessus les dix ans, dix mois se sont écoulés."
(*K*, p. 989) *balγasun-u γadana üldeǰü kögekü* "chasser hors de la ville."
Abl. (*BE*, p. 96) *qudalduqui-ača γadana* "aside from doing business."
(*MKB*, p. 95) *kemekü-eče γadana* "aside from saying."
(*CSN*) *süme-yi üǰegsen-eče γadana* "aside from seeing the monastery."
Kh. (*MKB*, p. 122) *eldew xor xiixiin gadana* "aside from doing all kinds of harm."
(*Kh*, p. 64) *ene utširaas gadana* "ausser diesem Umstand."
Ord. (*TOO*, p. 223) *ene Ģo't'ōō ĢaDana* "à l'extérieur de cette ville."
Bur. (*BMS*, p. 153) *tereenhee gadna* "aside from that."

39) *γarui* "more than."
(*ST*, p. 130, l. 15) *arban γarun üy-e* "more than ten generations."
(*CSN*) *dayisun-u doluγan saya γarui čerig* "more than seven million of the enemy's soldiers."
(*CSN*) *edüge doluγan tümen γarui kümün bolǰai* "[they] were now more than seventy thousand men."
Kh. (*MKB*, p. 127) *dzuu garan* "more than one hundred."
Ord. (*DO*, p. 295b) *Ģų'tš'in Džil Ģarų̄* "plus de trente ans."
(*DO*, p. 295b) *arwās Ģarų̄* "plus de dix."
Cf. (*DO*, p. 295b) *Ģarų̄ = Ģar^{u}ī*

40) *ilegü(ü) / ülegü(ü)* "more than; superfluous."
Cf. (*SH* § 203) *ken-eče hüle'u güčü ögüle'e* "rendered more service than anyone."
Cf. (*1338*, l. 8) *tümen ülegü sükes* "more than one myriad of lingots."
Cf. (*EE*, p. 2) *mingγan ilegüü temege mori-yi gegeǰü* "losing more than one thousand camels and horses."

Kh. (*Kh* [Rudnev], p. LXVII) *ald iluü* "more than an alda."
Ord. (*TOO*, p. 85) *χan yrit yrDīī Gäχalās ilgū GäχaDži* "l'empereur était encore plus étonné qu'il ne l'avait été les fois précédentes."
(*DM*, p. 106) *χarwanDza fuliū* "plus de dix."

41) *inadu* "in this direction; that which is here."
(*K*, p. 275) *nadača inadu* "jusqu'à moi, jusqu'à mon temps."

42) *inaγsi* "here, hither, up to here; from, since."
(*SH* § 239) *Bajigid-ača inaγsi* "diesseits der Badschigit."
(*ST*, p. 46, l. 7) *tere uu quluγana jil-eče inaγsi* "seit jenem U-Mause-Jahre."
(*OS*, p. 318) *bayiγuluγsan-ača inaγsi* "après que . . . [il] eut établi."
(*EE*, p. 34) *erte-eče inaγsi* "from antiquity till now."
(*EE*, p. 8) *samaγuraγsan-ača inaγsi* "since [the time] they quarreled."
(*DM*, p. 255) *Gurān uDurDza naGse* "depuis trois jours."

43) *inaru* "this side of; before, up to; from, since."
(*OS*, p. 326) *olan-iyar ergügdegsen qaγan saγulγaγsan-ača inaru* "ils mirent sur le trône [celui qu'on nomme] 'empereur promu par la multitude.' Plus tard . . ."
(*K*, p. 277) *ekilegsen-eče inaru* "depuis le commencement même."
(*K*, p. 278) *bi erdeni-yi abuγa inaru ülü qarimui* "je ne retournerai pas jusqu'à ce que je ne recois des pierres précieuses."
(*K*, p. 278) *ebderege inaru* "jusqu'il ne tombe en ruines."

44) *jabsar* "interval, crevice, space between; between."
(*SK*, p. 31) *aγula talayin jabsar idegen erijü oduγsan-dur* "so machte sie sich auf, um in der Richtung zwischen einem Berge und der Ebene Nahrung zu suchen."
(*ST*, p. 98, l. 10) *qara sira qoyar-un jabsar qarbu* "shoot between the black and the yellow (i.e., of the vulture's head)."
Kh. (*SMY*, p. 177) *ene xadnəi dzawsar* "through this cliff."

45) *jaγura* "between, among, in the interval; during."
Gen. (*SH* § 61) *Čegčer Čiqurγu qoyar-un ja'ura Onggiradai Dei Sečin-i jolγaba* "[il] rencontra, entre le [mont] Čäkčär et le [mont] Čiqurγu, l'Onggiradai Däi-säčän."
(*HsCh* 16b3) *tngri γajar-un jaγura* "in between Heaven and Earth."
(*1335*, l. 17) *γurban on-u jaγura* "during (lit., 'in the interval of') three years."
(*Hy* IIa 26v) *dörben tabun hon-u ja'ura* "during four or five years."
(*K*, p. 2254) *sanaqu-yin jaγura* "durant la méditation."

(*MKB*, p. 117) *Swičari ba Parančа ulus-ud-tu saγuqu-yin jaγura* "while [he] was living in Switzerland and France."

(*CSN*) *nutuγ-daγan bučaqu jam-un jaγura* "on the way back to one's native land."

Stem (*SH* § 46) *aqa de'ü ja'ura* "among [his] brothers."

(*SH* § 127) *Temüjin anda ba qoyar ja'ura* "entre l'anda Tämüjin et moi."

(*Hy* IIa Iv) *tenggiri γajar ja'ura* "between heaven and earth."

(*SH* § 200) *tere uγulja-yin miqa iden büküi ja'ura* "while [they] were eating the flesh of the *uγulja*."

(*SH* § 145) *üjetele edüi ja'ura* "pendant qu'ils auraient été occupés à regarder (= en un rien de temps)."

(*K*, p. 2254) *qariqu jaγura* "au retour, en revenant."

Kh. (*R*, p. 111) *dzam dzuur / dzaməin dzuur* "on the way."

(*R*, p. 111) *yawxəin dzuur* "while going."

(*MKB*, p. 111) *xiliin tšanad baix dzuur* "while being abroad."

Ord. (*TOO*, p. 657) *tš'aǥ DžU̯r* "sur-le-champ."

(*DO*, p. 219b) *tš'agīī DžU̯r* "sur-le-champ."

Bur. (*BMS*, p. 280) *garaxa dzuuraa* "when going out."

Mong. (*Monguor*, p. 156) *nDāni Ďźiōro* "parmi nous."

(*DM*, p. 91) *k'uni Ďźiōro sU̯-* "s'entremettre."

46) *jüg* "in the direction of; side, region; cardinal point."

(*SH* § 121) *Jamuγa-yin jüg mögören* "meuglant dans la direction de Jamuqa."

(*Arγun 1289*, l. 9) *Misir-ün jüg mörilebesü* "if [you] campaign in the direction of Egypt."

(*K*, p. 2417) *gindan-u ger-ün jüg güyüldükü* "courir vers la prison."

(*SH* § 119) *Jamuγa jüg gödölba* "[ils] se dirigèrent du côté de Jamuqa."

(*SH* § 100) *Burqan jüg γarba* "[ils] sortirent du côté du Burqan[-qaldun]."

(*SH* § 245) *e'üten jüg* "nach der Tür hin."

(*1338*, l. 10) *emün-e örön-e jüg* "in the southwestern quarter [outside of their city]."

(*ČQ*, p. 11, l. 9) *ger jüg qariju* "returning towards the yurt."

(*ST*, p. 74, l. 20) *urγuqui jüg odču* "going towards the east (i.e., 'the rising')."

(*MKB*, p. 133) *nigen nigen jüg yabuju* "[they] went in different directions."

(*MKB*, p. 140) *emüne jüg dutaγabai* "[they] fled south."

(*MKB*, p. 140) *jegün jüg yabuqu* "going eastwards."

Kh. (*Kh*, p. 75) *ger dzüg* "zum Hause."

(*EBQ*, l. 250) *Gerēə DZÜG* "in der Richtung nach seinem Hause."

(*R*, p. 111) *nar šingex dzüg* "westwards."

(*SMY*, p. 147) *naran garax* *dzüg* *yawaw* "[he] went towards the east."

47) *kiri* "measure, proportion; almost, nearly, in accordance with, up to; extent, volume, space."

(*MKB*, p. 132) *naran ǰirγaqu-yin kiri bosučaγaǰu* "[they] got up about the time the sun set."

(*K*, p. 2548) *üde-yin kiri* "vers le midi."

(*MKB*, p. 132) *ende-eče naiman modu-yin kiri* "about eight versts from here."

(*TOO*, p. 696) *oDō k'ereni* "jusqu'à present."

(*TOO*, p. 696) *nėge Dẑu χonogīī k'ere* "de cent jours environ."

48) *metü* "as, like, similar to; sort, kind; seemingly."

(*SH* § 78) *a'uri-yan darun yadaγu arslan metü* "like the lion who cannot repress his anger."

(*SH* § 31) *časun metü* "[dispersés et chassés] comme la neige [dans une têmpete]."

(*Arγun 1290*, l. 31) *silem-dür oraγsan metü ülügü bei* "is it not the same as being baptized?"

(*Ölǰeitu 1305*, l. 9) *oyir-a metü* "as if [they were] near."

(*1335*, l. 54) *kög daγun metü nayiraduγsabar sayin aburi inu erdeni metü degeǰilegdeǰügü* "because they were in harmony with one another like music, his good character was exalted like a jewel."

(*1362*, l. 11) *qalqan kemebesü gerisge metü γaǰiγu dayisun-i qalqalaǰu qariγulqu-yi kemeyü* "as for *qalqan*, it means to ward off and repel evil enemies like a windbreak."

(*ČT*, p. 70, l. 5) *kkib-ün ǰanggiya metü aldarasi ügei* "indestructible as the twist of silk."

(*ČT*, p. 73, l. 22) *yeke ulustur ayuqu metü tungγaγabai* "[I] have proclaimed it in a fearful manner to the empire."

(*ST*, p. 126, l. 9) *dalai metü yeke ulus* "the empire like the sea."

(*ST*, p. 90, l. 1) *ene kelen amin ügei görügesün ber eyin kümün metü mörgüküi anu yaγun* "was [mag es bedeuten] das dieses sprachlose Wild sich wie ein Mensch verbeugt?"

(*ST*, p. 102, l. 7) *urida-ki metü* "as formerly."

(*ST*, p. 130, l. 5) *kemen nomlaγsan metü* "seemingly he taught that . . ."

Cf. (*OS*, p. 321) *anabad dalai metü qorim* "banquet (copieux) comme la mer Anabat."

(*ÜD*, p. 134, l. 2) *miqan-iyan oγtaluγsan metü ǰoban* "suffering as though we had cut our own flesh."

(*EE*, p. 4) *doluγan dačang bayiγuluγsan metü* "seemingly he had seven temples built."

(*WY*, p. 112, l. 5) *uridaki metü* "as formerly."

Kh. (*MKB*, p. 65) *tšuluu met bat* "solid as stone."

(*SMY*, p. 159) *suman met türgen, xartsaga met xurdan* "quick as an arrow, swift as a hawk."

(*SMY*, p. 149) *üneg üxsen met xewtseer baiw* "the fox was lying as though dead."

(*SMY*, p. 161) *xürtš irsen galt tereg uul met ix atšaa buulgaw* "the arriving train unloaded freight as high as a mountain."

(*SMY*, p. 159) *xaluun dzürxnii tsus met* "like blood from a burning heart."

(*EBQ*, 1. 265) *t'sēl jiχχə ǤaDzrīg nisχə me't DeGDəw* "es (= das Pferd) erhob sich, als ob es flöge über das ferne, grosse Land."

Ord. (*TOO*, p. 78) *t'awu̯n öŋgīī soloŋgo mö't'ɯ* "[s'étendant] comme un arc-en-ciel de cinq couleurs."

(*TOO*, p. 104) *u̯su̯ mö't'ɯ u̯ru̯swā* "coula comme l'eau."

(*TOO*, p. 85) *k'ɯ mö't'ɯ* "comme [si j'étais son] fils."

(*TOO*, p. 313) *sa'ᵏχū̯s mö't'ɯ šɯ't'ɯj-Do* "je la vénérerai comme une divinité protectrice."

Bur. (*BMS*, p. 329) *urda mete* "as formerly."

Mong. (*Monguor*, p. 157) *Dal͡ʑni maDu* "comme la mer."

Note the plural noun form *metüs* "such people;" cf. (*SH* § 156) *inu metüs* "solche Leute wie er."

(*DM*, p. 229) *k'uni maDu t'iGī ʂGewa* "il est grand comme un homme."

49) *naγaγur* "along this side."

(*DO*, p. 480b) *maŋχā nāgū̯r jawu̯-* "faire route par ce côté-ci des dunes."

(*DO*, p. 480b) *ɯ'ᵏχɯ'ᵏχᵘīī nāgū̯r tš'āgū̯r Bol-* "être près de mourir."

50) *naγana* "on this side."

(*Kh*, p. 74) *uuləin naana* "diesseits des Berges."

(*R*, p. 133) *mal goləin naana biltšidž baina* "the cattle are grazing this side of the river."

(*KhN*) *noos ni tušaaxəin naana* "prior to delivering the wool."

51) *naγasi* "towards this side, hither."

Cf. (*Geserica*, p. 27) "die Formen *naγasi* und *čaγasi* gehen auf *inaγasi* und **tiγasi* (Primärstamm **ti-*) zurück und kommen in der Schriftsprache als Entlehnung aus der Umgangsprache vor."

Also (*K*, p. 612) *nasi (= nāsi) / inaγsi* "ici, en ce lieu."

(*DO*, p. 485a) *t'ɯ̄nes nāši ɯgᵘī* "cela n'arrivera pas avant cette [date]."

(*DO*, p. 487a) *χojor miŋga laŋgās nāši* "pour moins de deux mille onces d'argent."

52) *ögede* "up, above; upstream; in the direction of."

(*SH* § 32) *qoram atala Tünggelig γoroqan ö'ede niken gü'ün ayisun buyu* "nach einer kurzen Weile nahte sich ein Mann den Tunggelik-Bach aufwärts."

Kh. (*Kh*, p. 74) *ara öödö* "den nördlichen Abhang aufwärts."

Ord. (*TOO*, p. XXXIX) *Gerēᴅen* < *ger ögede-ben* "vers sa propre maison."

(*Ordos*) *ger ōᴅö jawu̧-* "to go towards the yurt."

(*DO*, p. 527a) *u̧su̧n ōᴅö jawu̧-* "aller contre le courant de l'eau."

(*DO*, p. 527a) *salᵏχin ōᴅö jawu̧-* "aller contre le vent."

Note *ögede* used as the predicate, (*DO*, p. 527a) *Ģal ōᴅö, u̧su̧ u̧rū̧* "la flamme monte, l'eau descend (dicton)." See also page 39.

Kalm. (*KD*, p. 303) *ūlᵘ ödᵒ* "bergauf."

53) *ögere / öbere* "otherwise, apart from; other different."

(*SH* § 156) *gü'ün ayima'ud-ača ö'ere bayiba* "un [jeune] homme était debout à part des divers clans."

(*SH* § 137) *örgen e'üden-eče činu ö'ere odu'asu* "s'ils vont au dehors de ta large porte."

(*ST*, p. 124, l. 9) *Juu oboγ-tu-yi alaqui-ača öber-e arγa ügei* "there is no way aside from killing the [man] from the Juu clan."

Kh. (*R*, p. 167) *tüünees öör* "aside from him."

(*TOO*, p. 105) *ene Ģu̧rwan ami't'anās ōrö jum-ugᵘī* "hormis ces trois êtres vivants il n'y a rien d'autre."

Cf. (*DO*, p. 538b) *naᴅās ōrö k'ɯn* "quelqu'un d'autre que moi."

54) *oyira* "near."

(*1335*, l. 55) *degedüs-ün oyir-a čaγada yabuγulǰuγui* "one had them serve in the presence of the Emperor."

(*MKB*, p. 140) *ǰam-un oyira* "near the road."

(*MKB*, p. 140) *tere utaγan-u oyira* "near the smoke."

Ord. (*TOO*, p. 41) *t'ere šilīn ȯg̊rȯ i'tš'iᵏχɯlē* "quand il arriva à proximité de cette colline."

(*TOO*, p. 40) *Ģaᴅžarīī ȯg̊rȯ* "proche de l'endroit."

(*TOO*, p. 196) *Gerīn ȯg̊rȯ iresẽ* "[qui] venaient dans le voisinage immédiat de la maison."

(*TOO*, p. 212) *t'ere mu̧ᴅu̧n ȯg̊rȯ* "près de cet arbre."

(*TOO*, p. 86) *u̧lān ȯg̊rȯ* "dans le voisinage de la montagne."

Kalm. (*KD*, p. 304) *gerīn ōrö* "in der nähe des hauses."

55) *qamtu* "together, conjointly; united, common."

(*SH* § 170) *tere ayisuqui-dur Jamuγa Ong-qan-lu'a qamtu ayisulčaǰu* "in jenem Zuge kam Dschamucha mit Ongchan zusammen daher."

(*SH* § 229) *kebte'ül-lü'e qamtu* "together with the guards."

(*SH* § 155) *güregen-lü'e qamtu* "en compagnie du gendre."
(*1338*, l. 33) *morid-luγa qamtu* "together with horses."
(*1362*, l. 51) *bii tas-tur qamtu* "on the stele together."
(*BE*, p. 96) *Kitad ulus-un qamtu* "together with the Chinese."
(*EE*, p. 27) *tegün-ü köbegün Γaldan Dorǰi-luγa qamtu* "together with his son Γaldan Dorǰi."
(*EE*, p. 39) *Qalq-a-yin qamtu* "together with the Qalqa."
(*EE*, p. 45) *oros-un elči Saba-luγa qamtu* "together with the Russian envoy Saba."
(*MKB*, p. 117) *nöküd-ün qamtu* "together with companions."
(*CSN*) *ayančin-u qamtu* "together with the traveler."
(*MKB*, p. 132) *ülegsen čerig-ün qamtu* "together with the troops left behind."
(*CSN*) *daγalduγčid-un qamtu* "together with [his] followers."
(*CSN*) *kögǰiǰü irekü-yin qamtu* "along with developing."
Kh. (*Kh*, p. 74) *nöxörteegöö xamta* "zusammen mit seinem Gefährten."
(*SMY*, p. 67) *nöxörtei xamt* "together with a companion."
(*Kh*, p. 143) *baawagai argata šara ünegetee xamta yawadži baital* "while the bear was traveling together with the sly yellow fox."
(*SMY*, p. 163) *öwgön Galdanəi xamt ordž irlee* "[he] entered together with the elder Galdan."
(*SMY*, p. 87) *ter dzaluugiin xamt* "[he went out] with that young man."
(*SMY*, p. 162) *xüü idžiin xamt baidžee* "the boy lived together with his mother."
Ord. (*DO*, p. 331b) *eDent'ī χamt'u̧ irelē* "il est venu ensemble avec ceux-ci."
Bur. (*BMS*, p. 545) *gerhee garaxatain' xamta boroo oroo* "as soon as he left the house, it rained."

56) *qoγorundu / qoγorumdu* "in the middle, between, among; while."
This seems to be a compound postposition made up of *qoγor* "between, in the middle," and *dumda* "between, among."
Cf. (*K*, p. 886) *qoγor dumda* "au milieu, au centre même, entre, entre soi." See also (*KD*, p. 192) *χōr dundᴰ* "in der mitte."
(*EE*, p. 18) *qalq-a-yin doloγan qosiγun-u qoγorumda-ban* "in the midst of the seven banners of the Qalqa."
(*WY*, p. 69, l. 13) *tegün qoγordumda* "meanwhile."
(*MKB*, p. 108) *qoyar-un qoγorumdu* "between the two."
Kh. (*DzDz*, l. 621) *xoyor uuləin xoorondo* "between two mountains."
(*R*, p. 267) *olon ulsəin xoorond* "among nations."
(*R*, p. 267) *ta bid xoyorəin xoorond* "among ourselves."
(*SMY*, p. 162) *Bügd Nairamdax Mongol ard uls Dundad Uls xoyorəin xoorond diplomatig xariltsaa baiguulax tuxai* "concerning the establishment of diplomatic relations between the Mongolian People's Republic and China."

(*Kh*, p. 152) *bulaatsaldaxiin xoorond* "while [they] were quarreling."

(*Kh*, p. 156) *tegexiin xoorond* "while that was going on."

(*R*, p. 267) *tanai irex xoorond* "until you come."

(*Kh*, p. 138) *edze-güi xoorondo* "while no one was at home."

Ord. (*TOO*, p. 31) *χojor χolbōlDžīī χōrgonDu̯* "entre deux collines voisines de même hauteur." Note (*TOO*, p. 685) *χōrgonDu̯* = *χōronDu̯*.

(*TOO*, p. 215) *Dži'tš'ik t'ūgēt ire'ᵏχīī χōrgonDu̯* "pendant que [la vieille femme] était partie pour aller cueillir des fleurs."

Kalm. (*KD*, p. 192) *modn̥ χōrn̥dᴰ* "zwischen dem holze."

57) *qoγorunduγur* "throughout, during."

(*Kh*, p. 152) *tere xooronduur* "during that [time]."

58) *qola* "far, distant."

(*SH* § 195) *ele teyin bögesü tede doromǰi-ača qolo bayiya* "in dem Falle wollen wir uns von diesen üblen Leuten etwas ferner halten."

(*TT*, p. 33, l. 1) *Qori-yin tayiša-ača qola negüdeg siltaγan-iyar* "by reason [of the fact] that [they] nomadized far from the *tayiša* of the Qori."

(*MKB*, p. 43) *ende-eče gola* "far from here."

Kh. (*MKB*, p. 30) *endees xol* "far from here."

(*MKB*, p. 30) *minii gerees xol* "far from my yurt."

Ord. (*Ordos*) *Gerēs χolo* "loin de la maison."

Bur. (*BMS*, p. 567) *xorin kilometrhee xolo* "twenty kilometers away."

Mong. (*Monguor*, p. 159) *BaDzarDza χuloni* "loin de la ville."

(*DM*, p. 181) *k'uDuDzanā χulo sūDźi* "il demeure loin de sa famille."

59) *qoyiγur* "along the rear; along the north (Khalkha), along the west (Ordos); after."

(*SMY*, p. 176) *baruun xoiguur* "along the northwest."

(*Kh*, p. 159) *yawasanaas xoiguur* "after [he] left."

60) *qoyina* "after, later, behind, beyond; afterwards; north (Khalkha), west (Ordos)."

(*SH* § 52) *Qabul Qahan-u qoyina* "après Qabul-qahan."

(*SH* § 12) *te'ün-ü qoyina* "par la suite."

(*1338*, l. 20) *kedün ödür-ün qoyina* "after several days."

(*ST*, p. 86, l. 22) *tegün-ü qoyina* "darnach."

(*ST*, p. 286, l. 2) *tegün-eče qoyina* "hierauf."

Nom. Verb (*SH* § 11) *Duwa Soqor ügei boluγsan-u qoyina* "nach dem Tode Duwas des Blinden."

(*SH* § 28) *naran šinggegsen-ü qoyina* "after the sun went down."

(*1335*, l. 28) *ǰob es-e boluγsan-u qoyina* "after [he] died."

(*1362*, l. 20) *bulγ-a-yi burčiγsan-u qoyina* "after [Atai Buqa] had put down the rebellion."

(*ST*, p. 122, l. 18) *ene keüken ösügsen-ü qoyina* "after this child has grown up."

(*EE*, p. 2) *mori barir-a iregsen-ü qoyina* "after having come to present horses."

(*EE*, p. 8) *bey-e künügegdegsen-ü qoyina* "after his person (lit., 'body') was tormented (i.e., after he was killed)."

(*MKB*, p. 101) *nasun-аča nögčigsen-u qoyina* "after [he] had passed away."

(*MKB*, p. 112) *kedün ǰil önggeregsen-ü qoyina* "after several years had passed."

(*BE*, p. 52) *Sanaγan-i ösügsen qoyina* "after Sanaγan had grown up."

(*K*, p. 299) *arban ilegüü qonuγsan qoyina* "après plus de dix jours."

Kh. (*MKB*, p. 111) *xeden dǯil öngörsnii xoino* "after several years had passed."

(*Kh*, p. 143) *yawasan xoino* "after [he] went."

(*EBQ*, l. 290) ɢarsɒ χöɢnɒ "nachdem [sie] herausgegangen waren."

(*EBQ*, l. 362) *urDīī t'àwɩli* ʙaesɒ χöenɒ "nachdem die Segensprüche der früheren [Wiedergeburten] ausgesprochen waren."

(*Kh*, p. 74) *geriin xoino* "hinter dem Hause."

Ord. (*TOO*, p. 251) *iresẽ χöŏno* "quand [ils furent] venus."

Also Ord. χöö't'ā̃ (< *qoyitai).[122]

(*TOO*, p. 38) *jawųsã* χöö't'ā̃ "après [ton] départ."

(*TOO*, p. 211) *ene* ʙarųų̃ χöö't'ā̃ "au sud-ouest d'ici."

(*DO*, p. 357a) ɯDīĩ χöö't'ā̃ "après midi."

Bur. (*BMS*, p. 574) *xadəin xoino* "behind the mountain."

Kalm. (*KD*, p. 194) *ükᵘsn̥ χönö* "nach dem tode."

Dag. (*Dagur*) ґēpī xoaiнă "behind the yurt."

Mong. (*Monguor*, p. 158) ɢor *uDurDza χueno* "après deux jours."

(*DM*, p. 177) *niũDurDza χueno* "dès aujourd'hui."

61) *qoyinaγsi* "towards the rear; afterwards, following; in the future."

(*K*, p. 853) *ene edür-eče qoyinaγsi* "dès à présent à l'avenir."

62) *qoyisi* "backwards; after, next; in the future; northwards (Khalkha), westwards (Ordos)."

(*EE*, p. 2) *egünče qoyisi* "since that [event]."

(*K*, p. 855) *egün-eče qoyisi* "à l'avenir."

(*K*, p. 855) *marγata-аča qoyisi* "après demain, dès demain."

(*TT*, p. 11, l. 1) *tegün-ece qoyisi* "after that."

Kh. (*KhN*) *tüünees xoiš* "after that."

(*KhN*) *ter tsagaas xoiš* "since that time."

(*KhN*) *xotnoos xoiš xorin tawan mil'* "twenty-five miles north of the city."

(*SMY*, p. 159) *Batəin yaria duussanaas xoiš* "after Bata had finished speaking."

(*SMY*, p. 139) *nar bür džargasnaas xoiš* "each time after the sun went down."

(*EBQ*, l. 364) *maχχɒ t'sussɒnɒ t'ɯrsnəs χoės* "nachdem man zu Leib und Blut geboren ist."

(*KhN*) *bagš bolsnoosoo xoiš* "after [I] became a teacher."

(*KhN*) *surguuli exelsnees xoiš* "after school began."

Note (*R*, p. 395), the Nomen Perfecti takes the ablative suffix with *xoiš* (as in the examples above); it takes the genitive suffix or it takes no suffix with *xoino* (see number 60).

Ord. (*TOO*, p. 690) *iDžūrās χöǧši* "depuis les temps anciens, depuis toujours."

(*TOO*, p. 136) *t'ɯ̄nēs χöǧši* "depuis lors."

(*TOO*, p. 166) *enɯ̄nēs χöǧši* "dorénavant."

(*TOO*, p. 106) *mani Gerēs χöǧši* "à l'ouest de notre maison."

Bur. (*BMS*, p. 575) *endehee xoiso* "from now on."

63) *selte* "together, conjointly, with."

(*SH* § 187) *haran selte* "with the people."

(*SH* § 162) *irge orγa selte* "avec ses gens et ses foyers."

(*SH* § 229) *qubčasun selte* "mitsamt der Kleidung."

(*1362*, l. 47) *bii tas-un ayalγus-i silüg selte ǰoqiyaǰu* "[I have] composed the text (lit., 'sounds') of the stele together with the verses."

(*O*, p. 57) *γaǰar ǰüg-ün eǰed selte ende iren orusi* "ensemble avec les esprits de la terre et des points cardinaux, venez et installez-vous ici."

(*O*, p. 57) *čingɡilǰeküi daγun selte eldeb ǰüil-ün takil-yi masi sayitur bisireǰü ergümüi-ǰa* "ensemble avec des sons retentissants, toutes ces différentes espèces d'offrandes, nous vous les offrons avec très grande dévotion."

(*ÜD*, p. 133, l. 4) *busu qamuγ nöküd selte* "with all [her] other companions."

64) *sidar* "near, next to."

(*K*, p. 1483) *aγula-dur sidar bolqu* "se trouver près d'une montagne."

65) *šiγ* ~ *šig* "like, similar, alike; row of five."

Cf. (*R*, p. 315) *šig* is called a postposition. It has no existence without a preceding noun or pronoun. Cf. (*Kh*, p. 96) *nama-šig* "wie ich," where N. N. Poppe lists it as a "particle." It is not to be confused with the diminutive suffix *-siγ* / *-sig* as found in such words as *bagašig* "smallish," *ixšig* "rather large," and *xaršig* "blackish," *metüsig* "à peu près comme."

(*SH* § 46) *noyanšiγ* "like a prince."

(*CSN*) *kürel sig küreng čirai-tai* "with a bronze-like dark complexion."

(*Kh,* p. 96) *xün-šig* "wie ein Mensch."

(*Kh,* p. 96) *modo-šig* "wie ein Baum."

(*Kh,* p. 144) *dalaišig* "like the sea."

(*Kh,* p. 144) *šaasan gadasa-šig* "like a driven stake."

(*Kh,* p. 162) *tunamal toli-šig* "like a clear mirror."

(*Kh,* p. 162) *ulaan linxuaayiin üner-šig* "like the smell of the red lotus."

(*Kh,* p. 157) *gaxai-šig* "like a pig."

(*SMY,* p. 136) *ööriin tawan xuruu šig mededž baix xeregtei* "you should know it like the five fingers of your hand."

(*KhN*) *tolind xaragsan šig* "[it was] like looking in the mirror."

(*KhN*) *öör šigee neg adžiltšintai xanilan suuw* "I married a worker like myself."

(*EBQ,* l. 441) *neg* ʙᴏᴅᴅɒχɒᴅ ᴅ*īlmər šik* "wenn man einmal denkt, ist es, als ob er siegen könnte."

66) *singgi* "as well as, similarly; like, as."

(*DO,* p. 621a) *mori šiŋᵏχᵘī* ɯᴅ*žiGDeDži wän* "on voit [dans le lointain] quelque chose qui ressemble à un cheval."

(*TOO,* p. 204) *t'ere šiŋgɯ* "semblables à celles-là."

(*BMS,* p. 714) *nege xün šengi* "like one person."

(*Buriat*) *šama-sińyī* χɯŋ "a person like thee."

(*KD,* p. 359) *narn̥-šiŋgᵊ* / *narᴰ-šiŋgᵊ* "wie die sonne."

67) *šitü* ~ *sitü* "like, as, in the manner of; seemingly."

(*SH* § 164) *γaγča kö'ün minu ügei šitü* "mein einziger Sohn ist, als ob ich keinen hätte (i.e., ist eine 'Null')."

(*HsCh* 6a2) *mölsün deger-e gečkikü sitü* "as if [ye] were treading on thin ice."

(*HsCh* 35a3-5) *sedkil-degen oyisiyaγsan-i qola ber bügesü oyir-a sitü sedkil-dür ele aγulbasu umartaqu üdür inu kejiy-e bolqu* "if, even though he be far, I but cause to be in [my] heart as if [he were] near [him] whom I have loved in my heart, when will the day arrive when I forget him?"

(*1338,* l. 9) *ečige eke-yügen kekiüdeglečegsen sitü emgenin ajuγu* "[the people of the district] grieved as if they had lost their father or mother."

Also Ord. *šint'ī* (< **sintei*).[123]

Cf. (*DO*, p. 620) *χoni* _*šint'ī*_ *jum* "quelque chose qui ressemble à un mouton."
Cf. (*DO*, p. 620) *oDō irep* _*šint'ī*_ *Bān* "je crois que maintenant ils sont arrivés."
Cf. (*TOO*, p. 175) *nɯDɯni Gem-ɯgᵘī Bāχu* _*šint'ī*_ "ses yeux pourtant ne sont pas malades."
(*TOO*, p. 21) *χojor nɯDɯni tš'olmō* _*šint'ī*_ *Bɯlt'īDži* "les deux yeux [qui brillaient] comme Vénus sortant de leurs orbites."
(*TOO*, p. 58) *ene* _*šint'ī*_ *sāχan* "si délicieux que ceux-ci."

68) *tedüi* "as much, so much; to the extent of; afterwards, then; almost; at once."
Cf. (*SH* § 103) *qarča-*_*yin*_ _*tedüi*_ *amin-iyan* "ma vie, qui [n']est [qu']autant qu'une sauterelle."[124]
Cf. (*'P*, p. 134) *arča-yin nabsin-*_*u*_ _*tedüi*_ *sikür-i egüdčü* "[if] he builds a parasol the size of a juniper leaf."*
(*EE*, p. 6) *üǰegsen-*_*ü*_ _*tedüi*_ "[it was] as if one saw [them alive]."
(*EE*, p. 39) *tobči-*_*yin*_ _*tedüi*_ *bičisgügei* "[I] shall write [in quantity only] so much [as that] of a *tobči* ('résumé')."
(*K*, p. 1715) *üčügen* _*tedüi*_ "tant soit peu, un peu."
Ord. (*DO*, p. 645b) *aliman* _*t'eDᵘī*_ "de la grandeur d'une pomme."
(*DO*, p. 654b) *amsasan t'ōn̄* _*t'eDᵘī*_ "assez pour pouvoir dire qu'on en a goûté." Note *t'ōn̄ < toγon-u*.

69) *tege < eteged* "side, direction."
These two words are doublets. The pronunciation *etgeed* in Khalkha is the result of a literary loan. The historically evolved form is *tee < eteged*. Cf. (*SH* § 213) *ete'ed*, (*Hy* II 8r) *etēd*. In spoken Khalkha the two forms have become semantically differentiated. The spelling *tege* is based on the spoken *tee*, whose long vowel is indicated by the intervocalic -g-. Cf. *Begeǰing* for *Pei-ching* 北 京.
(*SH* § 213) *Onggün Boro'ul qoyar bara'un ǰe'ün* _*ete'ed*_ *ta qoyar ba'určin ide'en tüke'erün* "wenn ihr beiden Köche, Onggur und Borochul, an der rechten und linken Seite das Essen so ausgebt."
(*SH* § 144) *Onan-*_*u*_ _*čanaǰi*_ _*ete'ed*_ "auf der anderen Seite des Onan."
(*1362*, l. 6) *baraγun* _*eteged*_ *Sartaγčin ayan ayalan yabuǰu* "[he] took the field (lit., 'went campaigning') against the Sartaγčin in the West."
(*Hy* II 8r) *urida bara'un* _*etēd*_ "in the southwest."
(*SME*, l. 2) *baraγun* _*eteged*_ *saγuǰu* "residing in the Western Quarter."
(*K*, p. 166) *ene* _*eteged*_ "de ce côté."
(*K*, p. 1768) *tere* _*tege*_ "de l'autre côté."

(*K*, p. 1774) *usun-u tertege (< tere tege)* "au delà de l'eau."

(*K*, p. 1774) *γol-un tertege* "de l'autre côté de la rivière."

Kh. (*R*, p. 226) *golɘin tertee* "on that side of the river."

(*MKB*, p. 42) *dzüün tee suu* "sit on the left side."

(*EBQ*, l. 571) *t'er't'ē ūlªīg derlēt* "[er] legte sich auf den Berg jenseits."

Ord. (*DO*, p. 654a) *k'ɯ̄ı̃ ᴅörwön t'ē sų̄ᴅži wān* "les gens sont assis à chacun des quatre côtés de la table."

(*DO*, p. 56b) *ʙarų̄nt'ā < *ʙarų̄ų̄ t'ē* "au Sud."

(*DO*, p. 225a) *ᴅzɯ̄nt'ē* "au nord."

(*DO*, p. 654a) *ɢolīn ene t'ē* "ce côté de la rivière."

Bur. (*BM*, par. 167) *baran tee* "on the right."

(*BM*, par. 167) *züün tee* "on the left."

70) *tegegür* "along the side."

(*MKB*, p. XI) *negen teegüür . . . nögöön teeguur* "on the one hand . . . on the other hand."

(*BM*, par. 167) *züün teegüür* "along the left side."

71) *tegesi / tesi (= tēsi)* "in the direction of, towards." This postposition is derived from the preceding one with the addition of the Lative suffix *-si*. The two forms above show the confusion arising from the lack of a precise symbol in the Classical Script to indicate long vowels.

(*K*, p. 1737) *öröne tegesi* "à l'occident, vers l'occident."

(*CSN*) *baraγun tesi* "towards the west."

(*K*, p. 1713) *Isarayil γaǰar oron tesi mordobai* "il s'en alla dans le pays d'Israël."

Kh. (*Kh*, p. 74) *ger teeši* "zum Hause."

(*Kh*, p. 138) *enedxeg džagaraas dzüün teeši* "to the east of India."

(*R*, p. 202) *gol tiiš* "to the river." Cf. (*R*, p. 227) *tiiš = teeš* and *tiišee = teešee*. Also in Buriat-Mongolian, *tiiše (< teyisi*; see below) has become habitual also for *teeše (< tegesi)*; i.e., the two postpositions have "fallen together."[125] Cf. Ord. (*DO*, p. 663a) *t'īš = t'ēš*.

(*HB*, p. LXI) *gal teesi / galiin teeši* "towards the fire."

(*R*, p. 202) *dzüün tiiš* "to the left."

(*R*, p. 202) *ger tiišee* "to one's home."

(*R*, p. 202) *surguul' tiišee* "to one's school."

(*R*, p. 202) *morin tiišee* "to one's horse."

Ord. (*DO*, p. 538b) *ȫrö t'ēši* "dans une autre direction."

(*DO*, p. 663a) *ȫrö t'īš* "à un autre endroit."

(*DO*, p. 661a) *k'ɯ̄ni t'ēš ɢar-* "prendre le parti de quelqu'un."

Bur. (*BMS*, p. 471) *aman teeše* "towards the mouth."

(*BMS*, p. 471) *baruun teeše* "towards the right."

(*BMS*, p. 59) *ara teešee* "backwards."

72) *tende* "there, at that place."
(*Kh*, p. 143) *baruun gadasanii tende* "there where the right stake is."
(*DO*, p. 657b) *Baǧšīĩ t'enDe* "chez le maître."
(*DO*, p. 657b) *t'ani t'enDe* "là-bas dans vos parages."

73) *teyisi* "to that place, there; (= *tegesi*) towards."
(*K*, p. 1685) *baraγun teyisi* "à droite; vers l'occident."
(*K*, p. 1685) *ǰegün teyisi* "à gauche; vers l'orient."
(*WY*, p. 112, l. 15) *qoyimar teyisi* "towards the rear of the yurt."

74) *tölöge* "in place of, for the sake of, in the name of; in order to; pay, payment."
(*Doc. C*, l. 24) *Sučungγa-u tölöge* "in place of Sučungγa."
(*K*, p. 1920) *tabunang-un tölöge* "au nom du tabunang."
(*K*, p. 1920) *kümün-ü tölöge yabuqu* "aller à la place d'un autre, ou pour un autre."
(*CSN*) *čilüge ba tusaγar toγtanil-un tölöge* "for the sake of freedom and independence."
Nom. Fut. (*CSN*) *ǰoriγa-yi beyelegülkü-yin tölöge* "in order to carry out our purpose."
(*CSN*) *tegün-i beyelegülkü-yin tölöge büküi küčün-ben dayičilaǰu bayina* "we are mobilizing all of our strength in order to accomplish that."
Kh. (*R*, p. 211) *ex ornəi tölöö* "for the sake of one's country."
(*KhN*) *enx taiwan baidləin tölöö* "for the sake of a peaceful state of affairs."
(*Kh*, p. 74) *adžiliin tölöö* "für die Arbeit."
(*SMY*, p. 159) *üriinxee tölöö* "for one's children."
(*SMY*, p. 161) *tsagiin baidal negent tügšüürtei tul, bi öwgönxöö tölöö dzowdž l suuw* "since times were bad, I was worried about my old man."
Nom. Fut. (*KhN*) *xamtran adžillaxəin tölöö* "in order to work together."
(*KhN*) *nairamdaltai baixəin tölöö* "in order to live peacefully."
(*KhN*) *ayuulgüi baidleig togtooxəin tölöö dzütgedž baina* "we are striving in order to establish security."
Ord. (*TOO*, p. 41) *tš'i mini t'ölō Bi'tš'ige Džowō* "ne t'inquiète pas de moi."
(*TOO*, p. 35) *jamar u'tš'irīĩ t'ölō* "pourquoi?"
(*TOO*, p. 215) *tš'ini t'ölō* "à ta place."

75) *tula* "for, for the sake of; because of, on account of; in order to."

(*SH* § 46) *noyan-siγ aburi-tu* tula "because his deportment was like [that of] a prince."

(*SH* § 46) *ide'en-e baruγ* tula "because [they] were greedy for food."

(*SH* § 46) *aqa de'ü ǰa'ura aduruγči* tula "since [he was] an *aduruγči* among his brothers."

(*EE*, p. 8) *ögkü ügei* tula "because [they] did not give [them]."

(*SH* § 82) *ǰöb ele eyimü arγatu-*yin tula "précisement parce que tu es ainsi un homme de ressource."

(*1335*, l. 44) *mön eǰen-*yügen tula "for his same lord."

(*1335*, l. 14) *kičiyenggü uγaγatu ünen ǰoriγ-tu-*yin tula "because he had zeal and intelligence and a sincere will."

(*SME*, l. 6) *činu sayin ǰoriγ-*un tula *qarimǰilamui* "[thus I] compensate (lit., 'answer') [thee] because of thy good will."

(*ST*, p. 274, l. 3) *teyimü-*yin tula "for that reason."

(*ST*, p. 290, l. 1) *tegün-ü köbegün ügei-*yin tula "because of his having no son."

(*SH* § 103) *Qo'aγčin eke-yi solangγa bolǰu sonosγu-*yin tula "parce que mère Qo'aγčin entend comme une belette."[126]

(*1335*, l. 41) *usγal aburi-tu bükü-*yin tula "because he had a gentle character."

(*1338*, l. 5) *erdem-tü bükü-*yin tula "because he was clever."

(*ČT*, p. 70, l. 1) *ulus-i amuγulqu-*yin tula "in order to pacify the people."

(*ČT*, p. 76, l. 18) *yeke ulus-i engkeǰigülkü-*yin tula "in order to make the Empire fortunate."

(*ST*, p. 262, l. 5) *šasin bariqu-*yin tula "pour gouverner la religion (= exercer le pouvoir suprême)."

(*OS*, p. 324) *yeke ulus törü-ben batudqaqu-*yin tula "en vue de rendre fort votre grand royaume."

(*AYM*, l. 5) *sira-yin šasin-i degedlekü-*yin tula "in order to venerate the yellow doctrine."

(*ÜD*, p. 132, l. 11) *ögkü-*yin tula "in order to give [his body to the tiger]."

(*CSN*) *dabsiqu-yi qoriγlaqu-*yin tula "in order to stop the advance."

(*MKB*, p. 132) *čöm-iyer bayiqu* tula "since [they] were complete."

(*WM*, p. 131) *nisün ülü čidaqu* tula "because [the bird] cannot fly."

(*SH* § 150) *Ong-qan-a abču ögügsen-*ü tula "because [he] took [them] and gave [them] to Ong-qan."

(*1335*, l. 54) *sayid üiles üiledügsen-ü* tula "because he performed good deeds."

(*1362*, l. 19) *kemegdegsen-*ü tula "because he said (lit., 'because it was said')."

(*ST*, p. 124, l. 19) *namayi J̌üge Noyan-i ergügsen-ü̲ tu̲l̲a̲* "[he is jealous] because I have promoted Jüge Noyan."

(*Geserica*, p. 170) *bui-y̲i̲n̲ t̲u̲l̲a̲* "infolge ihres Seins."

(*CSN*) *učir ni bükü kümün törölkiten-dü ayul-yi učiraγuluγči dayisun baraγun Ewöröpe-eče bosuγsan-u̲ t̲u̲l̲a̲ bolai* "the reason is because an enemy, bringing fear to all mankind, has arisen in (lit., 'from') Western Europe."

Kh. Cf. (*R*, pp. 394-396) *tul* preceded by a Nomen Verbale means "because." Preceded by the Nomen Futuri in the genitive case, *tul* means "in order to."

(*SMY*, p. 161) *boroo orson t̲u̲l̲* "because it was raining."

(*SMY*, p. 161) *šine üsgiig suraltsaxə̲i̲n̲ t̲u̲l̲ šiidwerteigeer temtsegtün* "struggle hard to master the new writing."

(*SMY*, p. 161) *gar xaduurəig džöw ašiglaxə̲i̲n̲ t̲u̲l̲ sain xurtslax xeregtei* "in order to make proper use of the sickle, it is necessary to sharpen it well."

(*KhN*) *šiidweriig biyelüülexi̲i̲n̲ t̲u̲l̲* "in order to carry out the decision."

(*KhN*) *atšiig ulam ixeer xariulaxə̲i̲n̲ t̲u̲l̲* "in order to show an even greater appreciation."

Ord. (*DO*, p. 678b) *t̲'̲u̲l̲a̲* "à cause de, pour (emprunt fait à la langue littéraire)."

76) *tuqai* "concerning, regarding, on the occasion of, about; occasion, favorable moment (= *tuq-a*)."

(*WY*, p. 98, l. 13) *egün t̲u̲q̲a̲i̲* "with regard to this."

(*CSN*) *amǰiltai-y̲i̲n̲ t̲u̲q̲a̲i̲* "with regard to the success."

(*K*, p. 1796) *ene t̲u̲q̲a̲i̲* "à present, à l'occasion présente."

(*MKB*, p. 123) *ǰobalang-tu bayidal-u̲n̲ t̲u̲q̲a̲i̲* "concerning a painful situation."

(*MKB*, p. 141) *ene edür-un bayilduγsan-u̲ t̲u̲q̲a̲i̲ seǰig-tei buyu, ügei-üü* "concerning the fighting [which took place] today, is there any doubt or not?

Kh. (*MKB*, p. 38) *gadaadəin baidlə̲i̲n̲ t̲u̲x̲a̲i̲ iltgel* "report on foreign affairs."

(*Kh*, p. 74) *adžili̲i̲n̲ t̲u̲x̲a̲i̲* "die Arbeit betreffend."

(*R*, p. 389) *malə̲i̲n̲ t̲u̲x̲a̲i̲* "concerning cattle."

(*SMY*, p. 161) *bi orondoo ordž xewteed surguuli̲i̲n̲ t̲u̲x̲a̲i̲ olon törliin yum bodsoor untdžee* "having gone to bed, while continuing to think of the many things connected with school, I fell asleep."

(*MKB*, p. 85) *sain ödöri̲i̲n̲ t̲u̲x̲a̲i̲* "on the occasion of a holiday."

(*KhN*) *uls ündestnii xamtəin adžillagaanə̲i̲ t̲u̲x̲a̲i̲ xelexdee* "while [they] discussed universal cooperation among nations."

(*KhN*) *Puškinəi üil yawdal dzoxioluudə̲i̲n̲ t̲u̲x̲a̲i̲ lekts* "a lecture on the life and works of Pushkin."

Ord. (*DO*, p. 160a) *meDe ʿᵏχī̲ī̲ D̲u̲χ̲ā̲* "pour savoir, dans le but de savoir."

Bur. (*BMS*, p. 451) *asuudal tuxai* "concerning the question."

77) *tursi* "during; length, measure, dimension, distance, space."
(*K*, p. 1894) *edür-ün tursi* "tout le jour."
(*CSN*) *olan ǰil-ün tursi* "during many years."
Kh. (*R*, p. 215) *šönö turš* "during the course of the night."
(*KhN*) *xeden džiliin turš* "during several years."
(*SMY*, p. 159) *xorin tawan džiliin turši* "during twenty-five years."
Ord. (*DO*, p. 166b) ᴜᴅᴜrīĩ ᴅy̨ši "pendant toute la journée."
(*DO*, p. 166b) *nasy̨n* ᴅy̨ši "pendant toute la vie."
(*DO*, p. 166b) ᴅžilīĩ ᴅy̨ši "pendant toute l'année."
(*DO*, p. 166b) ᴅžam ᴅy̨ši "tout le long de la route."
Kalm. (*KD*, p. 411) *neg ödṛrin turš* "den ganzen tag."

78) *tus* "facing, against, opposite; separate; concerning."
(*ST*, p. 260, l. 17) *ene burqan-u terigün tus süme-yin niruγun-a* "ausserhalb der Mauern dieses Tempels, dem Antlitz des Buddha gegenüber."
(*WY*, p. 89, l. 5) *tegün tus bügüde boluγsan bičilge-i tusiyaγsan bui* "as regards that, they exchanged correspondence on all that had happened."
(*MKB*, p. 61) *qubisqal-un tus* "concerning the revolution."
Kh. (*MKB*, p. 59) *xuw'sgalәin tus* "concerning the revolution."
Cf. (*Ordos*) ū̄ᴅen ᴅy̨st'y̨ *maŋχa't'ā̈* "vis-à-vis de la porte il y a des dunes."

79) *učir* "occasion, time, circumstance, relation; reason, cause, motive, principle."
(*EE*, p. 12) *törü-yin učir* "for affairs of the government."
(*KhN*) *gertee oluul utšir* "since there were many of us at home."
(*KhN*) *arwan neg nastai baisan utšir* "when [I] was eleven years old."
(*SMY*, p. 61) *tšono xowor utšir* "since there were few wolves."

80) *ügei* / *ügeigüi* "no, none, not; non-existence; poor, indigent; no distinction between; without."
(*Teheran* III, l. 12) *yosu ügegüi* "illegally."
(*1335*, l. 13) *baraši ügei* "without end."
(*1346*, l. 13) *uγaγ-a* [= *uqaγ-a*] *ügegü* "without intelligence."
(*1362*, l. 49) *qaltaril ügei* "without shirking."
(*ČT*, p. 74, l. 6) *tüdel ügei* "without delay."
(*OS*, p. 321) *tengsel ügei* "incomparable."
(*AYM*, l. 13) *čaγlaši ügei* "measureless."
(*EE*, p. 6) *toγ-a-yi bodoqu ügei* "without counting the number."
(*CSN*) *udaqu ügei* "without delaying."

(*K*, p. 556) *sayin maγu* <u>*ügei*</u> "le bien et le mal."
(*CSN*) *edür söni* <u>*ügei*</u> "day and night."
Kh. (*R*, p. 239) *bitšiš* <u>*ügüi*</u> "indescribable."
(*KhN*) *urid udzegdee* <u>*güi*</u> "previously unknown."
(*SMY*, p. 152) *uxaa*<u>*n*</u> <u>*güi*</u> "without knowledge."
(*SMY*, p. 122) *usa*<u>*n*</u> <u>*güi*</u> "without water."
(*R*, p. 239) *us* <u>*ügüi*</u> "without water."
Ord. (*DO*, p. 751b) *ɯDɯr söni-*<u>*ɯgᵘī*</u> "jour et nuit, sans cease."
(*DO*, p. 751b) *īrgẽ moŋgọl-*<u>*ugᵘī*</u> "Chinois et Mongols."
(*DO*, p. 751b) *öglō̈ ɯDeši-*<u>*ɯgᵘī*</u> "toute la journée."
Bur. (Cf. p. 36) *uha* <u>*ügei*</u> "dépourvu d'eau." Cf. *uha*<u>*n*</u> <u>*ügei*</u> "il n'y a pas d'eau."
Mong. (*Monguor*, p. 156) *uDur soni* <u>*uGuīni*</u> "jour et nuit."

81) *ulam* "gradually; more, by far; on account of, in consequence of; tradition."[127]

(*HsCh* 18a6-18b2) *boγda sayid qataγuǰil-*<u>*ača*</u> <u>*ulam*</u> *kündülemdegü bolqu-yi surγan čiqulalaqui-*<u>*ača*</u> <u>*ulam*</u> *čing ünen-iyer taγalaqu-yi surγan aǰuγui* "the Holy Worthies in consequence of circumspection [were] teaching [how] to be respectful and in consequence of affection were teaching [how] to love with sincere truth."

(*HsCh*, 19a) *tegüne*<u>*če*</u> <u>*ulam*</u> "in consequence of that."
(*1335*, l. 21) *ečige-*<u>*če*</u> <u>*inu*</u> <u>*ulam*</u> "in consequence of his father."
(*1335*, l. 22) *imada*<u>*ča*</u> <u>*ulam*</u> "on account of him."

(Žamcarano, p. 93) *buγu-yin miq-a-yi qubilan qubiyaqui-*<u>*ača*</u> <u>*ulam*</u> "on account of the sharing of the deer flesh."

(Vladimircov, p. 75) *tere muur segül tasuraγsan-*<u>*u*</u> <u>*ulam*</u> "the cat, in consequence of the fact that [its] tail had been broken."
Cf. (*R*, p. 230) *ulamaar* "in consequence of."

82) <u>*ülemǰi*</u> "much, more, much more; superior, remarkable."
(*K*, p. 1749) *tegün-*<u>*eče*</u> <u>*ülemǰi*</u> "plus que cela, d'autant plus."

83) *umara* / *ümere* "north."

(*SH* § 214) *ger-*<u>*ün*</u> <u>*ümere*</u> *Ǯetei Ǯelme qoyar muqular qara hüker ǰemlen alaǰu büküi-dür* "nördlich von der Yurte waren die Beiden Dschetei und Dschelme gerade beim Schlachten eines ungehörnten schwarzen Rindes für die Verpflegung."

84) *urida* / *urid* "before, in front, forward; previously, formerly; henceforth; south."
Cf. Stem (*SH* § 111) *türün* <u>*urida*</u> "im Anfang."
Cf. (*1335*, l. 35) *angqa* <u>*urida*</u> "in the very beginning."
(*R*, p. 235) *arwan džil* <u>*ur'd*</u> "ten years ago."
Cf. (*DO*, p. 738b) *ụrDa χojor ɯDɯr* "il y a deux jours."
Gen. (*SH* § 118) *terged-*<u>*ün*</u> <u>*urida*</u> *yabuǰu* "vor den Karren [dahergeritten] kamen."
(*WY*, p. 133, l. 7) *egün*<u>*ü*</u> <u>*urida*</u> "before this."

(*Kh*, p. 148) *tere xaanii xotonii urda* "before the city of the Khan."

(*DO*, p. 738b) *ɯDīn urDa* "avant midi."

(*BMS*, p. 485) *dainai urda* "before the war."

Verb. (*SH* § 90) *naran urγuqu-yin urida* "vor Sonnenaufgang."

(*K*, p. 441) *odqu-yin urida* "avant le départ."

(*K*, p. 440) *mordoqu-yin urid* "avant le départ."

(*TOO*, p. 23) *namǟ ǥarχᵃīn ụrDa* "avant ma naissance."

Abl. (*SH* § 240) *yeke čerig-eče urida yabura odču* "[als Borochul] anlangte, um vor dem Haupttrupp daher zu reiten."

(*Kh*, p. 155) *naranaas urda* "before the sun."

(*KhN*) *üünees ur'd* "before this."

(*KhN*) *xuw'sgalaas ur'd* (= *xuw'sgalaas ömnö*) "before the revolution."

(*Kh*, p. 138) *mongol oronoos baruun urda* "southwest of Mongolia."

(*DO*, p. 738b) *χamụǥās ụrDa* "avant toute autre chose."

(*BMS*, p. 485) *boldzorhoo urda* "before the appointed time."

Also Ord. *ụrt'ǟ* (< **uritai*).[128]

(*TOO*, p. 202) *mini ụrt'ǟ* "avant moi."

85) *uruγsi* "forward; towards the south (Khalkha); towards the east (Ordos)."

(*SH* § 142) *ede manglan-ača uruγsi basa qara'ul ilerün* "diese schickten vor der Spitze noch Späher voraus."

(*1362*, l. 22) *olan-ča uruγsi yabuǰu* "[because he] went more in advance than the multitude."

(*EE*, p. 5) *egün-eče uruγsi* "in the future."

(*CSN*) *Kan-ača baraγun uruγsi* "[advancing] north of Caen."

86) *uruγu* "downwards, downstream; (down) toward; eastwards (Ordos)."

(*SH* § 24) *Onan Müren huru'u* "[went] down the Onan river."

(*SH* § 81) *usun huru'u* "downstream."

(*ST*, p. 180, l. 1) *toloγai uruγu qalaγun čai asqaγad* (= *t'oloǥ̄ rụ̄ χalūū tš'ǟ asχāt*) "pouring hot tea on his head."

(*DO*, p. 742a) *ǥol ụrụ̄ jawụ-* "descendre une rivière."

(*DO*, p. 742a) *ene ụrụ̄* "vers l'est ici."

(*BMS*, p. 489) *uula uruu* "down the mountain."

(*HB*, p. LXI) *gal ruu / galiin ruu* "towards the fire."

Cf. also the postposition *ruu* "in the direction of."

(*Kh*, p. 74) *usa ruu* "das Wasser abwärts."

(*Khalkha*) *mori ruu* "towards the horse." *Ruu* does not follow vocalic harmony in Khalkha and Buriat, but in Ordos it is best classified as a suffix since it does follow vocalic harmony (cf. *TOO*, p. XXXIV, *-rụ̄ / -rṻ*).

(*Monguor*, p. 156) *ulani furu* "en bas de la montagne."

(B) WITH PRONOUNS

The numbers correspond to the numbers of the postpositions listed in (A).

1) *adali.*
   (*MSM*, p. 303b) *tüündü adali* "similar to it."
   (*SK*, p. 61) *nada adali* "gleich mir."
   (*SK*, p. 78) *nadur adali* "gleich mir."
   (*SMY*, p. 175) *nadtai adil* "like me."
   (*KD*, p. 21) *nandᴰtɛ̄ (nandᴰ / namlā̈) ädl̥ˈ* "wie ich, mir ähnlich."
   (*Ordos*) *tš'amalā aᴅali* "similar to thee."
   (*Kh*, p. 150) *tšamatai aw adilxan* "just like thee."
   (*KhN*) *tüüntei adil* "like him."
   (*KD*, p. 21) *tūndᵘ̈ ädl̥ˈ* "dem ähnelnd, gleich wie der."

4) *čaγada.*
   (*SH* § 226) *bidanu ča'ada* "on the other side of us."

6) *čaγana.*
Also Ord. *tš'ā't'ā̈ (< *čaγatai).*
   (*DO*, p. 697a) *t'ṻnēsen tš'ā't'ā̈n* "outre cela."

7) *čaγasi.*
   (*Kh*, p. 158) *ternees tsaiši* "beyond that [place]."

9) *činaγsi.*
   (*K*, p. 2131) *tegüneče činaγsi* "plus loin, outre cela."

10) *činana.*
   (*SH* § 142) *te'ün-ü činana* "au delà de celui-là."

12) *čuγ.*
   (*Kh*, p. 74) *tšamtai tsug* "mit dir zusammen."
   (*MKB*, p. 42) *tantai tsug* "together with you."
   (*Ordos*) *tš'umalā tš'ug̨* "together with thee."
   (*Buriat*) *nadatai sug iresen* "they came together with me."
   (*Buriat*) *tedenei sug huuži baina* "[he] lives together with them."

13) *daraγa.*
   (*K*, p. 1663) *tegün-ü daraγa* "à la suite, après, de suite."
Cf. (*KD*, p. 78) *tūnɛ̄ darūn* "nach ihm."
Cf. (*WY*, p. 98) *tegünü udaγa* "vsled za nimi."

14) *darui.*
   (*AYM*, l. 6) *tegünče darui* "immediately after that."
   (*WY*, p. 165, l. 3) *mön tere darui* "right after that."

(*R*, p. 68) *ter darui* "at that moment."
(*BMS*, p. 485) *tere darəi* "after that."

15) *degegsi.*
(*DM*, p. 418) *nDāDza t'ieṣe* "plus haut que moi."

16) *degegür.*
(*K*, p. 1743) *egün-ü degegür* "sur cela."

17) *degere.*
(*SH* § 272) *bidanu de'ere* "over us."
(*SH* § 205) *minu de'ere* "on me."
(*SMY*, p. 101) *nad deere* "to me."
(Ordos) naDaDār "on me."
(*BMS*, p. 336) *nam deere* "on me."
(Öljeitü 1305, l. 30) *anu degere* "against them."
(*SH* § 143) *anu de'ere* "sur eux."
(*SK*, p. 79) *tegün-ü degere* "darauf."
(*WY*, p. 98, l. 13) *tegün degere* "on it."
(*ST*, p. 126, l. 7) *tere degere* "on it."
(*EE*, p. 22) *ene deger-e* "in addition to this."
(Khalkha) tere deere "on it, on him, on her; on that."
(Khalkha) teren deere "on it, on him, on her; on that."
(Khalkha) terüün deere "on it, on her, on him; on that."
(*Kh*, p. 74) *tüün deere* "auf ihm, etc." Note that this is the preferred form in Khalkha.
(*TOO*, p. 223) *t'ere Dēre* "sur cela."
(*TOO*, p. 39) *t'erū̄ū̄ Dēre* "au dessus [du sommet]."
(Ordos) t'ū̄n Dēre "on it."
(*TOO*, p. 192) *mani Dēre* "sur nous."
(*TOO*, p. 5) *t'ani Dēre* "sur vous."
(*DM*, p. 49) *muni Dẹre* "sur moi, sur mon corps."
Also (*TOO*, p. XLI) *t'anāDār* "chez vous."
(*TOO*, p. XLI) *t'eDenīDēr* "chez eux."
(*DO*, p. 452b) *manāDār* "chez nous."
Also Ord. *Dē't'ī (< *degetei).*
(*TOO*, p. 137) *t'erū̄ū̄ Dē't'ī* "sur lequel."
Abl. (*R*, p. 86) *nadaas deer* "better than I."
(*DO*, p. 140b) *tš'amās Dēre* "meilleur que toi."
(*Monguor*, p. 158) *niänDza Dẹre* "outre ceci."

18) *dergede.*
(*MSM*, p. 119a) *bidanu dergede* "near us."
(*R*, p. 127) *minii derged* "near me."
(*TOO*, p. 32) *mini DergeDu* "chez moi."
(*KD*, p. 89) *mini dergəde* "bei mir."
(*ST*, p. 240, l. 19) *činu dergede* "in deiner Gegenwart."

(*WY*, p. 112, l. 5) *tegünü dergede* "near it."
(*R*, p. 221) *tüünii derged* "near him."
(*TOO*, p. 39) *t'erüü Dergede* "près de cette [dune]."
(*R*, p. 196) *tanai derged* "near you, beside you."
(*TOO*, p. 182) *t'ani Dergede* "près de vous."

22) *doora / dora.*
(*Khalkha*) *minii doro* "under me."
(*Ordos*) *mini Doro* "sous moi."
(*Monguor*, p. 156) *muni Dōro* "sous moi."
(*TOO*, p. 221) *tš'ini Doro* "sous tes ordres."
(*Khalkha*) *tere doro* "under it."
(*DO*, p. 152b) *ene Doro* "sous ceci."
(*BMS*, p. 734) *ene doro* "right here."
(*KD*, p. 95) *ter^ə dor^o* "da (wo sie waren), ebendort."
(*Khalkha*) *tüün doro* "under it."
(*Ordos*) *t'ūn Doro* "sous cela."
(*Khalkha*) *terüün doro* "under it."
(*TOO*, p. 135) *t'erüü Doro* "under it (i.e., the earth)."
(*HB*, p. 79) *teren doro* "under it."
(*HB*, p. 79) *eneen doro* "under this."
Abl. (*ST*, p. 130, l. 15) *čimača doora* "after thee (i.e., after your generation)."
(*SMY*, p. 160) *nadaas dor* "worse than I [am]."

24) *dorona.*
(*SH* § 190) *ene dorona* "east of here."
Cf. (*SH* § 260) *ene hörene* "im Westen."
Cf. (*Kh*, p. 152) *ene dzüün* "east of this." Note that these phrases are in effect quite similar to adverbial phrases such as *ene edür* "this day > today." (See chapter five, adverbs.)

26) *dotora.*
(*Buriat*) *minii soo* "in me."
(*HB*, p. XLVI) *nam soo* "in me."
(*Buriat*) *šama soo* "in thee."
(*Khalkha*) *minii dotor* "in me."
(*Ordos*) *mini Do't'oro* "in me."
(*SH* § 203) *tere dotora* "in it."
(*ST*, p. 288, l. 2) *tere dotora* "among them." *Tere* is used as a collective singular pronoun. Cf. (*Ordos*) *enūn Do't'or* "among these."
(*TOO*, p. 220) *t'ere Do't'oro* "là-dedans."
(*SMY*, p. 133) *ter dotor* "among them (i.e., the songs)."
(*WY*, p. 96, l. 7) *tegün dotora* "in it."
(*WM*, p. 34) *tegün dotora* "into it."
(*Khalkha*) *tüün dotor* "in it."

(*Ordos*) *t'ūn* *Do't'oro* "in it."
(*HB*, p. XLVI) *tüün soo* "in it."
(*Khalkha*) *terüün dotor* "in it."
(*Ordos*) *t'erūū* *Do't'oro* "in that."
(*Khalkha*) *teren dotor* "in that."
(*HB*, p. LX) *teren soo* "in it."
(*HB*, p. 55) *teren dotor* "in it."
(*SK*, p. 79) *tegün-ü dotora* "im Inneren desselben (= Königspalast)."
(*KhM*, p. 35) *tüünii dotor* "in jenem [schachtel]."
(*KhN*) *tüünii dotor* "within that."
(*KhN*) *tüünii dotor* "among them (i.e., the medicines)."
(*SMY*, p. 162) *üünii dotor* "among them."
(*Ordos*) *enūn* *Do't'or* "among these."
(*WY*, p. 116, l. 4) *bidan dotora* "among us."
(*EE*, p. 16) *teden-ü dotora* "within those."
(*MKB*, p. 140) *teden-ü dotora* "in those [tents]."
(*KhN*) *tednii dotor* "among them."
(*Ordos*) *t'eDeni Do't'oro* / *t'eDen Do't'oro* "among them."
(*BMS*, p. 404) *teden soo* "among them."
(*SK*, p. 4) *bügüde dotora* "in Gegenwart aller."
(*K*, p. 238) *egün-ü dotora* "de ceux-ci, au nombre de ceux-ci."
(*KhM*, p. 8) *enüünii dotor* "in diesem [kästlein]."
(*DM*, p. 434) *t'ani t'uro k'än muDiäm* "qui de vous le sait?"

27) *dumda*.
(*WY*, p. 98, l. 2) *tegün-ü dumda* "in the midst of them."
(*MKB*, p. 112) *teden-ü dumda* "among them."
(*MKB*, p. 111) *tednii dunda* "among them."
(*KhN*) *ednii dund* "among these [persons]."
(*KhN*) *tednii dund* "among them."

31) *emüne*.
(*SH* § 218) *minu emüne* "vor mich."
(*R*, p. 165) *minii ömnö* "before me, in my presence."
(*CSN*) *bidan-u emüne* "before us."
(*SMY*, p. 159) *manai ömnö* "[problems are placed] before us."
(*KhN*) *tednii ömnö* "in front of them."
(*TOO*, p. 210) *tš'ini ömönö* "devant toi."
(*DM*, p. 237) *muni mieșe* "devant moi."
Abl. (*DM*, p. 237) *nDāDza mieșe* "[il est sorti] avant moi."

32) *ende*.
(*TOO*, p. 705) *mani enDe* "ici chez nous."
(*TOO*, p. 222) *tš'i mini enDe sū* "reste ici chez moi."
(*R*, p. 327) *manai end* "here at our place."
(*DzDz*, l. 280) *tanää ende* "here where you are."

35) *γadaγa.*
(*DO*, p. 284a) *mani* *ɢaDā* "outside of us (i.e., outside of our yurt)."

36) *γadaγsi.*
(*MKB*, p. XI) *tüünii gadagš* "beyond it."

37) *γadaγur.*
(*TOO*, p. 197) *t'erūūū ɢaDūr* "autour de ce [doigt]."

38) *γadana.*
(*EE*, p. 42) *čimača γadana* "except thee."
(*K*, p. 238) *egünče γadana* "hormis cela."
(*EE*, p. 6) *egün-eče γadana* "in addition to this."
(*MKB*, p. 78) *tegün-eče γadana* "aside from that."
(*MKB*, p. 87) *egün-eče γadana* "aside from this."
(*KhN*) *üünees gadna* "aside from this."
(*Kh*, p. 74) *tüünees gadana* "ausser ihm, ausserdem."
(*BMS*, p. 153) *tereenhee gadna* "aside from that."

40) *ilegü(ü) / ülegü(ü).*
Cf. (*SH* § 203) *ken-eče hüle'ü küčü ögüle'e* "[he] rendered more service than anyone."
(*TOO*, p. 88) *Bi enūūnēs ilgūū tš'aŋɢa Džūχū* "je to mordrai encore plus fort que cette fois-ci."
(*TOO*, p. 75) *t'ūūnēs ilgūū arwã χuwi* "dix fois plus."

41) *inadu.*
(*K*, p. 275) *nadača inadu* "jusqu'à moi, jusqu'à mon temps."

42) *inaγsi.*
(*K*, p. 8) *egünče inaγsi* "depuis ce temps, à l'avenir."
(*DM*, p. 255) *niänDza naɢse* "dorénavant."

44) *ǰabsar.*
(*KhN*) *ene dzabsar* "during this period." Cf. the adverbial phrase *ene edür* "this day > today." See section on adverbs in chapter five.

45) *ǰaγura.*
(*SH* § 281) *bidan-u ǰa'ura* "between us."
(*Ölǰeitü 1305*, l. 30) *bidan-u ǰaγura* "among us."
(*Monguor*, p. 156) *nDāni Dźioro sū* "assieds-toi parmi nous."

46) *ǰüg.*
(*CSN*) *tegün-ü ǰüg očiqu* "to go in the direction of it."
(*Kh*, p. 75) *tüünii dzüg* "in der Richtung zu ihm."

48) *metü.*
(*SH* § 162) *ene metü* "de même manière."

(*SH* § 177) *činu metü* "like thee."
(*SH* § 203) *minu metü* "wie ich."
(*DM*, p. 229) *muni maᴅu* "comme moi."
(*Hy* IIa 4v) *tere metü* "like that."
(*SK*, p. 81) *tere metü* "ihm gleich."
(*K*, p. 2012) *bi metü* "comme moi."
(*1338*, l. 5) *mön ene kü metü* "even like this."
(*ST*, p. 122, l. 6) *ene metü* "thus."
(*K*, p. 2012) *tere metü* "de cette manière; tel."
(*WY*, p. 112, l. 7) *tere metü* "in a manner similar to that."
(*R*, p. 132) *ene met* "similar to this; thus."
(*TOO*, p. 178) *ene me't'ɯ* "à ce point."
(*KD*, p. 262) *ter*^{ə} *met*^{ə} "wie dies, so."
(*Monguor*, p. 157) *t'ieni maᴅú* "comme cela."

50) *naγana.*
(*DzDz*, l. 69) *tüünii naana* "this side of him."

51) *naγasi.*
(*DO*, p. 485a) *t'ɯ̄nēs nāši* ɯg^{u}ī "cela n'arrivera pas avant cette date."

52) *ögede.*
(*SH* § 88) *tere ö'ede* "up that [valley]."
(*DO*, 527a) *mani ȫᴅö* "dans notre direction."
(*DO*, p. 240a) *enēᴅɯ* < *ene ögede* "vers ici."
(*DO*, p. 660b) *t'erēᴅɯ* < *tere ögede* "vers là."

53) *ögere / öbere.*
(*K*, p. 1749) *tegün-če öbere* "étranger à cela."
(*R*, p. 167) *tüünees öör* "besides him."
(*DO*, p. 538b) *naᴅās ȫrö* "autre que moi."

54) *oyira.*
(*SK*, p. 7) *tegün-ü oyira* "in seiner Nähe."
(*KD*, p. 304) *mini ȫrö* "bei mir."
(*BMS*, p. 365) *tereenəi oiro* "near him."

55) *qamtu.*
(*MKB*, p. 43) *nada-luγa qamtu* "together with me."
(*Ordos*) *eᴅenlē χamt'u̯* "together with them."
(*DO*, p. 331b) *eᴅent'ī χamt'u̯* "ensemble avec ceux-ci."
(*KhN*) *nadtai xamt* "together with me."
(*SMY*, p. 159) *nadtai xamt* "together with me."
(*KD*, p. 271) *nanlē χamt*^{ɒ} "zusammen mit mir."

56) *qoγorundu.*
(*WY*, p. 69, l. 13) *tegün qoγordumda* "meanwhile."
(*R*, p. 267) *ta bid xoyorəin xoorond* "among ourselves."

(*Kh*, p. 140) *tere xoorondo* "unterdessen, inzwischen."
(*TOO*, p. 178) *t'ere χōrg̣onDu̜* "entretemps."
Note (*TOO*, p. 685) *χōrg̣onDu̜* = *χōronDu̜*
(*KD*, p. 192) *manᴅ̈ χōrn̥dɒ* "unter uns."

57) *qoγorunduγur*.
(*Kh*, p. 152) *tere xooronduur* "during that [time]."

60) *qoyina*.
(*SH* § 12) *te'ün-ü qoyina* "par la suite."
(*1335*, l. 19) *tegün-ü qoyina* "after that."
(*ST*, p. 86, l. 22) *tegün-ü qoyina* "darnach."
(*ST*, p. 286, l. 2) *tegün-eče qoyina* "hierauf."
(*WY*, p. 66, l. 3) *tegünü qoyina* "after that."
(*WY*, p. 66, l. 1) *tegünče qoyina* "after that."
(*MKB*, p. 132) *tegün-ü qoyina* "after that."
(*Kh*, p. 154) *ööröö xoino* "behind himself."
(*TOO*, p. 159) *ene χȯg̈no* "à l'est d'ici."
(*KD*, p. 194) *tün̄ɛs χȫnᵒ̈* "nachdem, nach diesem."
Also Ord. (*TOO*, p. 36) *t'erɯ̄ɯ̄ χȯg̈'t'ˆ̄* "après cela."
(*TOO*, p. 161) *mini χȯg̈'t'ˆ̄* "derrière moi."
(*DM*, p. 177) *muni χuēno* "derrière moi."

61) *qoyisi*.
(*EE*, p. 2) *egünče qoyisi* "since that [event]."
(*TT*, p. 11, l. 1) *tegün-eče qoyisi* "after that."
(*MKB*, p. 112) *egünče qoyisi* "after this."
(*Kh*, p. 74) *tüünees xoiši* "nachdem, nach diesem, darauf."
(*KhN*) *tüünees xoiš* "after that."
(*Kh*, [Rudnev,] p. LXVII) *terüünees xoiš* "after that."
(*TOO*, p. 136) *t'ɯ̄nēs χȯg̈ši* "depuis lors."
(*TOO*, p. 62) *t'erɯ̄nēs χȯg̈ši* "à partir de ce moment."
(*TOO*, p. 166) *enɯ̄nēs χȯg̈ši* "dorénavant."
(*BMS*, p. 34) *ternehee xoišo* "after that."

65) *sig*.
(*Kh*, p. 96) *nama-šig* "wie ich."
(*Khalkha*) *nada-šig* "wie ich."

66) *singgi*.
(*TOO*, p. 204) *t'ere šiŋgɯ* "semblables à celles-là."
(*Ordos*) *Bi šiŋgɯ* "like myself."
(*Buriat*) *šama-šinyi* "like thee."

67) *sitü*.
(*TOO*, p. 34) *Bi šint'ī* "comme moi."
(*TOO*, p. 58) *ene šint'ī* "[si délicieux] que ceux-ci."

69) *tege.*

(K, p. 1786) *tere* *tege* "au delà, de l'autre côté."

(*R,* p. 226) *tertee* "there, on that side."

(*SMY*, p. 177) *tertee* "on that side."

(*SMY*, p. 177) *enetee* "on this side."

71) *tegesi.*

(Khalkha) nama *teeši* "towards me."

(Khalkha) nada *teeši* "towards me."

(Khalkha) minii *teeši* "towards me."

(*SMY*, p. 118) *manai* *tiiš* "towards us."

(*SMY*, p. 138) *biden* *tiiš* "towards us."

(*DO*, p. 663a) *t'ani* *t'ĭšēē* "dans vos parages."

(Ordos) mani *t'ēš* "in the direction of us."

(*BMS*, p. 336) *nam* *teeše* "towards me."

(*BMS*, p. 308) *man* *teeše* "towards us."

(*BMS*, p. 426) *tan* *teeše* "towards you."

(Khalkha) tüün *teeši* "towards it, him, etc."

(*BMS*, p. 460) *tüün* *teeše* "towards him."

(*Buriat*) *teden* *teeše* "towards them."

72) *tende*

(DzDz, l. 287) *manää* *tende* "there where we live."

(*R,* p. 263) *manai* *tend* *tšono xowor* "there [where] we [live] the wolves are few."

(*KD*, p. 391) *tanā̈* *tendə* "dort, wo ihr seid; bei euch, in eurem haus oder land."

(*DO*, p. 657b) *t'ani* *tenDe* "là-bas dans vos parages."

74) *tölöge.*

(*R,* p. 211) *minii* *tölöö* "for me, in place of me."

(*R,* p. 211) *yuunəi* *tölöö* "for what purpose?"

(*SMY*, p. 100) *tanai* *tölöö* "for your sake."

(*TOO*, p. 71) *mini* *t'ölō̈* "à cause de moi."

(*TOO*, p. 215) *tš'ini* *t'ölō̈* "à ta place."

(*TOO*, p. 8) *jɯ̄ɯ̄* *t'ölō̈* "pourquoi?"

(*TOO*, p. 8) *t'ɯ̄ɯ̄* *t'ölō̈* "pour cette [affaire]."

(*TOO*, p. 71) *mini* *t'ölō̈* *Bi'tš'ige ṳ̄r k'ɯrēt wā̈* "ne vous fâchez pas à cause de moi."

(*KD*, p. 406) *mini* *tölɛ̄* "statt meiner."

(*KD*, p. 406) *jūnɛ̄* *tölɛ̄* "warum?"

75) *tula.*

(*SH* § 91) *minu* *tula* "à cause de moi."

(*MSM*, p. 97b) *tüüni* *tula* "because of that."

(*SK* , p. 5) *ay-a minu* *tula* *buu uyila* "weine doch um meinetwillen nicht!"

(*ST*, p. 142, l. 1) *yaγun-u* *tula* "why?"

(*ST*, p. 130, l. 10) *tegün-ü tula* "because of that."
(*ÜD*, p. 133, l. 10) *minu tula* "for my sake."
(*AYM*, l. 7) *teyimü-yin tula* "for that reason."
(*Doc. B*, l. 11) *egün-ü tula* "for him (i.e., in place of him)."
(*K*, p. 1848) *ken-ü tula* "pour qui."
(*WY*, p. 45, l. 11) *tegün-ü tula* "because of that."
(*Kh*, p. 74) *tüünii tula* "deswegen."
(*KD*, p. 409) *jūnɛ̄ tulᵘ* "warum?"
Cf. (*DO*, p. 678b) *t'ula* "à cause de, pour (emprunt fait à la langue litteraire)."

76) *tuqai*.
(*K*, p. 1796) *ene tuqai* "à présent, à l'occasion présente."
(*WY*, p. 98, l. 13) *egün tuqai* "with regard to this."
(*KhN*) *ene tuxai* "concerning this."
(*Khalkha*) *minii tuxai* "concerning me."
(*Khalkha*) *tüün tuxai* "concerning that, him, etc."
(*Khalkha*) *tüünii tuxai* "concerning that, him, etc."
(*Khalkha*) *terüün tuxai* "concerning that, him, etc."
(*BMS*, p. 688) *šam tuxai* "concerning you."
(*BMS*, p. 191) *eneen tuxai* "concerning this."
(*BMS*, p. 308) *man tuxai* "concerning us."

78) *tus*.
(*WY*, p. 89, l. 5) *tegün tus* "with regard to that."

80) *ügei*.
(*BMS*, p. 734) *eneen güi* "without this."

81) *ulam*.
(*HsCh*, 19a) *tegüneče ulam* "in consequence of that."
(*1335*, l. 22) *imadača ulam* "on account of him."

82) *ülemǰi*.
(*K*, p. 1749) *tegün-eče ülemǰi* "plus que cela, d'autant plus."

84) *urida*.
(*WY*, p. 133, l. 7) *egünü urida* "before this."
(*R*, p. 247) *üünii ur'd* "before this."
(*MKB*, p. 121) *enüünii urida* "before this."
(*SMY*, p. 178) *ene urd* "south of here."
(*KhN*) *üünees ur'd* "before this."
(*BMS*, p. 485) *minii urda* "before me."
(*DO*, p. 738b) *mini u̯rDa* "avant moi."
(*DO*, p. 738b) *t'ere u̯rDa* "autrefois."
Also Ord. (*TOO*, p. 202) *mini u̯rt'ā̈* "avant moi."

85) *uruγsi*.
(*EE*, p. 5) *egün-eče uruγsi* "henceforth."

(*EE*, p. 27) *tegün-če uruɣsi* "southward from here."
(*Doc. C*, l. 9) *egünče uruɣsi* "from now on."

86) *uruɣu*.
(*TOO*, p. 214) *ene yrū* "vers l'est d'ici."
(*Khalkha*) *nama ruu* "towards me."
Cf. (*Ordos*) *naDa-rū* "towards me."
(*Buriat*) *teree ruu* "towards that."

Additional information on postpositions may be obtained from A. R. Rinčine, *Učebnik mongol'skogo yazïka* (Moscow, 1952). The following excerpts are taken from this publication:

Ömnö "before, up to," is preceded by the Ablative Case, when the meaning is temporal; it is preceded by the Genitive Case, when the meaning is spatial (p. 47).
xitšeelees ömnö "before the lesson" (p. 47).
baišingiin ömnö "in front of the building" (p. 47).
minii ömnö "before me" (p. 47).
However, this postposition (i.e., *ömnö*) even in its temporal meaning sometimes takes the Genitive Case, thereby substituting the Genitive Case for the Ablative Case. In modern Khalkha Mongolian, the Genitive Case is used more often with postpositions than formerly, thus tending to replace other cases (p. 47).
xitšeeliin ömnö "before the lesson." However, it is still more usual to use *xitšeelees ömnö* "before the lesson" (p. 47).
xitšeeliin daraa "after the lesson" (p. 47).
Cf. *xitšeelees xoiš* "after the lesson" (p. 106).

Minimal Form Postpositions:
minii daraa "after me" (p. 47).
Cf. *daraa bid uuldzana* "we shall meet later" (p. 37).
nom deer "in the book" (p. 200).
xural deer "at the meeting" (p. 49).
ter sandal' deer suu "sit on that chair" (p. 30).
arwan neg deer xorin gurwəig nembel xed bolox we "if you add twenty-three to eleven, what is the result?" (p. 74).
tsaasan dor "under the paper" (p. 46).
booltšlogtšdəin esreg - - - temtsliig xiidž "struggling - - - against the enslavers" (p. 175).
ter nom unššnaas gadna "aside from reading that book" (p. 166).
dörwön dzuun dalan tawan saya garui "more than 475,000,000" (p. 74).
xoyor sar ilüü "for more than two months" (p. 186).
dzagas met šumbadž "plunging [in the water] like a fish" (p. 187).

yuunəi ömnö "above all" (p. 178).
garaxəin ömnö "before going out" (p. 92).
gurwanəi neg xuw' ortšim "about one third" (p. 74).
xoyor džil šaxam "for about two years" (p. 187).
tawan dzuun saya šaxam "almost 500,000,000" (p. 74).
bid bol tüün-šig baix yostoi "we must be like him" (p. 88).
širee tiišee "to his table" (p. 198).
utga dzoxiol, šii ba xögdžmiin tuxai yaria xiiw "[we] talked about literature, the theater, and music" (p. 71).
xüiten bolsnoos xoiš "after it became cold" (p. 166).
tüünees xoiš "after that" (p. 187).

Noun Postpositions:

bi tšinii xelsen yosoor biyee dzasiyaa "I'll fix myself up in the manner you have stated" (p. 204).
adžlaa amdžilt-taigaar yawuulsnəi atšaar ülemdžxen toonəi mal ösgöw "as a result of the fact that they successfully carried out their work, they raised a large number of cattle" (p. 113).

Verb Postpositions:

širee xürtel "up to the table" (p. 46).
surguul' xürtel "to school" (p. 46).
gadaa ix tsas orsnoos boldž dzam xaragdaxgüi bolow "because much snow was falling outside, the road was invisible" (p. 166).
Cf. *tšinii irsend bi ix bayarlaw* "I was very glad that you came" (p. 166).

NOTES

The system for transcribing names and titles in Russian is that described on page 363 of "La Gest du prince Igor'," *Annuaire de l'Institut de Philologie et d'Histoire Orientales et Slaves,* Tome VIII (New York, 1945-1947).

1. P. E. Skačkov, *Vnutrennyaya Mongoliya* "Inner Mongolia" (Moscow, 1933), pp. 10-13.
2. O. Lattimore, *Mongols of Manchuria* (New York, 1934), pp. 24-25.
3. F. Lorimer, *Population of the Soviet Union* (Geneva, 1946), pp. 59-60.
4. N. N. Poppe, *Buryat-mongol'skoe yazïkoznanie* (Leningrad, 1933).
5. B. Vladimircov, *Le régime social des Mongols* (translated by M. Carsow from Russian), Paris, 1948.
6. I.e., "Red Hero," formerly called *Da Küriye(n)* "Great Monastery," and by the Chinese, *Ta K'u-lun* 大庫倫. The Russian name for it was *Urga* < *ergüge* "residence," *örgöö* in Khalkha.
7. Reported by Choibalsang, and printed in *Pravda,* Nov. 26, 1949.
8. Ma Ho-t'ien, *Chinese Agent in Mongolia,* a translation from Chinese by John de Francis, Baltimore, 1949. Ma Ho-t'ien 馬鶴天, a political agent and specialist on frontier affairs, took notes on a journey which he made to Outer Mongolia during 1926 to 1927. The published notes were originally called 內外蒙古考察日記 ("Journal of Investigations in Inner and Outer Mongolia"). They appeared in *Hsin Ya-hsi-ya hsüeh-hui* [*New Asia Society*], during December, 1932. They give a detailed account of the Mongolian People's Republic *(Bügüde Nayiramdaqu Mongɣol Arad Ulus)* during its formative years.
9. D. Diringer, *The Alphabet* (New York, 1948).
10. "T'a-t'a T'ung-a chuan" 塔塔統阿傳, *Yüan shih* 124. Cf. Lin Yün-t'ao 林韻濤, "Meng-ku yung Weiwu tzu chih yüan-yin" 蒙古用畏兀字之原因 ["Origin of the Use of Uigur Script among the Mongols"], *Yü Kung* 禹貢 *(The Chinese Historical Geography)* 5(1936).21-24. Cf. Paul Pelliot, "Notes sur le 'Turkestan' de M. W. Barthold," *TP* 27(1930).34-35, n. 1.
11. Called Kanbalu (= Qan-balïq) by Marco Polo.
12. *'Phags-pa* is a Tibetan title meaning "honorable, noble." It is a translation of the Sanscrit word *arya* meaning the same thing.
13. See N. N. Poppe, *Kvadratnaya pis'mennost'* (Leningrad, 1941). This work gives a comprehensive treatment of the *'Phags-pa* texts.
14. N. N. Poppe, *Buryat-mongol'skoe yazïkoznanie* (Leningrad, 1933).
15. N. N. Poppe, "Remarks on the Vocalism of the Second Syllable in Mongolian," *HJAS* 14(1951).189-207.
16. B. Ya. Vladimircov, *Sravnitel'naya grammatika mongol'skogo pis'mennogo yazïka i halhaskogo narečiya* (Leningrad, 1929).

17. E. Haenisch, *Mangḥol un niuca tobca'an* (Leipzig, 1935).

18. See n. 13.

19. E. N. Setälä, "Über Transkription der Finnisch-Ugrischen Sprachen," *Finnisch-Ugrische Forschungen* 1(Helsingfors, 1901).

20. G. J. Ramstedt, *Kalmückisches Wörterbuch* (Helsinki, 1935).

21. N. N. Poppe, *Khalkha-Mongolische Grammatik* (Wiesbaden, 1951). This is the most complete and up-to-date description of spoken Khalkha, the language of the cultural center of Mongolia.

22. See n. 16.

23. See n. 21.

24. "As in English," "similar to English" are mere approximations and do not indicate phonetic equivalents.

25. For a complete treatment of orthographic rules concerning əi, cf. Rinčine, *Kratkiy mongol'sko-russkiy slovar'* (Moscow, 1947).362-364.

26. Additional signs used for transcription purposes: /e/ is also used to indicate the short neutral vowel (= ă / ĕ) front or back in non-initial syllables. Its quality is slightly front or back depending on the vocalic harmony of the word. /˘/ over a vowel means that it is short. /ʾ/ over a vowel means that it is fronted. /ʻ/ after a consonant indicates aspiration. /´/ over a syllable indicates accent (of any kind). A few other conventional phonetic symbols are occasionally used.

27. N. N. Poppe, "Beiträge zur Kenntnis der altmongolischen Schriftsprache," *AM* 1(1924).668-675.

28. G. J. Ramstedt, "Das Schriftmongolische und die Urgamundart," *JSFOu* 21(1902).50.

29. K. Grønbech, "Der Akzent im Türkischen und Mongolischen," *ZDMG* 94(1940), Heft 3.

30. A. Mostaert, *Textes oraux ordos*, pp. X and XX.

31. P. Pelliot, "Les mots à *h* initiale aujourd'hui amuie dans le mongol des XIIIe et XIVe siècles," *JA* (Avril-Juin 1925).193-263. G. J. Ramstedt, "Ein anlautender stimmloser Labial der mongolisch-türkischen Ursprache," *JSFOu* 32.2(1916-1920).

32. A. de Smedt et A. Mostaert, *Dictionnaire monguor-français* (Peking, 1933).

33. A. Mostaert, "The Mongols of Kansu and Their Language," *Bulletin No. 8 of the Catholic University of Peking* (Peking, 1931).75-89.

34. G. J. Ramstedt, "Zur Geschichte des labialen Spiranten im Mongolischen," *Festschrift Vilhelm Thomsen* (1912).

35. F. W. Cleaves, "The Mongolian Names and Terms in the *History of the Nation of the Archers* by Grigor of Akanc'," *HJAS* 12(1949).400-443.

36. See n. 29.

37. B. Vladimircov, *op. cit.*, pp. 223-234.

38. Cf. the section on short vowels, p. 22.

39. Rinčine, *op. cit.*, pp. 405-411.

40. Cf. N. N. Poppe, "The Groups **uγa* and **üge* in Mongol Languages," *Studia Orientalia* 14(1950).3-15.

41. Rinčine, *op. cit.*, p. 339.

42. N. N. Poppe, "Voprosï grammatiki mongol'skogo yazïka," *Zapiski Instituta Vostokovedeniya A. N.* 2(1922).

43. G. J. Ramstedt, *op. cit.*, p. 53.

44. A. Mostaert, *Textes oraux ordos*, pp. VII-VIII.

45. A. Mostaert, "Le dialecte des Mongols Urdus (Sud)," *Anthropos* 21(1926).167.

46. N. N. Poppe, "Remarks on the Vocalism of the Second Syllable in Mongolian," *HJAS* 14(1951). 189-207.

47. I. Ya. Šmidt, *Grammatika mongol'skago yazïka* (St. Petersburg, 1832).

48. N. N. Poppe, "O častyah reči v mongol'skom yazïke," *Sovetskoe Vostokovedenie A. N. USSR* (Moscow, 1940). 147-173.

49. O. Kovalevsky (= Kowalewski), *Kratkaya grammatika mongol'skago knižnego yazïka* (Kazan', 1835).

50. A. Popov, *Grammatika kalmïckago yazïka* (Kazan', 1847).

51. A. Rudnev, *Lekcii po grammatike mongol'skago pis'mennago yazïka* (St. Petersburg, 1905).

52. A. de Smedt et A. Mostaert, *Le dialecte monguor parlé par les Mongols du Kansou occidental, IIe Partie, Grammaire* (Peking, 1945).

53. O. Jespersen, *The Philosophy of Grammar* (New York, 1924), p. 91.

54. See nn. 21 and 48.

55. N. N. Poppe, "Die Nominalstammbildungssuffixe im Mongolischen," *KSz* 20(1923-1927). 89-125. G. Ramstedt, "Zur Verbstammbildungslehre der mongolisch-türkischen Sprachen," *JSFOu* 28. 3(1912).

56. M. Lewicki, "Przyrostki przysłowkowe *-ra ~ -rä, -ru ~ -rü, rï ~ -ri* w jezykach ałtajskich," *Collectanea Orientalia*, Nr. 15 (Wilno, 1938).

57. N. N. Poppe, *Khalkha-Mongolische Grammatik* (Wiesbaden, 1951), p. 74.

58. G. Ramstedt, "Über die Konjugation des Khalkha-Mongolischen," *MSFOu* 19(1903). 56.

59. A. von Gabain, *Alttürkische Grammatik* (Leipzig, 1950), p. 86.

60. N. N. Poppe, *op. cit.*, p. 64.

61. A. Mostaert, *Textes oraux ordos*, pp. xxiv-xxxi.

62. Wł. Kotwicz, "Contributions aux études altaiques. IV. Sons intercalaires," *Rocznik Orjentalistyczny* 12(Lwow, 1936). Cf. also N. N. Poppe, "Osnovï okančivayuščiesya na *n* v mongol'skih yazïkah," *Sovetskoe Yazïkoznanie* I. 167-171. Cf. also N. N. Poppe, "Über die Sprache der Daguren," *AM* 10(1935). 213.

63. A. von Gabain, *op. cit.*, pp. 86-99.

64. G. J. Ramstedt, "Mogholica," *JSFOu* 23(1906). 59.

65. N. N. Poppe, "Geserica," *AM* 3(1926). 16.

66. See n. 62.

67. The abbreviations in parentheses are listed with their equivalents in full form on pages xiii-xvi.

68. B. Ya. Vladimircov, *Sravnitel'naya grammatika mongol'skogo pis'mennogo yazïka i halhaskogo narečiya. Vvedenie i fonetika* (Leningrad, 1929), pp. 353-354.

69. A. Rudnev, *Hori-buryatskiy govor*, Vip. I-III (Petrograd, 1913-1914).

70. A. Rudnev, *op. cit.*, p. 122.

71. A. Mostaert, *op. cit.*, p. XXXIV.

72. A. Mostaert, "Sur quelques passages de l'*Histoire secrète des Mongols* (I)," *HJAS* 13(1950). 357.

73. This whole passage on the indefinite case is taken from N. N. Poppe's *Khalkha-Mongolische Grammatik* (Wiesbaden, 1951), p. 62.

74. From *Čaγan teüke* in *Mongol'skie letopisi XVII veka* (Moscow-Leningrad, 1936, p. 76) by C. Z. Žamčarano. The passage which includes ***namabar*** is given on p. 291 of "Sur quelques passages de l'*Histoire secrète des Mongols* (I)" by A. Mostaert, *HJAS* 13(1950).

75. G. J. Ramstedt, "Über mongolische pronomina," *JSFOu* 23. 3(1906). 1-20.

76. N. N. Poppe, *Mongol'skiy slovar' Mukaddimat al-Adab* (Moscow-Leningrad, 1938). The forms from the stem *čina-* are given in the glossary of *Ibn-Muhanna* on page 435. The *Mukaddimat al-Adab* is an Arabic-Persian-Chagatai-Mongolian dictionary compiled in the fourteenth century. The glossary of *Ibn-Muhanna* is given as Supplement IV to Professor Poppe's edition of the *Mukaddimat al-adab* given above.

77. The translation is that of the Reverend Antoine Mostaert as found in "Sur quelques passages de l'*Histoire secrète des Mongols* (I)," *HJAS* 13(1950).343.

78. A. Mostaert, "Sur quelques passages de l'*Histoire secrète des Mongols* (Suite)," *HJAS* 14(1951).345.

79. Translation given in "The Expression *Jöb Ese Bol-*" by Professor Cleaves, *HJAS* 11(1948).320.

80. M. Lewicki, *La langue mongole des transcriptions chinoises du XIVe siècle. Le Houa-yi yi-yu de 1389* (Wrocław, 1949).

81. N. N. Poppe, "Beiträge zur Kenntnis der altmongolischen Schriftsprache," *AM* 1(1924).668-675. *Ima* is mentioned on page 672. Note *Sidintü Kegür-ün čadig* (Peking, no date), p. 5a, l. 8, *nima tegün-i üǰeged* [= *ima üǰeged*] "l'ayant vu." *Nima* is a mistake for *ima,* since there should be no point at the left of the "head" of the initial letter.

In a letter to me dated October 29, 1952, Professor Poppe pointed out the following concerning *ima*:

1) The *ima* mentioned by Ramstedt (see p. 49) occurs in Jülg's *Kalmuk Siddhi Kür,* and not in the *Mongolian* version.

2) There is a difference between *nama* and *nima* (= *ima)* used alone and the use of *ima* (Ramstedt's example) as the first member of a group.

3) As the first member of a group *ima γurban* is like *üker morin γurban-i*. This makes *ima* an equal member of a syntactic group. Cf. *egün tegün-i* (with *-i* common to both of them).

4) That *ima* is singular is not puzzling since *ene γurban* and *ede γurban* mean the same thing ("these three"). In preclassic language there was more agreement between an attribute and the word defined by it. Cf. *tede olan iregsed nököd* "those many comrades who have come." The modern version would be *tere olan iregsen nököd* (or even *nökör,* because *olan* by itself shows that there are "many").

5) At the present time pronouns are the only part of speech that agree in number, but this also is not obligatory. Therefore, *ima γurban* is as "grammatical" as *tede γurban.* One might suppose that an even more "grammatical" form would have been **an γurban-i* "the three of them (acc.)."

82. Suggested in a letter to me dated 9 March 1952 from Professor Poppe.

83. J. Whatmough, "Natural Selection in Language," *Scientific American* 186.4(1952).83.

84. See n. 56.

85. A. Bobrovnikov, *Grammatika mongol'sko-kalmïckago yazïka* (Kazan', 1849). V. L. Kotvič, *Lekcii po grammatike mongol'skago yazïka* (St. Petersburg, 1902). A. D. Rudnev, *Lekcii po grammatike mongol'skago pis'mennago yazïka* (St. Petersburg, 1905).

86. See nn. 47, 49, and 50.

87. A. Mostaert, "Sur quelques passages de l'*Histoire secrète des Mongols* (Suite)," *HJAS* 14(1951).376.

88. N. N. Poppe, "O častyah reči v mongol'skom yazïke," *Sovetskoe Vostokovedenie* 1(1940).147-173.

89. B. H. Todaev, *Grammatika sovremmennogo mongol'skogo yazïka* (Moscow, 1951), pp. 154-158.

90. In a letter to me dated 9 March 1952, Professor Poppe pointed out the following:

"I think *doora* is better than *doura,* and this is why: even if it were *doura,* this form before contracting into D*oro* or Dō*š* had to pass the secondary stage **doora.* The form *doγoγsi* is doubtlessly from **doγaγsi.* The form *doora* is **do-ra* and **o* is the primary vowel. The spelling *doora* may be a peculiarity of the spelling, instead of *dora,* in order to make it different from *dura* 'mind.'

Cf. *doora* "below."
dura "mind."
qoora "poison."
qura "rain."

Do-ra is from **dora* and *doγoγsi* is from **doγaγsi.*"

91. A. Mostaert, "Sur quelques passages de l'*Histoire secrète des Mongols* (Suite)," *HJAS* 14(1951).374.

92. Letter to me dated 9 September 1951 from the Reverend Antoine Mostaert.

93. N. N. Poppe, *Grammatika buryat-mongol'skogo yazïka* (Leningrad-Moscow, 1938).

94. A. D. Rudnev, *Hori-buryatskiy govor* (Petrograd, 1913-1914), p. 122.

95. B. H. Todaev, *op. cit.,* pp. 158-163.

96. Todaev does not discuss *-n* stems in connection with postpositions.

97. Example taken from a letter to me dated 25 May 1952 from Professor Poppe.

98. Pointed out to me in a letter dated 31 December 1951 from Professor Poppe.

99. Rinčine, *op. cit.,* pp. 394-396.

100. N. N. Poppe, *Kvadratnaya pis'mennost'* (Moscow-Leningrad, 1941), p. 158.

101. G. J. Ramstedt, "Mongolische Briefe aus Idiqut Schähri bei Turfan," *Sitzungsbericht der K. Preuss. Akad. der Wissensch.,* 1909, XXXII, T II. D 224.

102. N. Poppe, "Die Nominalstammbildungssuffixe im Mongolischen," *KSz* 20(1923-1927).

103. B. H. Todaev, *op. cit.,* p. 156.

104. See n. 58.

105. N. Poppe, *op. cit.,* p. 97.

106. N. Poppe, *op. cit.,* p. 102.

107. G. K. Zipf, *The Psycho-Biology of Language* (Boston, 1935), pp. 226-227.

108. G. K. Zipf, *op. cit.,* pp. 227-229.

109. A. D. Rudnev, *Hori-buryatskiy govor* (Petrograd, 1913-1914), pp. LVI and LX.

110. G. J. Ramstedt, *Kalmückisches Wörterbuch* (Helsinki, 1935).

111. G. K. Zipf, *op. cit.,* p. 38.

112. Paul Pelliot, *Histoire secrète des Mongols,* restitution du texte mongol et traduction française des chapitres i à vi (Paris, 1949).

113. Erich Haenisch, *Die geheime Geschichte der Mongolen aus einer mongolischen Niederschrift des Jahres 1240 von der Insel Kode'e im Keluren-Fluss erstmalig übersetzt und erläutert;* zweite verbesserte Auflage (Leipzig, 1948).

114. Antoine Mostaert, C. I. C. M., *Folklore ordos (Traduction des Textes oraux ordos)*, *MS* Monograph XI (Peking, 1947). *Dictionnaire ordos*, vols. I-III (Peking, 1941-1944).

115. See n. 72.

116. See p. 65.

117. Professor F. W. Cleaves kindly allowed me to use his unpublished translation of the *Erdeni-yin Erike* and his unpublished translation of the Mongolian text of the *Hsiao ching*.

118. See p. 65.

119. See n. 90.

120. A. Mostaert, "Sur quelques passages de l'*Histoire secrète des Mongols* (Suite)," *HJAS* 14(1951).370-380.

121. See n. 101.

122. See p. 65.

123. See p. 65.

124. A. Mostaert, "Sur quelques passages de l'*Histoire secrète des Mongols* (I)," *HJAS* 13(1950).319-323.

125. N. N. Poppe, *Grammatika buryat-mongol'skogo yazïka* (Leningrad-Moscow, 1938), paragraph 168.

126. See n. 124.

127. F. W. Cleaves, "The Sino-Mongolian Inscription of 1338 in Memory of J̌igüntei," *HJAS* 14(1951).94-95, n. 110.

128. See p. 65.

BIBLIOGRAPHY

Abbreviations for Titles of Periodicals

AM	*Asia major*
HJAS	*Harvard Journal of Asiatic Studies*
JA	*Journal asiatique*
JAOS	*Journal of the American Oriental Society*
JSFOu	*Journal de la Société Finno-Ougrienne*
KSz	*Keleti Szemle*
MS	*Monumenta Serica*
RO	*Rocznik Orjentalistyczny*
TP	*T'oung pao*
ZDMG	*Zeitschrift der Deutschen Morgenländischen Gesellschaft*

1) Books.

Bleichsteiner, R., und Heissig, W., unter Mitwirkung von W. A. Unkrig, *Wörterbuch der heutigen mongolischen Sprache mit kurzem Abriss der Grammatik und ausgewählten Sprachproben* (Wien-Peking, 1941).

Bobrovnikov, A., *Grammatika mongol'sko-kalmïckago yazïka* (Kazan', 1849).

Deny, J., *Grammaire de la langue turque (dialecte osmanli)*, Paris, 1921.

Diringer, D., *The Alphabet* (New York, 1948).

Francis, John de, *Chinese Agent in Mongolia* (Baltimore, 1949).

Gabain, A. von, *Alttürkische Grammatik* (second edition, Leipzig, 1950).

Grønbech, K., *Der türkische Sprachbau* (Copenhagen, 1936).

Hambis, L., *Grammaire de la langue mongole écrite (première partie)*, Paris, 1946.

Haenisch, Erich, *Manghol un niuca tobca'an (Yüan-ch'ao pi-shi). Die geheime Geschichte der Mongolen, aus der chinesischen Transkription (Ausgabe Ye Têh-hui) im mongolischen Wortlaut wiederhergestellt* (Leipzig, 1935).

———, *Wörterbuch zu Manghol un niuca tobca'an (Yüan-ch'ao pi-shi), Geheime Geschichte der Mongolen* (Leipzig, 1939).

———, *Die geheime Geschichte der Mongolen aus einer mongolischen Niederschrift des Jahres 1240 von der Insel Kode'e im Keluren-Fluss erstmalig übersetzt und erläutert* (Leipzig, 1941), zweite verbesserte Auflage, Leipzig, 1948.

Heissig, Walter, *Bolur Erike "Eine Kette aus Bergkristallen" (eine Mongolische Chronik der Kienlung-Zeit von Rasipungsuγ, 1774/75)* [= *MS* Monograph X], Peking, 1946.

Jespersen, Otto, *The Philosophy of Grammar* (first published in New York, 1924; reprinted in London, 1948).

Jülg, Bernhard, *Mongolische Märchen-Sammlung (die Neun Märchen des Siddhi-kûr ... und die Geschichte des Ardschi-Bordschi Chan), Mongolisch mit deutscher Übersetzung*, etc. (Innsbruck, 1868).
Kotvič, V. L., *Lekcii po grammatike mongol'skago yazïka* (St. Petersburg, 1902).
Kovalevsky (= Kowalewski), O., *Kratkaya grammatika mongol'skago knižnego yazïka* (Kazan', 1835).
Kowalewski (= Kovalevskiy), Joseph Etienne, *Dictionnaire mongol-russe-français (Mongol'sko-russko-francuzskiy slovar')*. Kazan', 3 vols., 1844, 1846, 1849.
Lattimore, O., *Mongols of Manchuria* (New York, 1934).
Lewicki, Marian, *La langue mongole des transcriptions chinoises du XIVe siècle. Le Houa-yi yi-yu de 1389* [= Travaux de la Société des Sciences et des Lettres de Wrocław, Seria A, Nr. 19], Wrocław, 1949.
Lorimer, F., *Population of the Soviet Union* (Geneva, 1946).
Mostaert, Antoine, C. I. C. M., *Dictionnaire ordos*, vols. I-III (Peking, 1941-1944).
———, *Textes oraux ordos, recueillis et publiés avec introduction, notes morphologiques, commentaires et glossaire* (Peking, 1937).
———, *Folklore ordos (Traduction des Textes oraux ordos)*, Peking, 1947.
Pelliot, Paul, *Histoire secrète des Mongols* (Paris, 1949).
Popov, A., *Grammatika kalmïckago yazïka* (Kazan', 1847).
Poppe, N. N., *Kvadratnaya pis'mennost'. Istoriya mongol'skoy pis'mennosti* (Moscow-Leningrad, 1941).
———, *Mongol'skiy slovar' Mukaddimat al-Adab*, Parts I-III (Moscow-Leningrad, 1938-1939).
———, *Učebnik mongol'skogo yazïka (Mongol kele biçig suralcakada yzeke debter)*, Leningrad, 1932.
———, *Khalkha-Mongolische Grammatik, mit Bibliographie, Sprachproben und Glossar* (Wiesbaden, 1951).
———, *Grammatika buryat-mongol'skogo yazïka* (Moscow-Leningrad, 1938).
———, *Buryat-mongol'skoe yazïkoznanie* (Leningrad, 1933).
———, *Buryat-mongol'skiy fol'klornïy dialectologičeskiy sbornik* [= Obrazcï Narodnoy Slovesnosti V] (Moscow-Leningrad, 1936).
———, *Letopisi Horinskih Buryat. Vip. I* [= Trudï Instituta Vostokovedeniya IX] (Moscow-Leningrad, 1935).
———, *Letopisi Horinskih Buryat. Perevod* N. N. Poppe [= Trudï Instituta Vostokovedeniya XXXIII] (Moscow Leningrad, 1940).
———, *Dagurskoe narečie* [= Materialï Komissii po Issledovaniyu Mongol'skoy i Tannu-tuvinskoy Narodnïh Respublik i Buryat-Mongol'skoy ASSR, v. 6], Leningrad, 1930.
Pozdneev, A. M., *Mongol'skaya letopisъ „Erdeniynъ-yin erike". Podlinnïy tekst sъ perevodomъ i poyasneniyami, zaklyučayuščimi vъ sebe materialï dlya istorii Halhi sъ 1636 po 1736 g.* (St. Petersburg, 1883).
Ramstedt, G. J., *Kalmückisches Wörterbuch* (Helsinki, 1935).
Rinčin (= Rinčine), *Qan qan-köbegün qoyar* [= A translation of a story by Maxim Gorky, forming part of a series called *Ewöröpe dakin-u uran ǰokiyal*] (Ulan Bator, 1948).
Rinčine, A. R., *Kratkiy mongol'sko-russkiy slovar'* (Moscow, 1947).
Rudnev, A. D., *Hori-buryatskiy govor. Opït issledovaniya, tekstï, perevod i primečaniya. Vip. I-III* (Petrograd, 1913-1914).
———, *Lekcii po grammatike mongol'skago pis'mennago yazïka* (St. Petersburg, 1905).
Shiratori Kurakichi 白鳥庫吉, *Onyaku Mōbun Genchō Hishi* 音譯蒙文元朝秘史 *A Romanized Representation of the Yüan-ch'ao pi-shih (A Secret History*

of the Mongols in its Original Mongolian Sound), Tōyō Bunko Publications Series C, Volume VIII (Tokyo, 1942).

Skačkov, P. E., *Vnutrennyaya Mongoliya* (Moscow, 1933).

Smedt, A. de, et Mostaert, A., *Le dialecte monguor parlé par les Mongols du Kansou occidental, IIe partie, Grammaire* (Peking, 1945).

———, *Le dialecte monguor parlé par les Mongols du Kansou occidental, IIIe partie, Dictionnaire monguor-français* (Peking, 1933).

Šmidt (= Schmidt), I. Ya., *Grammatik der mongolischen Sprache* (St. Petersburg, 1831).

———, *Geschichte der Ost-Mongolen und ihres Fürstenhauses, verfasst von Ssanang Ssetsen Chungtaidschi der Ordus. Aus dem Mongolischen übersetzt und mit dem Originaltexte, nebst Anmerkungen, Erläuterungen und Citaten aus anderen unedirten Originalwerken herausgegeben von ...* (St. Petersburg, 1829).

———, *Grammatika mongol'skago yazïka* (St. Petersburg, 1832).

Todaev, B. H., *Grammatika sovremmenogo mongol'skogo yazika* (Izdatel'stvo Akademii Nauk SSSR, Moscow, 1951).

Tšeremisov, K. M., i Tsïdendambaev, Ts. B., *Buryat-mongol'sko-russkiy slovar'* (Gosudarstvennoe Izdatel'stvo Inostrannïh i Nacional'nïh Slovarey, Moscow, 1951).

Vladimircov, B. Ya., *Sravnitel'naya grammatika mongol'skogo pis'mennogo yazïka i halhaskogo narečiya. Vvedenie i fonetika* (Leningrad, 1929).

———, *Obrazcï mongol'skoy narodnoy slovestnosti (Severo-Zapadnaya Mongoliya)*, Leningrad, 1926.

———, *Le régime social des Mongols (Le féodalisme nomade)*, Traduction par Michel Carsow (Paris, 1948).

———, *Mongol'skiy sbnornik razskazov iz Pančatantra* (Petrograd, 1921).

Žamcarano, C., i Rudnev, A. D., *Obrazcï mongol'skoy narodnoy literaturï. I. Halhaskoe narečie* (St. Petersburg, 1908), *lith.*

Žamcarano, C. Ž., *Mongol'skie letopisi XVII veka* [= Trudï Instituta Vostokovedeniya XVI] (Moscow-Leningrad, 1936).

Zipf, G. K., *The Psycho-Biology of Language* (Boston, 1935).

2) Articles.

Bambaev, B. B., "Otčet o komandirovke v Mongoliyu letom 1926 goda," *Predvaritel'nïy otčet lingvističeskoy ekspedicii v Severnuyu Mongoliyu za 1926 god* (Izdatel'stvo Akademii Nauk SSSR, Leningrad, 1929).

Cleaves, Francis Woodman, "The Sino-Mongolian Inscription of 1335 in Memory of Chang Ying-jui," *HJAS* 13(1950).1-131.

———, "The Sino-Mongolian Inscription of 1338 in Memory of J̌igüntei," *HJAS* 14(1951).1-104.

———, "The Sino-Mongolian Inscription of 1346," *HJAS* 15(1952).1-123.

———, "The Sino-Mongolian Inscription of 1362 in Memory of Prince Hindu," *HJAS* 12(1949).1-133.

———, "The Sino-Mongolian Edict of 1453," *HJAS* 13(1950).431-446.

———, "The Mongolian Names and Terms in the *History of the Nation of the Archers* by Grigor of Akanc'," *HJAS* 12(1949).400-443.

———, "A Chancellery Practice of the Mongols in the Thirteenth and Fourteenth Centuries," *HJAS* 14(1951).493-526.

———, "The Expression *Jöb Ese Bol-* in the *Secret History of the Mongols*," *HJAS* 11(1948).311-320.

Cleaves, Francis Woodman, "Review of E. Haenisch's *Die Geheime Geschichte der Mongolen*," *HJAS* 12(1949).497-534.

Dragunov, A., "The *h*Phags-pa Script and Ancient Mandarin," *Izvestiya Akademii Nauk* (1930).627-747, 775-797.

Fuchs, Walter, und Mostaert, Antoine, "Ein Ming-Druck einer chinesisch-mongolischen Ausgabe des Hsiao-ching," *MS* 4(1945).325-329.

Grønbech, K., "Der Akzent im Türkischen und Mongolischen," *ZDMG* 94(1940), Heft 3.

Haenisch, Erich, "Zu den Briefen der mongolischen Il-khans Argun und Öljeitü an den König Philipp den Schönen von Frankreich (1289 u. 1305)," *Oriens* 2(1949).216-235.

_____, "Die viersprachige Gründungsinschrift des Tempels An-yüan-miao in Jehol v. Jahre 1765," *Abhandlungen der Geistes und Sozialwissenschaftlichen Klasse,* Jahrgang 1950, Nr. 15 (Akademie der Wissenschaften und der Literatur, Wiesbaden, 1950).

Hung, William, "The Transmission of the Book Known as *The Secret History of the Mongols*," *HJAS* 14(1951).433-492.

Kotwicz, Wł., "En marge des lettres des il-khans de Perse retrouvés par Abel Rémusat," *Collectanea Orientalia* 4(Lwow, 1933).

_____, "Contributions aux études altaiques. IV. Sons intercalaires," *RO* 12(1936).

_____, "Sur les modes d'orientation en Asie Centrale," *RO* 5(1927).68-91.

Laufer, B., "Skizze der mongolischen Literatur," *KSz* 8(1907).165-261.

Lewicki, Marian, "Przyrostki przysłowkowe *-ra ~ -rä, -ru ~ -rü, -rï ~ -ri* w jezykach ałtajskich," *Collectanea Orientalia* 15(Wilno, 1938).

Lin Yün-t'ao 林韻濤, "Meng-ku yung Weiwu tzu chih yüan-yin 蒙古用畏兀字之原因 ["Origin of the Use of Uigur Script among the Mongols"], *Yü Kung* 禹貢 *(The Chinese Historical Geography)* 5.12(Peking, 16 August 1936).21-24.

Menges, K. H., "Recent Publications in the Field of Mongolian Studies," *JAOS* 63.1(1943).17-24.

Mostaert, Antoine, "Sur quelques passages de l'*Histoire secrète des Mongols* (I)," *HJAS* 13(1950).285-361.

_____, "Sur quelques passages de l'*Histoire secrète des Mongols* (Suite)," *HJAS* 14(1951).329-403.

_____, "A propos du mot *širolγa* de l'*Histoire secrète des Mongols*," *HJAS* 12(1949).470-476.

_____, "The Mongols of Kansu and Their Language," *Bulletin No. 8 of the Catholic University of Peking* (Peking, 1931).

_____, "Ordosica," *Bulletin No. 9 of the Catholic University of Peking* (Peking, 1934).

_____, "L''ouverture du sceau' et les adresses chez les Ordos," *MS* 1(1935-1936).315-337.

_____, "Le dialecte des Mongols Urdus (Sud)," *Anthropos* 22(1927).160-186, 851-869.

Pelliot, Paul, "Les systèmes d'écriture en usage chez les anciens mongols," *AM* 2(1925).284-289.

_____, "Les documents mongols du Musée de Ṭeherān," *Aṯhār-é-Īrān* 1(1936).37-44.

_____, "Les Mongols et la Papauté," extrait de *la Revue de l'Orient Chrétien,* 3e série, T. III (XXIII), Nos 1 et 2 (1922-23).3-30.

_____, "Notes sur le 'Turkestan' de M. W. Barthold," *TP* 27(1930).34-35.

_____, "Les mots à *h*-initiale aujourd'hui amuie dans le mongol des XIII-e et XIV-e siècles," *JA* (Avril-Juin 1925).193-263.

Poppe, N. N.,"Geserica. Untersuchung der sprachlichen Eigentümlichkeiten der mongolischen Version des Gesserkhan," *AM* 3(1926).1-32, 167-193.

_____, "Zum Khalkhamongolischen Heldenepos," *AM* 5(1928).183-213.

_____, "O častyah reči v mongol'skom yazïke," *Sovetskoe Vostokovedenie* 1(1940).147-173.

_____, "Voprosï mongol'skoy grammatiki," *Zapiski Instituta Vostokovedeniya* II (Leningrad, 1933).

_____, "Die Nominalstammbildungssuffixe im Mongolischen," *KSz* 20(1923-1927).

_____, "Beiträge zur Kenntnis der altmongolischen Schriftsprache," *AM* 1(1924).668-675.

_____, "The Groups **uγa* and **üge* in Mongol Languages," *Studia Orientalia* 14(1950).3-15.

_____, "Remarks on the Vocalism of the Second Syllable in Mongolian," *HJAS* 14(1951).189-207.

_____, "Über die Sprache der Daguren," *AM* 10(1935).1-32, 183-220.

_____, "Russische Arbeiten auf dem Gebiet der Mongolistik 1914-1924," *AM* 1(1924).676-681.

_____, "Russische Arbeiten auf dem Gebiet der Mongolistik während der Jahre 1926-1927," *AM* 5(1928).214-224.

_____, "Otčet o poezdke na Orhon letom 1926 goda," *Predvaritel'nïy otčet lingvističeskoy ekspedicii v Severnuyu Mongoliyu za 1926 god* (Izdatel'stvo Akademii Nauk SSSR, Leningrad, 1929).

_____, "Review of *Oeuvres posthumes de Paul Pelliot. I. Histoire secrète des Mongols*," *HJAS* 13(1950).262-268.

_____, "Osnovï okančivayuščiesya na *n* v mongol'skih yazïkah," *Sovetskoe Yazïkoznanie* I. 167-171.

Ramstedt, G. J., "Mongolische Briefe aus Idiqut Schähri bei Turfan," *Sitzungsbericht der K. Preuss. Akad. der Wissensch.* (1909).838-848.

_____, "Zur mongolisch-türkischen Lautgeschichte," *KSz* 15(1914-1915).135-150; *KSz* 16(1915-1916).66-84.

_____, "Über die Zahlwörter der altaischen Sprachen," *JSFOu* 24.1(1907).

_____, "Ein anlautender stimmloser Labial der mongolisch-türkischen Ursprache," *JSFOu* 32.2(1916-1920).

_____, "Zur Geschichte des labialen Spiranten im Mongolischen," *Festschrift Vilhelm Thomsen* (1912).

_____, "Zur Verbstammbildungslehre der mongolisch-türkischen Sprachen," *JSFOu* 28.3(1912).

_____, "Über mongolische pronomina," *JSFOu* 23.3(1906).

_____, "Das Schriftmongolische und die Urgamundart phonetisch verglichen," *JSFOu* 21(1902).

_____, "Über die Konjugation des Khalkha-Mongolischen," *MSFOu* 19(1903).

_____, "Mogholica. Beiträge zur Kenntnis des Moghol-Sprache in Afghanistan," *JSFOu* 23.4(1906).I-III, 1-60.

Setälä, E. N., "Über Transkription der Finnisch-Ugrischen Sprachen," *Finnisch-Ugrische Forschungen* 1(Helsingfors, 1901).

Smedt, A. de, et Mostaert, A., "Le dialecte monguor parlé par les Mongols du Kansu occidental," *Anthropos* 24(1929), 25(1930).

Vladimircov, B. Ya., "Mongol'skie literaturnïe yazïki," *Zapiski Instituta Vostokovedeniya* (1932).1-17.

Whatmough, Joshua, "Natural Selection in Language," *Scientific American* 186.4(1952).82-86.

APPENDIX A

XVII

ORDOS

TRANSCRIPTION. *

Pour les détails de la phonétique du dialecte des Ordos du Sud, voir mon étude intitulée *Le dialecte des Mongols Urdus (Sud)* (1). Dans ce travail, je me suis servi de l'alphabet Anthropos. Dans le présent ouvrage, une notation quelque peu simplifiée a été adoptée. Je me sers de la transcription employée par la Société finno-ougrienne (2), à l'exception de quelques légères modifications, qui ont été introduites pour des raisons typographiques et pratiques.

Consonnes.

Vélaires		(*k̭*) ɢ̭ *g̭*			*χ*		*g̭*
Médio-gutt.	*k*‘	(*k*) ɢ *g*	$^{k}\chi$		*χ*		*g*
Prégutt.							*j*
Palatales			*tš*‘	ᴅ*ž*	*š*		*ž*
Dent. alv.	*t*‘	(*t*) ᴅ		ᴅ*z*	*s*		*z*
Dentilab.					*f*		
Bilab.	*p*‘	(*p*) ʙ *b*				ᴡ	*w*

Liquides : ʟ, *l*, *r*.
Nasales : *η*, *n*, *m*.

Voyelles.

Position supérieure	*ų*	*u*			*ɯ*	*ü*	*i*	
Position moyenne	*o*	*ȯ*			*ö*		*e*	*ė*
Position inférieure	*å*		*a*	*ȧ*	ӛ		*ä*	

(1) Anthropos, vol. XXI-XXII, 1926-1927 (correct. vol. XXV, p. 725)
(2) Voir E. N. Setälä, *Über transskription der finnisch-ugrischen sprachen. Historik und vorschläge,* dans Finnisch-ugrische Forschungen, Band I, Heft 1, 1901, p. 15.

* [Corrigenda: N. B. Le groupe $\chi^k\chi$ (χ^k) est à changer partout en ‘$^k\chi$ (‘^{k}).]

Remarques. I. Consonnes.

Les petites capitales G, G̨, D, B transcrivent des explosives douces assourdies; W est la fricative bilabiale douce assourdie; L est la forme assourdie de *l*.

g et *g̨* intervocaliques sont des fricatives à détroit fricatif étroit.

χ figure une fricative médio-gutturale dans l'affriquée $^{k}\chi$, dans le groupe $\chi^{k}\chi$ (le *χ* précédant l'affriquée appartient à la syllabe précédente; l'occlusion du ^{k} de l'affriquée est faible et de peu de durée — excepté dans la désinence du nomen futuri, le groupe $\chi^{k}\chi$ permute, même chez le même individu, avec *ʿkʿ*, le *k* étant fortement aspiré—), ainsi que dans les cas où *χ* représente la fricative précédant l'affriquée $^{k}\chi$ disparue par apocope ou réduite par syncope. Dans tous les autres cas, le signe *χ* transcrit une fricative vélaire à bruit de friction fort. Ainsi il est médio-guttural dans des mots tels que *eχ*^{k}*χener*, *Dżaχ*^{k}*χilā*, *eη*^{k}*χe*, *DżöDʿ*^{k}*χör*, *sā̈χ* (~ *sā̈χ*^{k}*χi*), *jāχ*^{k}*san* (~ *jāχ*^{k}*χisan*); tandis qu'il est vélaire dans des mots tels que *χara*, *awχu̯*, *aχa*, *iDeʿtšχu̯lā*, *Darχat*, *alχu̯χu̯*, *Dżaηgiraχ-im*, *lamā̈ēχās*. Le *χ* est vélaire aussi dans les mots d'emprunt. Ex.: *χ*^{u}*ār* «fleurs» (< chin.), *χui̯ʿtšʿaη* «espèce de violon à quatre cordes» (< chin.).— Dans les interjections *joχ*, *pʿaχ*, *pʿɯχ* etc., la nature de la fricative est déterminée par la voyelle qui la précède: vélaire après une voyelle postérieure (p. ex. dans *joχ*, *pʿaχ*), médio-gutturale après une voyelle antérieure (p. ex. dans *pʿɯχ*).

η est vélaire devant les consonnes vélaires; dans les autres cas, il est médio-guttural. *n* est alvéolaire. *r* est alvéolaire et roulé. Le timbre de *l* varie d'après la nature des voyelles qui l'accompagnent. L'assourdissement des dernières vibrations de *l* et *r* devant les dures ou une pause n'a pas été marqué. La liquide *l* (L) fonctionnant comme consonne-voyelle n'a pas reçu de signe spécial.

II. Voyelles.

a = *a* pur de l'italien «padre».

ȧ = *a* antérieur du français «madame».

ä = *ä* ouvert finnois. Dans les mots empruntés au chinois, *ä* est souvent un peu plus bas et un peu plus ouvert, quand il rend la voyelle chinoise qui dans la romanisation française (Couvreur) est représentée par *a* ou *(i)e*, *(iu)e* devant *n*.

å sonne entre *a* et *o* ouvert.

e transcrit un *e* postérieur ouvert et prononcé avec la langue quelque peu retirée et n'adhérant pas aux dents inférieures.

ė = *e* antérieur fermé. Dans la diphtongue *ȧe̯* le *e* antérieur asyllabique est transcrit par le signe plus simple *e̯*.

i sert à figurer deux espèces de voyelles. Notre dialecte distingue en effet deux espèces de *i*. L'un antérieur (le *i* fermé de l'allemand «ihn»), l'autre postérieur, un peu plus ouvert que le premier et prononcé avec la langue quelque peu retirée. Le premier est toujours bref et ne se rencontre que dans des mots de la classe antérieure, de même que dans les monosyllabes et devant *i* de la seconde syllabe (Ex.: *šine, Bi'tš'ik, Džil, mini*). Le second, étant bref, ne s'entend que dans les mots de la classe postérieure (Ex.: *šinag̡a, irōl, miŋg̡an, Gilōn, Birṵ̄*); sous sa forme longue, ou l'entend dans les mots des deux classes (Ex.: *minīχᵏχi, nī't'e, narīχan*).

u̯ = voyelle à timbre sourd sonnant entre *o* et *u*. Dans la prononciation de ce son, la langue est plus retirée que pour le *u* du français «pour»; ce mouvement de recul intense de la langue est cause d'un abaissement energique du larynx. L'allongement et l'arrondissement des lèvres sont faibles.

u a sa valeur ordinaire; seulement dans la prononciation de cette voyelle, l'allongement et l'arrondissement des lèvres sont assez faibles.

ɯ = *u* fermé prononcé avec la langue plus avancée que pour *u* français; probablement à identifier avec le *u* du norvégien «hus».

o = *o* ouvert.

ȯ = *o* antérieur qui tout en étant un *o* nettement ouvert, est cependant un peu plus fermé que la voyelle précédente; dans la prononciation de *ȯ* la langue est aussi un peu plus avancée que pour *o*.

ü transcrit deux sons. Après les affriquées palatales, *ü* figure le *ü'* fermé du français «reçu», «plus» (Ex.: *Džüi̯l, Džǖl*); dans tous les autres cas, il figure un *ü* postérieur qui a l'ouverture et la position de langue du *i* postérieur. Dans ce dernier cas, il ne se rencontre que sous sa forme longue (Ex.: *k'ǖ't'ön, nǖlgön*).

ö = un *ö* prononcé avec la langue retirée; les lèvres sont quelque peu allongées et arrondies, avec une ouverture de grandeur moyenne. Cette voyelle se rencontre aussi comme partie asyllabique de la diphtongue *öö̯*.

ɔ̈ ne s'entend que sous la forme longue: *ɔ̈̄*. Par ce signe je transcris un *ö* très ouvert dans l'articulation duquel la langue a la même position que pour la voyelle *ā*. L'allongement et l'arrondissement des lèvres sont faibles.

En vue de simplifier la transcription, les voyelles réduites, qui se rencontrent dans les syllabes brèves non accentuées et qui d'ailleurs, en notre dialecte, ne le sont pas à un degré tel qu'elles ne laissent plus aisément reconnaître leur timbre original comme il arrive dans beaucoup d'autres dialectes mongols, ont été transcrites au moyen des mêmes signes que les voyelles non réduites de la première syllabe.

Les voyelles réduites affectées de nasalité ont été marquées par un tilde au dessus.

Les voyelles glissantes varient quelque peu de nuance d'après la nature des sons avoisinants ; ce qui se remarque surtout pour la voyelle glissante ᵘ (par ex. dans les mots *jawu̯χᵘīn, ɯgᵘī*).

La voyelle brève de la dernière syllabe s'allonge facilement dans le discours emphatique et peut, dans ce cas, même changer de qualité. Ex. : *jawu̯ᴅžī ʙā̃ʿtʿar* « pendant qu'il s'avançait (ainsi à son aise) »; *öʿtʿölᴅžī* « il est devenu vieux », *ʙī = ʙi* « je, moi » ; *ʙėrē = ʙėre* « bru » ; *ɢėšēk = ɢėšik* « bienfait » ; *awu̯rāl = awu̯ral* « délivrance, salut, secours qui sauve ».

L'accent dynamique frappe régulièrement la première syllabe. Il est moins fort que celui des autres dialectes de la Mongolie du Sud et des dialectes khalkha.

---

§ 9. Mentionnons aussi les enclitiques *-tʻan (-tʻen), -jan-tʻan, -jān* qui indiquent la catégorie des êtres qui ont une certaine relation de famille, de voisinage, de similitude etc. avec le concept indiqué par le nom auquel elles se joignent. Dans une énumération de noms propres, *-tʻan* est souvent simplement l'équivalent de la particule coordinative française « et ». Ex.: *maši-tʻan* « Machi et les gens de sa famille, les gens qui sont venus avec lui, qui demeurent non loin de lui etc. » (*maši* nom propre d'homme); *tšʻilū-jan-tʻan irewū* « Tchilu et ses gens sont-ils arrivés? » (*tšʻilū* nom propre d'homme et de femme); *tšʻagān oχᵏχī-jan-tʻanāt* (ou *tšʻagān oχᵏχin-tʻan tʻere ɢerūt*) *iʻtšʻij* « j'irai chez Tchaghan Okin et chez ses voisins » (*tšʻagān oχᵏχin* nom propre d'homme et de femme); *šaralᴅā-jāā ɢerūᴅēs kʻɯn irēᴅᵘī wān* « personne n'est encore venu de chez Charaldai et de chez les gens de son voisinage » (*šaralᴅā* nom propre d'homme); *ene kʻɯn ölᴅžī ʙaʻtʻu-jānās ᴅēre* « cet homme-ci vaut mieux que Öldjei Batu et les gens de son espèce » (*ölᴅžī ʙaʻtʻu* nom propre d'homme); *noχᵃsu mū šara-tʻan* « Nokhaisu et Mu Chara » (*noχᵃsu* nom propre d'homme, *mū šara* id.); *ölᴅžī ᴅžaʙ χara kʻū-tʻenī irēᴅᵘī* « les gens de Öldjei Djap et de Khara Kü ne sont pas encore arrivés » (*ölᴅžī ᴅžaʙ* nom propre d'homme, *χara kʻū* id.).

Déclinaison.

§ 10. 1) Noms terminés par une voyelle brève.

Nom.	*ʙagši* « maître »	*šili* « colline »
Gén.	*ʙagšīn*	*šilīn*
Dat.-Loc.	*ʙagšiᴅu*	*šiliᴅɯ*
Acc.	*ʙagšīg* (*ʙagšī*)	*šilīg* (*šilī*)
Abl.	*ʙagšⁱās*	*šilēs*
Instr.	*ʙagšⁱār*	*šilēr*
Com.-Soc.	*ʙagšilā, ʙagšiʻtʻā*	*šililē, šiliʻtʻī*

Nom.	*eme* « femme »	*ʙölö* « enfants issus de sœurs »
Gén.	*emīn*	*ʙölīn*
Dat.-Loc.	*emeᴅɯ*	*ʙölöᴅɯ*
Acc.	*emīg* (*emī*)	*ʙölīg* (*ʙölī*)
Abl.	*emēs*	*ʙölös*
Instr.	*emēr*	*ʙölör*
Com.-Soc.	*emelē, emeʻtʻī*	*ʙölölö, ʙölöʻtʻī*

Nom.	*nastʻu̯* «vieillard, vieille femme»	*śɯrɯ* la nommée Chūrū
Gén.	*nastʻᵘīn*	*śɯrᵘīn*
Dat.-Loc.	*nastʻu̯ᴅu̯*	*śɯrɯᴅɯ*
Acc.	*nastʻᵘīg (nastʻᵘī)*	*śɯrᵘīg (śɯrᵘī)*
Abl.	*nastʻᵘās*	*śɯrᵘēs*
Instr.	*nastʻᵘār*	*śɯrᵘēr*
Com.-Soc.	*nastʻu̯lā, nastʻu̯ʻtʻa̿*	*śɯrɯlē, śɯrɯʻtʻī*

Nom.	*aχa* « frère aîné »	*ʙoro* le nommé Boro
Gén.	*aχa̿n*	*ʙorᵃ̿n*
Dat.-Loc.	*aχaᴅu̯*	*ʙoroᴅu̯*
Acc.	*aχa̿g (aχa̿)*	*ʙorᵃ̿g (ʙorᵃ̿)*
Abl.	*aχās*	*ʙora̿s (ʙorōs)*
Instr.	*aχār*	*ʙora̿r (ʙorōr)*
Com.-Soc.	*aχalā, aχaʻtʻa̿*	*ʙorola̿ (ʙorolō), ʙoroʻtʻᵃ̿*

§ 11. 2) Noms terminés par une voyelle longue.

Nom.	*ᴅā* «grand-chef de conféderation»	*kʻɯ̄* « fils »
Gén.	*ᴅāgīn*	*kʻɯ̄gīn*
Dat.-Loc.	*ᴅāᴅu̯*	*kʻɯ̄ᴅɯ*
Acc.	*ᴅāgīg (ᴅāgī)*	*kʻɯ̄gīg (kʻɯ̄gī)*
Abl.	*ᴅāg̡ās*	*kʻɯ̄gēs*
Instr.	*ᴅāg̡ār*	*kʻɯ̄gēr*
Com.-Soc.	*ᴅālā, ᴅāʻtʻa̿*	*kʻɯ̄lē, kʻɯ̄ʻtʻī*

Nom.	*rašisō* la nommée Rachiso	*kʻöᴅȫ* « steppe désertique et sablonneuse »
Gén.	*rašisōgīn*	*kʻöᴅȫgīn*
Dat.-Loc.	*rašisōᴅu̯*	*kʻöᴅȫᴅɯ*
Acc.	*rašisōgīg (rašisōgī)*	*kʻöᴅȫgīg (kʻöᴅȫgī)*
Abl.	*rašisōg̡a̿s (rašisōg̡ōs)*	*kʻöᴅȫgȫs*
Instr.	*rašisōg̡a̿r (rašisōg̡ōr)*	*kʻöᴅȫgȫr*
Com.-Soc.	*rašisōla̿ (rašisōlō), rašisōʻtʻᵃ̿*	*kʻöᴅȫlȫ, kʻöᴅȫʻtʻī*

§ 12. 3) Noms terminés primitivement par une diphtongue en *-i*, que celle-ci se soit conservée comme telle ou qu'elle se soit changée en une voyelle longue.

Nom.	*ᴅu̯g̡ᵘī* « circonscription »	*kʻī* « air » (mo. *kei*)
Gén.	*ᴅu̯g̡ᵘīn*	*kʻīn*
Dat.-Loc.	*ᴅu̯g̡ᵘīᴅu̯*	*kʻīᴅɯ*
Acc.	*ᴅu̯g̡ᵘīgīg* (*ᴅu̯g̡ᵘīgī*)	*kʻīgīg* (*kʻīgī*)
Abl.	*ᴅu̯g̡ᵘīg̡ās*	*kʻīgēs*
Instr.	*ᴅu̯g̡ᵘīg̡ār*	*kʻīgēr*
Com.-Soc.	*ᴅu̯g̡ᵘīlā*, *ᴅu̯g̡ᵘīʻtʻa̿*	*kʻīlē*, *kʻīʻtʻī*

Nom.	*g̡aχa̿* « porc » (mo. *γaqai*)	*noχᵃ̿* « chien » (mo. *noqai*).
Gén.	*g̡aχa̿n*	*noχᵃ̿n*
Dat.-Loc.	*g̡aχa̿ᴅu̯*	*noχᵃ̿ᴅu̯*
Acc.	*g̡aχa̿gīg* (*g̡aχa̿gī*)	*noχᵃ̿gīg* (*noχᵃ̿gī*)
Abl.	*g̡aχa̿g̡ās*	*noχᵃ̿g̡a̿s* (*noχᵃ̿g̡ōs*)
Instr.	*g̡aχa̿g̡ār*	*noχᵃ̿g̡a̿r* (*noχᵃ̿g̡ōr*)
Com.-Soc.	*g̡aχa̿lā*, *g̡aχa̿ʻtʻa̿*	*noχᵃ̿la̿* (*noχᵃ̿lō*), *noχᵃ̿ʻtʻᵃ̿*

§ 13. 4) Noms terminés par une consonns autre que *n*.

Nom.	*ᴅżaŋ* « caractère, naturel »	*em* « médecine »
Gén.	*ᴅżaŋgīn*	*emīn*
Dat.-Loc.	*ᴅżaŋᴅu̯*	*emᴅɯ*
Acc.	*ᴅżaŋgīg* (*ᴅżaŋgī*)	*emīg* (*emī*)
Abl.	*ᴅżaŋg̡ās*	*emēs*
Instr.	*ᴅżaŋg̡ār*	*emēr*
Com.-Soc.	*ᴅżaŋlā*, *ᴅżaŋtʻa̿*	*emlē*, *emtʻī*

Nom.	*g̡ol* « rivière »	*ᴅżis* « cuivre rouge »
Gén.	*g̡olīn*	*ᴅżisīn*
Dat.-Loc.	*g̡oltʻu̯* (*g̡olᴅu̯*)	*ᴅżistʻɯ* (*ᴅżisᴅɯ*)
Acc.	*g̡olīg* (*g̡olī*)	*ᴅżisīg* (*ᴅżisī*)
Abl.	*g̡ola̿s* (*g̡olōs*)	*ᴅżisēs*
Instr.	*g̡ola̿r* (*g̡olōr*)	*ᴅżisēr*
Com.-Soc.	*g̡olla̿* (*g̡ollō*), *g̡oltʻᵃ̿*	*ᴅżislē*, *ᴅżistʻī*

Nom.	*ʙar* « tigre »	*ᴅżɯɢ* « direction »
Gén.	*ʙarīn*	*ᴅżɯgīn*
Dat.-Loc.	*ʙart‘ų*	*ᴅżɯɢ‘t‘ɯ*
Acc.	*ʙarīg* (*ʙarī*)	*ᴅżɯgīg* (*ᴅżɯgī*)
Abl.	*ʙarās*	*ᴅżɯgēs*
Instr.	*ʙarār*	*ᴅżɯ̥gēr*
Com.-Soc.	*ʙarlā*, *ʙart‘a̿*	*ᴅżɯglē*, *ᴅżɯɢ‘t‘ī*

Nom.	*sāᴅ* « obstacle »	*öʙ* « biens »
Gén.	*sāᴅīn*	*öwīn*
Dat.-Loc.	*sāᴅt‘ų*	*öʙ‘t‘ɯ*
Acc.	*sāᴅīg* (*sāᴅī*)	*öwīg* (*öwī*)
Abl.	*sāᴅās*	*öwō̿s*
Instr.	*sāᴅār*	*öwō̿r*
Com.-Soc.	*sāᴅlā*, *sāᴅt‘a̿*	*öblō̿*, *öʙ‘t‘ī*

§ 14. 5) Noms terminés au cas absolu par *n*.

Nom.	*χān* « empereur »	*oron* « endroit »
Gén.	*χāni*	*oroni*
Dat.-Loc.	*χānᴅų*	*oronᴅų*
Acc.	*χānīg* (*χānī*)	*oronīg* (*oronī*)
Abl.	*χānās*	*oronă̄s* (*oronōs*)
Instr.	*χānār*	*oronă̄r* (*oronōr*)
Com.-Soc.	*χānlā*, *χānt‘a̿*	*oronlă̄* (*oronlō*), *oront‘ŏ̄*

Nom.	*īrgen* « Chinois »	*örö‘t‘ön* « créanciers, créancier »
Gén.	*īrgeni*	*örö‘t‘öni*
Dat.-Loc.	*īrgenᴅɯ*	*örö‘t‘önᴅɯ*
Acc.	*īrgenīg* (*īrgenī*)	*örö‘t‘önīg* (*örö‘t‘önī*)
Abl.	*īrgenēs*	*örö‘t‘önō̿s*
Instr.	*īrgenēr*	*örö‘t‘önō̿r*
Com.-Soc.	*īrgenlē*, *īrgent‘ī*	*örö‘t‘önlō̿*, *örö‘t‘önt‘ī*

§ 15. 6) Noms qui au cas absolu se terminent par une voyelle, mais prennent un *n* au génitif, au datif-locatif, à l'ablatif et au comitatif-sociatif en *-lā* (*-lē*, *-lā̄* etc.),— de même qu'au directif (voir § 26).

a) Noms terminés par une voyelle brève.

Nom.	*χaᴅa* «rocher»	*ʙᴏᴅᴏ* «pièce de gros bétail»
Gén.	*χaᴅan*	*ʙᴏᴅᴏn*
Dat.-Loc.	*χaᴅanᴅu̯*	*ʙᴏᴅᴏnᴅu̯*
Acc.	*χaᴅā̄g* (*χaᴅā̄*)	*ʙᴏᴅ$^{\bar{\bar{a}}}$g* (*ʙᴏᴅ$^{\bar{\bar{a}}}$*)
Abl.	*χaᴅanās*	*ʙᴏᴅᴏnā̄s* (*ʙᴏᴅᴏnōs*)
Instr.	*χaᴅār*	*ʙᴏᴅā̄r* (*ʙᴏᴅōr*)
Com.-Soc.	*χaᴅanlā*, *χaᴅaʿtʿā̄*	*ʙᴏᴅᴏnlā̄* (*ʙᴏᴅᴏnlō*), *ʙᴏᴅᴏʿtʿ$^{\bar{\bar{a}}}$*

Nom.	*mori* «cheval»	*ɢɯʿtšʿi* «force»
Gén.	*morin*	*ɢɯʿtšʿin*
Dat.-Loc.	*morinᴅu̯*	*ɢɯʿtšʿinᴅɯ*
Acc.	*morīg* (*morī*)	*ɢɯʿtšʿīg* (*ɢɯʿtšʿī*)
Abl.	*morinā̄s* (*morinōs*)	*ɢɯʿtšʿinēs*
Instr.	*mor^{i}ā̄r* (*mor^{i}ōr*)	*ɢɯʿtšʿēr*
Com.-Soc.	*morinlā̄* (*morinlō*), *moriʿtʿ$^{\bar{\bar{a}}}$*	*ɢɯʿtšʿinlē*, *ɢɯʿtšʿiʿtʿī*

Nom.	*elege* «foie»	*šölö* «bouillon de viande»
Gén.	*elegen*	*šölön*
Dat.-Loc.	*elegenᴅɯ*	*šölönᴅɯ*
Acc.	*elegīg* (*elegī*)	*šölīg* (*šölī*)
Abl.	*elegenēs*	*šölönȫs*
Instr.	*elegēr*	*šölȫr*
Com.-Soc.	*elegenlē*, *elegeʿtʿī*	*šölönlȫ*, *šölöʿtʿī*

Nom.	*mu̯ᴅu̯* «bois»	*ɯsɯ* «lait»
Gén.	*mu̯ᴅu̯n*	*ɯsɯn*
Dat.-Loc.	*mu̯ᴅu̯nᴅu̯*	*ɯsɯnᴅɯ*
Acc.	*mu̯ᴅ^{u}īg* (*mu̯ᴅ^{u}ī*)	*ɯs^{u}īg* (*ɯs^{u}ī*)
Abl.	*mu̯ᴅu̯nās*	*ɯsɯnēs*
Instr.	*mu̯ᴅ^{u}ār*	*ɯs^{u}ēr*
Com.-Soc.	*mu̯ᴅu̯nlā*, *mu̯ᴅu̯ʿtʿā̄*	*ɯsɯnlē*, *ɯsɯʿtʿī*

b) Noms terminés par une voyelle longue.

Nom.	*sanā* « pensée »	*t'emē* « chameau »
Gén.	*sanān*	*t'emēn*
Dat.-Loc.	*sanānᴅų*	*t'emēnᴅɯ*
Acc.	*sanāgīg (sanāgī)*	*t'emēgīg (t'emēgī)*
Abl.	*sanānās*	*t'emēnēs*
Instr.	*sanāg̨ār*	*t'emēger*
Com.-Soc.	*sanānlā, sanā't'ā*	*t'emēnlē, t'emē't'ī*

Nom.	*t'og̨ō* « marmite »	*ᴅörȫ* « étrier »
Gén.	*t'og̨ōn*	*ᴅörȫn*
Dat.-Loc.	*t'og̨ōnᴅų*	*ᴅörȫnᴅɯ*
Acc.	*t'og̨ōgīg (t'og̨ōgī)*	*ᴅörȫgīg (ᴅörȫgī)*
Abl.	*t'og̨ōnās (t'og̨ōnōs)*	*ᴅörȫnȫs*
Instr.	*t'og̨ōg̨ār (t'og̨ōgōr)*	*ᴅörȫgȫr*
Com.-Soc.	*t'og̨ōnlā (t'og̨ōnlō), t'og̨ō't'ā*	*ᴅörȫnlȫ, ᴅörȫ't'ī*

§ 16. Remarques.

1) La voyelle glissante *ᵘ* appartenant au nom décliné disparaît parfois devant l'initiale vocalique du suffixe casuel. Cela arrive le plus souvent dans une prononciation peu soignée. Ex.: *marg̨ā't'ᵘīn* ~ *marg̨ā't'īn* gén. de *marg̨ā't'ų* « demain »; *mųᴅᵘār* ~ *mųᴅār* instr. de *mųᴅų* « bois »; *āwār* instr. de *āwų* « père, grand-père ».

2) Le génitif des noms dont la déclinaison a été décrite sous § 14, est parfois en *-ā (-ī, -ā)*. Ex. *nojonā ᴅžarlik* « l'ordre du prince » *(nojon); k'enī jųnā sųwųrg̨a* « de qui est ce stūpa et quelle espèce de stūpa est-ce? » *(k'en)* (chanson). Chez les noms dont la déclinaison a été décrite sous § 15, le génitif est parfois en *-n-i* (cf. mo. *-n-u, -n-ü)* et même en *-n-ā*. Ainsi on entend *sųmųni ɢer* « étui à flèches » *(sųmų); mini ʙėjeni k'erek* « mon affaire personnelle » *(ʙėje); sawani k'ėr* « saletés adhérant à la paroi intérieure d'un vase » *(sawa); ᴅaχᵏχilg̨anā t'ɯrɯ̄* « chef préposé au culte » *(ᴅaχᵏχilg̨a)*. Pour le suffixe *-ā*, voir aussi §§ 30, 40, 44, 48.

3) Dans notre dialecte, le suffixe de l'accusatif *-īg* est sporadiquement remplacé par *-īgī*. Ex.: *ɯsᵘīgī* acc. de *ɯsɯ* « lait ».

[Noms à double déclinaison.]

	g̨oʿtʿo « enclos pour le bétail »	*g̨oʿtʿo* « ville »
Gén.	*g̨oʿtʿon*	*g̨oʿtʿɔ̄n*
Dat.-Loc.	*g̨oʿtʿonᴅu̯*	*g̨oʿtʿoᴅu̯*
Abl.	*g̨oʿtʿonās* (*g̨oʿtʿonōs*)	*g̨oʿtʿās* (*g̨oʿtʿōs*)
Com.-Soc.	*g̨oʿtʿonlā* (*g̨oʿtʿonlō*)	*g̨oʿtʿolā* (*g̨oʿtʿolō*)

	tʿerge « voiture »	*tʿerge* «la ville de Houa ma tch'eu (Ninghia)»
Gén.	*tʿergen*	*tʿergīn*
Dat.-Loc.	*tʿergenᴅɯ*	*tʿergeᴅɯ*
Abl.	*tʿergenēs*	*tʿergēs*
Com.-Soc.	*tʿergenlē*	*tʿergelē*

Il en est de même des autres noms de cette même catégorie chaque fois qu'ils sont employés comme noms de personne. Exemple :

	tśʿilū̯ « pierre »	*tśʿilū̯* le nommé Tchilu
Gén.	*tśʿilū̯n*	*tśʿilū̯gīn*
Dat.-Loc.	*tśʿilū̯nᴅu̯*	*tśʿilū̯ᴅu̯*
Abl.	*tśʿilū̯nās*	*tśʿilū̯g̨ās*
Com.-Soc.	*tśʿilū̯nlā*	*tśʿilū̯lā*

Cf. aussi la forme spéciale du génitif dans beaucoup de noms d'endroit. Ex. : *u̯nag̨āē burᴅɯ* nom d'endroit (*oʿtʿok̯*), litt. « l'étang du poulain », en regard de *u̯nag̨an ᴅżɯsɯ* « le pelage du poulain » ; *tśʿonɔ̄ō kʿöᴅō̈* nom d'endroit (*ɯ̄šin*), litt. « la steppe déserte des loups », en regard de *tśʿonon aru̯su̯* « peau de loup » ; *kʿɯrēgīī šili* nom d'endroit (*ɯ̄šin*), litt. « la colline de l'enclos », en regard de *kʿɯrēn ɯ̄ᴅe* « la porte de l'enclos » etc., etc.

A comparer : *öǫ̈rās* « d'un endroit peu éloigné » en regard de *öǫ̈ronās* « depuis quelque temps », de *öǫ̈ro* « proche, près ».

§ 18. Il y a en outre pour quelques mots des fluctuations et incertitudes se limitant d'ailleurs le plus souvent à un ou deux cas pour le même mot. Ainsi, chez le même individu, on peut entendre *öröndɯ* et *öröᴅɯ* (datif de *örö* « dette »), *u̯rᴅu̯nᴅu̯* et *u̯rᴅu̯ᴅu̯* (datif de *u̯rᴅu̯* « palais »), *ū̯lān* et *ū̯lan* (génitif de *ū̯la* « montagne ») etc.

§ 19. Dans les expressions ayant un caractère plus ou moins technique, telles qu'on en rencontre dans la langue administrative, les mots appartenant à la catégorie en question font parfois leur génitif sur le modèle de *ʙag̨ši, šili* etc.

APPENDIX C

KHALKHA-MONGOLIAN PAGRADIGMS[a]

1) Short vowel stem.

Nom.	*sara* "month"
Gen.	*sariin*
D.-Loc.	*sarada*
Acc.	*sariig*
Ind.	*sara*
Abl.	*saraas*
Instr.	*saraar*
Com.	*saratai*

2) Long vowel stem.

Nom.	*böö* "shaman"
Gen.	*böögiin*
D.-Loc.	*böödö*
Acc.	*böög*
Ind.	*böö*
Abl.	*böögöös*
Instr.	*böögöör*
Com.	*böötee*

3) Diphthong stem.

Nom.	*dalai* "sea"
Gen.	*dalain*
D.-Loc.	*dalaida*
Acc.	*dalaig*
Ind.	*dalai*
Abl.	*dalaigaas*
Instr.	*dalaigaar*
Com.	*dalaitai*

4) Consonant stem.

Nom.	*gar* "hand"
Gen.	*gariin*
D.-Loc.	*garta*
Acc.	*gariig*
Ind.	*gar*
Abl.	*garaas*
Instr.	*garaar*
Com.	*gartai*

5) -*n(g)* stem.

Nom.	*dzan(g)* "character"
Gen.	*dzangiin*
D.-Loc.	*dzan(g)da*
Acc.	*dzangiig*
Ind.	*dzan(g)*
Abl.	*dzangaas*
Instr.	*dzangaar*
Com.	*dzan(g)tai*

6) Absolute -*n* stem.

Nom.	*noyon* "prince"
Gen.	*noyonii*
D.-Loc.	*noyondo*
Acc.	*noyoniig*
Ind.	*noyon*
Abl.	*noyonoos*
Instr.	*noyonoor*
Com.	*noyontee*

[a]The paradigms are from *Khalkha-Mongolische Grammatik* by Nikolaus Poppe (Weisbaden, 1951), pp. 66-68.

7) Conditional *-n* stem.
a) With short vowels.

8) Conditional *-n* stem.
a) With long vowels.

	7a) short vowels	8a) long vowels
Nom.	*mori* "horse"	*galuu* "goose"
Gen.	*morinii*	*galuunii*
D.-Loc.	*morindo*	*galuunda*
Acc.	*mor'iig*	*galuug*
Ind.	*mori*	*galuu*
Abl.	*morinoos*	*galuunaas*
Instr.	*mor'oor*	*galuugaar*
Com.	*moritee*	*galuutai*

APPENDIX D

LISTS OF POSTPOSITIONS CITED

(I) MINIMAL FORM POSTPOSITIONS

The numbers correspond to the numbered postpositions in chapter six.

1) *adali*
2) *alus*
3) *aru*
4) *čaγada*
5) *čaγadu*
6) *čaγana*
7) *čaγasi*
8) *činadu*
9) *činaγsi*
10) *činana*
11) *činegen*
12) *čuγ*
13) *daraγa*
14) *darui*
15) *degegsi*
16) *degegür*
17) *degere*
18) *dergede*
19) *dergedegür*
20) *doγoγsi*
21) *doγoγur*
22) *doora/dora*
23) *doroγsi*
24) *dorona*
25) *dotoγur*
26) *dotora*
27) *dumda*
28) *dumdaγur*
29) *ebür/öbür*
30) *ečine*
31) *emüne*
32) *ende*
33) *esergü(ü)*
34) *eteged*
35) *γadaγa*
36) *γadaγsi*
37) *γadaγur*
38) *γadana*
39) *γarui*
40) *ilegü(ü)/ülegü(ü)*
41) *inadu*
42) *inaγsi*
43) *inaru*
44) *ǰabsar*
45) *ǰaγura*
46) *ǰüg*
47) *kiri*
48) *metü*
49) *naγaγur*
50) *naγana*
51) *naγasi*
52) *ögede*
53) *ögere/öbere*
54) *oyira*
55) *qamtu*
56) *qoγorundu*
57) *qoγorunduγur*
58) *qola*
59) *qoyiγur*
60) *qoyina*
61) *qoyinaγsi*
62) *qoyisi*
63) *selte*
64) *sidar*
65) *šiγ/šig*
66) *singgi*
67) *šitü/sitü*
68) *tedüi*
69) *tege*
70) *tegegür*
71) *tegesi/tesi*
72) *tende*
73) *teyisi*
74) *tölöge*
75) *tula*
76) *tuqai*
77) *tursi*
78) *tus*
79) *učir*
80) *ügei*
81) *ulam*
82) *ülemǰi*
83) *umara/ümere*
84) *urid(a)*
85) *uruγsi*
86) *uruγu*

(II) NOUN-POSTPOSITIONS

Only the noun-postpositions given in examples are listed.

a) Noun-postpositions whose minimal form is primarily neither an adverb nor a postposition.

ači-bar	*ǰaqa-da*	*tala-γar*
alda-da	*oron-da*	*učir-a*
angi-da	*qaǰaγu-da/qaǰau-da*	*üre-iyer*
aru-da	*siltaγa-bar*	*yosu-γar*
ǰabsar-a		

b) Noun-postpositions whose minimal form is primarily used as an adverb or a postposition.

degere-eče	*emüne-eče*	*qoyinaγsi-da*
dora-ača	*inaγsi-da*	*tula-da*
dotora-ača	*qoyina-ča*	

(III) VERB-POSTPOSITIONS

Only the verb-postpositions given in examples are listed.

a-tala	*ekile-n*	*orči-n*
bayi-tala	*ǰori-n*	*siqa-n*
bol-tala	*kür-tele*	*toγori-n*